NEWS OF PARIS

NEWS OF PARIS

*American Journalists in the
City of Light Between the Wars*

RONALD WEBER

Ivan R. Dee
CHICAGO 2006

www.ivanrdee.com

Library of Congress Cataloging-in-Publication Data:
Weber, Ronald, 1934–
    News of Paris : American journalists in the city of light between the wars / Ronald Weber.
        p. cm.
    Includes bibliographical references and index.
    ISBN 1-56663-676-0 (cloth : alk. paper)
    1. French periodicals—Foreign language press—History—20th century. 2. American periodicals—France—Paris—History—20th century. 3. Journalists—United States—Biography. 4. Americans—France—Paris—History—20th century. I. Title.
PN5184.F62E54 2006
070'.92'31304436—dc22

                                                                        2005022989

For Pat

Contents

NEWS OF PARIS

Jake's Work

All along people were going to work. It felt
pleasant to be going to work. I walked across
the avenue and turned in to my office.
—ERNEST HEMINGWAY,
The Sun Also Rises

ARRIVAL. Jake Barnes's work in Ernest Hemingway's novel is newspaper work, though we only glimpse him at it—reading French morning papers, turning to the typewriter and getting off his daily duty of rewrite for dispatch by weekly mail from Gare St. Lazare, attending a briefing at the Quai d'Orsay—before he is off from Paris for the Lost Generation escapades in Spain. Jake remarks that it is important in the newspaper business never to seem to be working, an aim he effortlessly realizes. Nonetheless a working newspaperman he is, as his friend Bill Gorton exuberantly reminds him during their fishing idyll in Burguete when he brings into a passing literary conversation Jake's ambition to become a writer. "There you go," says Bill. "And you claim you want to be a writer, too. You're only a newspaper man. An expatriated newspaper man."

Unlike Jake, Hemingway had not remained in France after war service, but he was another expatriated American newspaperman with ambition as a writer. "Everything is very lovely and we're getting off in excellent style," he wrote in a letter in December 1921, informing his family back in Illinois that he and his new wife, Hadley, were about to embark from New York to Le Havre on their way to Paris. He was just twenty-two yet already an experienced journalist with work behind him on the *Kansas City Star*, the *Toronto Star*, and a Chicago magazine, the *Cooperative Commonwealth*. Awaiting him in Paris was a space-rate job, plus expenses in gathering material, writing feature stories for the Toronto paper.

France as a European destination was a recent choice, replacing Italy, the change made possible by the Toronto job but inspired by a friendship with Sherwood Anderson. The older writer, whom Hemingway had come to know in Chicago, had returned from Paris with a glowing account of the City of Light as the place a writer, if he was serious about his work, had to go. As yet Hemingway had published nothing, but there was no question he was serious about writing, and after some hesitation he acted on Anderson's advice. Before Hemingway left New York, Anderson generously provided him with letters of introduction to Gertrude Stein, Ezra Pound, Sylvia Beach, and Lewis Galantière.

"Well here we are," Hemingway wrote back to Anderson as soon as he reached Paris. After describing the winter cold of the city and the warmth of charcoal braziers outside the cafés, he reported that already he was "earning our daily bread on this write machine," meaning he was churning out stories for the *Toronto Star*. In his first two months in Paris he would mail the *Star* thirty feature stories, leading to a lament to Anderson that "this goddam newspaper stuff is gradually ruining me—but I'm going to cut it all loose pretty soon and work for about three months." Not until the beginning of 1924, and after a four-month interlude at the home office of the *Toronto Star* while he and Hadley awaited the birth of a son, did he finally make his break with newspaper work. With the appearance of *The Sun Also Rises* in 1926, the transformation from journalist to writer was complete.

INVADING PARIS. Though "Fame became of him," as Archibald MacLeish would famously write, distancing him forever from his fellows, the Hemingway of 1921 was merely one of a large number of American journalists, amateurs and professionals, the raw and the seasoned, who made their way to Paris between the two world wars. Here they joined a relatively permanent American colony that numbered perhaps (it was always a hazy matter) six thousand when Hemingway arrived, thirty thousand and rising by the middle of the decade, sixty thousand in all of France. Thanks to postwar American prosperity coupled with the fallen value of the French franc, Paris provided the exiles with an inexpensive place to live, as Hemingway was soon hammering home in the Toronto paper: "Paris in the winter is rainy, cold, beautiful and cheap. It is also noisy, jostling, crowded and cheap. It is anything you want—and cheap."

For the journalists among the exiles, the city had an even more important advantage. It was what Vincent Sheean—Hemingway's exact contemporary, a fellow Midwesterner from Illinois, and a young journalist with literary ambition also newly arrived in Paris— called "the centre of American journalism in Europe" (and, for Hemingway at least, Canadian journalism), with editorial jobs available on English-language daily newspapers; as Paris-based foreign correspondents; as writers and editors for magazines and press services; as proofreaders and freelancers and odd-job writers of assorted kinds. (As the center of French journalism as well, Paris at the time was said to possess more newspapers in relation to population than any city in the world, with Frenchmen typically buying three to five a day.)

Just how large was the number of journalists flocking to Paris? An answer of sorts was given by Jimmie Charters, the amiable British barman of the Dingo and other Montparnasse drinking establishments favored by expatriates, in his 1934 memoir *This Must Be the Place*—edited by one American newspaperman, Morrill Cody, and with an introduction by another, Hemingway. Charters calculated that the largest part of his clientele, 40 percent, was made up of artists, writers, *and* newspapermen. Al Laney, an expatriate newspaperman and eventually the author of an informal history of one of the Paris-American papers, went considerably further, maintaining that the "American invasion of Paris, which began to roll up in waves about 1924, was led by newspapermen. They were, at any rate, the advance guard, patrols thrown ahead by this invading army."

Paul Scott Mowrer, a veteran Paris correspondent of the *Chicago Daily News*, remembered the city during the post–World War I period "filling up with . . . young men and women whose dollar checks were barely enough to live on, even when turned into francs. Most of these young folks seemed to want to do newspaper work. To eke out the little they had, they were willing to work for little, just to be able to stay in Paris." William L. Shirer, who went on to honored careers as a correspondent, radio commentator, and historian of the Third Reich, learned firsthand the invading army's size. While hunting for a newspaper job on a Paris-American paper he was shown an applicant file said to have a thousand names in it; on a second paper, its file nearly as thick, his name was taken but no hope held out for a job.

In *The Twenties*, a comprehensive study of the decade, Frederick J. Hoffman surveyed some eighty-five American expatriates in the period 1915–1930 and found, among sixty-five for whom information was available, that nearly two-thirds financed their European days with editing, journalistic writing, and daily journalism. Many others, Hoffman added, "used this way occasionally for making up deficits or meeting bills." The Anglo-American Press Association, founded in Paris in 1907, would offer a more exact indication of the number of American journalists in Paris, despite the limitation that its membership consisted largely of correspondents and included relatively few working newspapermen on Paris-American dailies or freelance writers working on their own. Regrettably, the group's membership rolls were lost when it returned to Paris from London after World War II.

During the interwar years the AAPA sponsored weekly Wednesday luncheons featuring invited speakers, with Hemingway a regular at the gatherings soon after his Paris arrival. Here, his *Toronto Star* readers learned, journalists in their shoptalk dissected the news "as they saw it as human beings watching human beings instead of newspapermen with diplomas." In *The Sun Also Rises*, Krum, the correspondent Jake Barnes shares a taxi with while returning from a government briefing, says, "See you at the lunch on Wednesday," to which Jake replies, "You bet."

Hemingway also attended the AAPA's annual banquets at Paris hotels or nightclubs, where champagne flowed and entertainment continued into the wee hours. "Big time at the Anglo American annual dinner," he reported in a letter after one extended evening. "Got in at seven A.M. this morning." Harold Stearns, the legendary expatriate with a walk-on part in *The Sun Also Rises* as Harvey Stone, had fond memories of the yearly frolics, which he attended while working as a Paris correspondent for the *Baltimore Sun*. On one occasion, after falling "weepingly and demonstratively in love" with a French singer who was part of the entertainment, he had to be taken home and put to bed, "still weeping out of strong emotion (and considerable liquor). But the dinner was a great success, nevertheless. Most of those annual dinners, in my time, were."

The Paris prefect of police was routinely a guest of honor at the banquets, lending them a measure of respectability and, perhaps more to the point of his presence, seeing to the safe transit home of journalists in a weakened condition. In a memoir of Paris days, Harold Ettlinger, a staff member of a Paris-American paper and later a wire-service correspondent, has a scene in which the prefect instructs his underlings about their duties in the aftermath of the tipsy affair:

> "*Messieurs*," said the Prefect, "tonight is the party of the
> American journalists. They have it every year, you know.
> They are friends of ours, these journalists. Courtesy must be

extended. We must see that there is no trouble. These Americans, they are a little—how shall I say?—impulsive. They are easily carried away by the charms of sociability. Some of them may have a little too much to drink? Do I make myself clear?"

Uniformed police are told to wait by the taxi stand to make certain drivers understand where the journalists wish to be taken. If one of them is uncertain of his destination, he is to be taken to the Dôme café, a place familiar to Americans that may refresh his memory. At the Dôme other policemen are to ensure that taxi drivers do not overcharge. For journalists who are truly "beyond comprehension momentarily," cots will be set up in the Rue Delambre *commissariat* that will allow them to sleep until they are in condition to go home. There is no question of their being under arrest, and they "must be made to feel—if they are not beyond feeling temporarily—that they are in the hands of friends, not officers of the law."

REGULAR JOBS. Harold Stearns, in the early thirties out of work but reluctant to leave the city, offered the paradoxical remark that "Paris is a wonderful place in which to loaf, if you also have a regular job." The present book has its origin in Stearns's emphasis on work together with Frederick J. Hoffman's survey and a passage in the 1934 edition of Malcolm Cowley's classic Lost Generation memoir, *Exile's Return*. In an epilogue, Cowley lists matters he failed to write about, the first being "I haven't told enough about the way young writers earned the money on which they lived":

> I haven't told how they managed to stay for years in Europe.
> Most of them were poor, and their trip abroad was financed in
> all sorts of accidental ways, fellowships, loans, prizes,
> commissions to write for magazines, a book unexpectedly
> published—there are a hundred stories here that cast a light
> on the times and shouldn't be forgotten.

This book follows the money in that it concentrates on a central way in which writers, young and not so young, financed their Paris days in the two decades between the wars—as working journalists of one sort or another. Their jobs sometimes came about in the accidental ways Cowley mentions, yet they were real jobs for real money. And they were jobs that were socially acceptable in the eyes of the Left Bank art-and-literature crowd, assuming the jobs were taken only from need and worked at without excessive zeal. "It was all right," remarked one of the journalists, Edmond Taylor, "to be a tourist guide—if one had the panache to carry off such a preposterous role—but not a clerk at the American Express. Newspaper work was countenanced, except in the most arcane intellectual circles."

In their own eyes the journalists saw their work—together with the effort spent on private writing projects, if only in anticipating them—as firmly setting them apart from the fabled rootless expatriates of the Paris period, tourists on sex-and-alcohol holidays, and the permanent American colony in general. As one of their number, Whit Burnett, would put it, while many Americans "were then cluttering up the Dôme and the Select and contemplating art and their navels and the pearly drink called Pernod," there were others "working, like us, more or less hard, at that journalism which, being Paris-American and founded on boom and amity, has since had no historic duplicate." Eric Sevareid, a latter-day Paris-American newspaperman who went on to a noteworthy career in broadcast journalism, made the same distinction between the café Americans and the working newsmen: "I was impressed at first by their bérets and beards and their careless way of tossing a French phrase into an English conversation . . . but very soon I felt a certain embarrassment on their behalf and the desire to escape them on the café terraces. And besides, I had little time for this. I was working."

WRITERS-IN-WAITING. An eagerness to work for a living as journalists was hardly at the forefront of their minds as young men and women ventured to Paris. Many if not most saw themselves as writers-in-waiting, marking time in journalism only until they made their names as poets, novelists and short-story writers, translators, critics, or nonfiction authors, a type of newsman common at the time and not unknown in the current age of high solemnity about journalism as a profession. Their news work was simply a reasonably interesting way of earning a living, bare bones though it usually was, in the company of colorful fellow workers in the setting of a magnificent city until the literary breakthrough came, if only making the popular magazines back home. They agreed with the view later expressed by Mavis Gallant, the Paris-Canadian short story writer who moved to Paris in the fifties and remained, when she said of her early years on a newspaper that "journalism was a life I liked, but not the one I wanted."

Kenneth Stewart, in the late twenties a copyreader on a Paris-American newspaper and later with *Literary Digest*, the *New York Times*, and *PM*, remembered that nearly every journalist of his era "had the notes for a novel, the synopsis of a play, inspirational clippings, secret jottings of poetry, rejected manuscripts or published works tucked away somewhere in desk drawers or on shelves at home. The flow of words rarely stopped when the office typewriter was covered for the day." Eugene Jolas, who labored on another Paris-American paper before founding the literary journal *transition*, said that during his newsroom days "we were all trying to write novels or poems of our own, and literary discussions interested us more than technical debates about headlines and news-stories." "Like all newspaper men," Jake Barnes acknowledges in material cut from *The Sun Also Rises*, "I have always wanted to write a novel"—and adds, in the newsman's self-deprecating manner, that the novel will likely have "that awful taking-the-pen-in-hand quality that afflicts newspaper men when they start to write on their own book."

For journalists with literary dreams, Paris was an obvious destination. It was the literary capital of the world—where James Joyce was and where *Ulysses* was published, in time where Hemingway, Scott Fitzgerald, Ezra Pound, John Dos Passos, and other literary luminaries had been. In the broadest and grandest sense, Paris was where the twentieth century was, as Gertrude Stein proclaimed. There were, to be sure, a spectrum of other attractions: the available jobs; the favorable postwar exchange rate; the city's physical beauty and ancient charm; the freedom from rigid back-home views of drink and sex; the sizable American colony that gave expatriates the agreeable sense—as Janet Flanner pointed out—that they were living a double life of home and abroad; and the not insignificant fact that nearly everyone else was going there. Nonetheless, in the interwar years the city's overwhelming draw for journalist-writers was its charged air of cultural excitement. In *Americans Abroad*, Peter Neagoe's 1932 anthology of work by writers living and working in Europe, fourteen of the fifty-two contributors identified themselves as journalists, seven as journalists working—now or in the past—in Paris. (Hemingway, prominently represented by "Big Two-Hearted River," included himself in neither group.)

READ COPY? Al Laney, trying to recreate his initial impressions of Paris, circa 1924, imagined a newly arrived journalist lost in literary reverie on the terrace of the Dôme:

> No more than a few hundred yards away from here, James Joyce might be dining that night, and if one sat long enough Gertrude Stein would surely show up. Over there was a chap named Hemingway, said to be working on something revolutionary, and at another table sat Harold Stearns, the young hopeful of the *New Republic*, who had just abandoned America with a fanfare of trumpets for a life of creation in Montparnasse.

Near the young man an older figure reads a Paris-American newspaper: "He was not only reading it, but making marks upon its front page with a pencil that clearly came from a newspaper's copy desk. He was immediately identified as an employee of the paper, probably a copyreader. Here," decides the young hopeful, "was destiny beckoning." He moves to the man's table and talks of himself. He has been living in Paris for months and wants to stay on but is out of money. Might there be an opening on the man's paper? "Read copy?" asks the man. "Always looking for copyreaders. Reporters a dime a dozen. You can just about live on the pay. Lousy sheet, but it's going to get better. Can't miss with all these people coming over. Just going down now. Want to come along and have a try?"

In Paris it was that easy—or made to appear so in Laney's recollection—to land a job on a newspaper, to rub shoulders with the literary great, to work at becoming a writer yourself. In that city, in those days, the pathway from journalism to literature seemed obvious and accessible, as perhaps it never would again with quite the same compelling clarity.

Of course, Paris-American journalists were not equally fired with literary ambition, or equally disciplined in its pursuit. For some, Paris days were simply a lark and a binge, a brief fling with the excess that followed the slaughter of World War I before returning home to dutiful lives in and out of journalism. And there was always within the community of journalists, especially those working as correspondents for major newspapers, magazines, and news services back home, men and women who considered news work their life's work and gave the products of Paris-American journalism whatever professional gloss they possessed. For them, said a managing editor of a Paris-American paper, a newspaper job "was a passport to all the pleasures of Paris, an identification, however ephemeral for most, with a new generation of writers and artists, and a chance to learn the trade of journalism in gay and glamorous circumstances."

It is true as well that, in time, many of the journalist-writers confronted the commonplace but no less dispiriting reality that newspaper offices are the graveyards of literary dreams and fell back on journalism as a career. Harold Stearns—as Laney's passage above suggests, once the great hope of the transatlantic exodus, later a ready illustration of its perils—even wondered if Paris itself served literary hopefuls badly by delaying a hard-eyed appraisal of their talent and dedication:

> . . . in Paris men could delude themselves for a longer time—perhaps the pathos of distance, I don't know—and believe that soon recognition would come. In Paris, also, the American will (at least the American will-to-work) is enfeebled, and many a man, who, had he remained at home and worked hard with what special capacity he had, would have made a modest second-rate success, suffered just a sufficient sea-change to let the will, competent in the home environment to generate some activity, relapse into mere wishing and dreaming. It was a tragedy, when you looked below the surface. . . .

But such hindsight would come later, after the heady promise of the twenties faded into the economic gloom of the thirties and the specter of a second war, sending home many of the literary-minded journalists, leaving the careerists—or, as often the case, simply American journalists married to French wives—to labor on. At the bright beginning when they steamed off to France, the journalists were joyously part and parcel of what in 1924 Ford Madox Ford called the "exodus of the young American writing class to Paris," hoping to find in the brilliant center of artistic activity their own burst of inspiration. "I thought with satisfaction of my trip," Stearns remembered of that moment. "I should finish my book in Paris; I should add to my correspondence jobs; I should make lots of money and send for my mother to come over on a summer vacation."

Even when they managed no such things and came home sober and wiser, Paris-American journalists bore a badge of distinction—if only in the eyes of those still eager to make the transatlantic journey themselves. One of them recalled of the returned exiles that they had "a Paris mark on them . . . that set them apart, perhaps

above. They not only knew foods and wines in the manner of connoisseurs but they were in many subtle ways more civilized, more
elite, more discerning." There could also be a practical benefit, as
two others noted, in that newspaper work abroad "clings to them
like an aureole of Continental glory and often insures them better
jobs in the States than they would have got by staying at home and
plugging away."

THE GRAND DISPLAY WINDOW. Largely from recollections of such
figures as Al Laney, Kenneth Stewart, Paul Scott Mowrer, Harold
Ettlinger, William L. Shirer, Edmond Taylor, Whit Burnett, Eric
Sevareid, and Harold Stearns—recollections, from those who
paused to recollect, in the form of memoirs, letters, articles, and fictional writings—this book takes its shape as a portrait of American
journalists and journalism in Paris (and a few continental locales
just beyond) in the glory years between the wars. Given the brevity
of a period that begins with the armistice of 1919, reaches a high-
water mark in the mid-twenties, loses steam in the depression thirties, and ends conclusively with the German occupation of Paris in
1940, the available material is surprisingly large, if never as large as
one might wish or—when writing about figures who dealt with
words for a living—expect. Surprisingly, too, it has drawn only passing notice in the ample commentary on the expatriate period.

There is, admittedly, an overriding reason for the limited
attention—one that was pointed to by the Canadian writer Morley
Callaghan in a memoir about a summer in Paris in the twenties.
Callaghan, who once worked with Hemingway on the *Toronto Star*,
tries to capture the lure of the expatriate period by calling it "the
one grand display window for international talent, and if you were
at all interested in the way the intellectual cloth of the time was being cut you had to be there, even if you couldn't do more than press
your nose against the window." For Paris-American journalists of
the interwar years, the metaphor is usefully kept in mind.

The major imaginative book of the first part of the period, Hemingway's *The Sun Also Rises*, came from a young Paris newspaperman and has as its narrator a Paris correspondent with literary hopes. The major book of the second part, Henry Miller's *Tropic of Cancer*, came from an older figure who worked briefly as a proofreader on a Paris-American newspaper, contributed feature articles to it, and in the fictionalized autobiography that made his name casts the newspaper work as a major feature of his Paris experience. Hemingway and Miller are, properly, two of the seven major literary and artistic figures singled out in George Wickes's important 1969 book *Americans in Paris*.

Yet with the two giant exceptions, Paris-American journalists of a literary sort contributed only marginally to the lasting literary record of the period. Rather than cutting the intellectual cloth, they were for the most part—as Bill Gorton reminds Jake Barnes—only expatriated newspapermen who pressed their noses to that grand display window that was Paris between the wars. In journalistic terms, their story is a shirttail to the lead story that has captured attention—the story datelined Paris that, for Americans, centers on Hemingway, Miller, Fitzgerald, Ezra Pound, Gertrude Stein, John Dos Passos, e. e. cummings, Glenway Westcott, Kay Boyle, William Carlos Williams, Archibald MacLeish, Hart Crane.

For the dedicated journalists within the expatriate community, the story belongs higher on the page if their careers are viewed as a whole. Several went on to notable achievement in print and broadcast journalism and produced books important in their time and recalled still—among them Vincent Sheean, William L. Shirer, Ned Calmer, John Gunther, Leland Stowe, Eric Sevareid. Paris-American journalism itself, however—the newspapers, magazines, and various news outlets and services that made Paris the center of American journalism in Europe—was on the whole a modest affair that left little mark in the annals of the press. "Amusing Period in History of U.S. Journalism Ended" was the faint praise in a headline—or "amusing" merely a word that fit the headline count—when one of the Paris-American papers folded in the mid-thirties.

Of course the *International Herald Tribune*, with roots well beyond the interwar years, thrives from its suburban Paris headquarters as a newspaper of high quality, and Paris is still considered a plum assignment for correspondents. But such matters belong to another story—of Americans in Paris after the curtain rose again following World War II.

The effort in what follows is not to calculate the importance of Paris-American journalists and journalism in literary or journalistic terms. Rather, it is to add to the familiar portrait of the expatriate period by recounting the experience of Americans like Jake Barnes who turned to journalistic work each day while living at the center of cultural creativity and heightened existence. "From newspaper shops all over America they came," Al Laney says of the great exodus to Paris at the beginning of his account, and goes on to portray a fabled era when "to be on a newspaper published in Paris in times such as these, and to be young and in revolt was all that the heart could wish." This is a story—broadened to include not only newspapers but Paris-American journalistic activity in general—of that time and place.

CHAPTER ONE

The Dear Paris *Herald*

She rarely read french newspapers,
she never read anything in french, and
she always read the Herald.
—GERTRUDE STEIN,
The Autobiography of Alice B. Toklas

PAPER OF CHOICE. During the lush days of the mid-twenties, house ads in the *New York Herald*'s European edition published in Paris routinely trumpeted that the newspaper was "read every day by more Americans than any other newspaper published outside of the U.S.A., English newspapers included." With thinly veiled reference to the paper's Paris-American rivals, the ads also pointed out the *Herald* was "sold on its own merit and is not given away or distributed in hotels as a common handbill."

At the time the *Herald* had two rivals, the independent *Paris Times* and the European edition of the *Chicago Tribune*. (A third English-language paper, the *Continental Daily Mail*, established in 1905 as the Paris edition of the *London Daily Mail*, was heavily filled with material from the parent paper but modestly sought American readers by, among other things, running baseball stories—leading to a *Tribune* staffer's quip that "possibly some Americans did buy the

Mail for this reason since baseball stories written by Britons who believed that baseball was a backwoods form of cricket were worth the price of the paper.") In his sprightly, richly anecdotal history of the paper commonly known as the Paris *Herald*, Al Laney—a skilled, soft-spoken newsman who joined the paper in 1924 and stayed nearly a decade as a dependable deskman, reporter, and night editor—airily dismisses them both: The *Times* "had only a tiny circle of readers, was not distributed widely even in Paris and amounted to nothing as a rival to the *Herald*." The *Tribune* "was a lively paper, now and then brilliant, but it was not read. Even at the height of the boom, with Americans swarming everywhere, it had to be given away to the hotels. It was one of the mysteries of the time that Americans refused to read this paper because, although quite often something of an atrocity, it was by all odds more entertaining than the *Herald* over the years."

The *Times* and *Tribune* were more serious contenders than Laney allows, the *Tribune* especially, and the *Herald*'s management kept a watchful eye on both. Still, as its house ads declared, the *Herald*, with a history of continuous publication since 1887, was clearly the Paris-American newspaper of choice. It would be the sole paper left standing at the end of the interwar period. The *Times*, an underfinanced afternoon upstart begun in 1924, was gone with the coming of the depression in 1929. The *Tribune*, better financed and staffed and a head-to-head competitor with the *Herald* as a morning paper, had a longer run yet was always on the losing end of competition for circulation, advertising, and the general regard of the Paris-American colony. Insofar as readers in the permanent Right Bank enclave had a hometown paper, "the dear Paris *Herald*"—in Janet Flanner's phrase—was it.

For newsmen searching for work in Paris, the *Herald* was ordinarily the paper of first call. Along with longevity, market dominance, and a reputation that reached back to campuses and editorial offices in America, it had the allure of offering the best salaries among Paris-American papers, if not by much. It had as well an appealing location (before a move to new quarters late in 1930) in leased space—though, unlike its competitors, with its own printing presses—close by the overflowing activity, pungent odors, and workingmen's bistros of Les Halles, the city's central marketplace. Finally, it had in its favor the stability of unusually long tenures among its two top editorial figures.

Small, dapper, British-born Eric Hawkins joined the paper in 1915 and stayed for forty-five years, thirty-six of them as managing editor. At last eased out of his position as the top editor of what had evolved into the *International Herald Tribune*, he produced his memoirs in 1963 to accompany the paper's seventy-fifth anniversary. Like Laney's *Paris Herald*, *Hawkins of the Paris Herald* is an invaluable account—if a less detailed and more guarded one—of the paper through the interwar years.

Laurence Hills, as mercurial as Hawkins was even-tempered, was a former head of the Washington bureau of the *New York Sun* who had come to Paris as the paper's chief correspondent at the Versailles peace conference following World War I. Installed as the *Herald*'s director when the paper was purchased in 1920 by the media mogul Frank Munsey, who earlier had bought the *Sun*, Hills was kept in the position when, four years later, Munsey sold the Paris property to the *New York Tribune*. He was still in charge when German troops marched into Paris in 1940 and the *Herald* shut down for the duration of the occupation.

SMALL-TOWN STUFF. The various elements that made for the *Herald*'s dominance failed, however, to coalesce into a distinguished newspaper. At best the *Herald* was a mediocre affair, content to carry on as an insular American paper largely detached from the rich life and creative vitality of interwar Paris. Laney, who knew the paper during the best of those years and thought fondly of it, acknowledged that it "was never very good, often quite bad." Kenneth Stewart, with the paper for two years in the same period, was concise: "The *Herald* was worse than any paper I had ever worked for." Eric Sevareid, who arrived in the late thirties when the *Herald* was the sole Paris-American paper, called it a "rather absurd little house organ for the diminishing American colony, which made ample room for the resort and fashion-house advertisements and as a kind of afterthought squeezed in the news." Janet Flanner's reference to "the dear Paris *Herald*" was not in tribute but an amused mention of how, at the time of Charles Lindbergh's epic Paris landing in 1927, the paper had accidentally joined two nonsense lines in a story about the airman's upbringing: "Downstairs a family had a larger self than most boys. He was never a angora cat."

In 1931 the *Herald* was rudely dissected in H. L. Mencken's *American Mercury* by two former staff members, Whit Burnett and Martha Foley, as a cobbled-together paper with a front page of news followed by several more of rewrite and reprint. The news came from skeletonized cables sent from New York and expanded in the Paris office to full-blown stories; rewrite was drawn from French papers and reprint clipped from London and New York papers mailed to Paris and appearing well after original publication. Local coverage, such as it was, was limited to boat trains, hotels, the diplomatic run, and the cozy doings of the Paris-American colony.

Overall, said Burnett and Foley, the *Herald* was dull, cautious, impersonal, and wholly removed from the sophisticated city in which it appeared. "We have got to take the attitude," Laurence Hills was quoted as saying, "that this is a town of about 20,000 people, kind of like a town in Ohio or New York. It's a small town. Give them small-town stuff." In its editorial voice the paper did just that, pursuing no causes and standing "on every fence that was ever erected." Books, music, and art were largely ignored. The paper's soul, concluded Burnett and Foley, was essentially "up-State New York."

A lone feature that came in for the pair's passing praise was the Mailbag, the *Herald*'s occasionally lively letters-to-the-editor column. Yet here as well the paper often gave off a frivolous, period-piece air that recalled the epistolary style of the Old Philadelphia

Lady and the long shadow of the imperious publisher who gave her ongoing life.

THE COMMODORE OF PARIS. Four years after inheriting the *New York Herald* from his father, James Gordon Bennett, Jr., removed himself to Paris in the wake of a scandal that left him at odds with polite society. During a New Year's Eve party in the Manhattan home of his fiancée's family, he had drunkenly urinated before mixed company in either the fireplace or the grand piano—accounts differ—and was subsequently horsewhipped in front of the Union Club by the young woman's brother. In Paris, where he had grown up, he lived in expatriate grandeur for the rest of his days while keeping tight control via cable of his New York paper. Around the clock someone was kept on hand in the home office to receive his frequent instructions.

Various reasons are advanced for why, on October 4, 1887, the Commodore—so called after the yachting enthusiast was elected as a young man to the rank by the New York Yacht Club—launched a Paris edition of the *Herald*. Thanks to competition, Atlantic cable rates had come down, and Paris was a central location for transmitting international news stories back to New York. At the same time improvements in sea and rail travel made European tours more appealing for well-heeled Americans who, while away, presumably wished to keep up with events back home. It may have been, as some speculated, that, living in Paris himself, Bennett simply wanted to keep busy with a paper near at hand.

He had tried and failed to buy *Galignani's Messenger*, a lingering Paris-American institution since 1814, but had more luck with a second English-language paper, the *Morning News*, which had begun appearing in 1874 in both English and French editions. The owner, William Alonzo Hopkins of Brattleboro, Vermont, sold Bennett the English edition while retaining the French edition under the name *Le Matin*, in time to become one of the country's leading newspapers.

For his renamed paper Bennett quickly gathered a mainly British staff—favoring them since they were easily found and, so it was said, travel home was short when they were fired. Before the *Herald*'s inaugural issue the staff was invited to the owner's quarters for a luncheon and a speech that would take on legendary status. "I want you fellows," said the Commodore,

> to remember that I am the only reader of this paper. I am the only one to be pleased. If I want it to be turned upside down, it must be turned upside down. I consider a dead dog in the Rue du Louvre more interesting than a devastating flood in China. I want one feature article a day. If I say the feature is to be Black Beetles, Black Beetles it's going to be.

The four-page daily was unquestionably Bennett's. In it he indulged whims and pet convictions, including printing part of the paper in French, apparently under the peculiar belief that French and English speakers liked reading the news both ways. One of his more celebrated whims involved a deadpan letter to the editor that appeared in the paper's Mailbag column on Christmas Day, 1899:

> I am anxious to find out the way to figure the temperature from Centigrade to Fahrenheit and vice-versa. In other words, I want to know, whenever I see the temperature designated on Centigrade thermometer, how to find out what it would be on Fahrenheit's thermometer.
>
> "Old Philadelphia Lady"
> Paris, December 24, 1899

When the letter appeared a second time, possibly due to a printer's error, the Commodore—a weather connoisseur who likely had written it himself—ordered it run every day, which it was for the next two decades. The repetition both maddened and delighted readers, especially when someone, happening upon the letter for the first time, tried to provide a serious answer.

ITS FINEST HOUR. Bennett's paper was not entirely a rich man's toy. He poured in money for, on the printing side, high-quality paper and ink supplies and the introduction of Linotype machines, and, on the editorial side, bringing to European journalism such innovations as heavy use of cable material, color engravings and halftone news photos, special supplements, and comic pages. Vigorously promoted by Bennett with inventive schemes, the paper was soon a success with tourists and the international set and grew steadily in circulation and advertising. In quality it was a faint shadow of the strong parent paper in New York.

But with the new century the *New York Herald* had slid into serious decline, due in part to money siphoned off by the Paris edition. By the start of World War I circulation had plunged dramatically from a half-million to sixty thousand. In contrast the Paris *Herald* was entering its finest hour. After German troops advanced on Paris and the French government and several French papers fled to Bordeaux, Bennett kept the *Herald* in the city and, in a show of solidarity with the nation, paid full salaries to the wives of his French printers who joined the military. With much of his British staff returned to England, he came to the office each day and, age seventy-four, worked side by side with a skeleton crew to put out a paper that eventually was reduced to a single sheet, English on the front and French on the back, yet an invaluable source of war information.

With American entry into the war in 1917, a significant competitor emerged in the Paris edition of the *Chicago Tribune*. But with the huge influx of English-speaking readers, eventually including some two million troops of the American Expeditionary Forces, together with the advertising that was quick to follow, there was more than enough room for two Paris-American papers. The military's *Stars and Stripes* was also in the mix, an eight-page weekly that appeared for seventy-one weeks in 1918 and 1919 and tried to distinguish itself from the *Herald* and the *Tribune*. "They don't give us what we want," complained a military press officer;

"we don't want hotel arrivals in Paris and society news." Thanks to a flood of advertising and a circulation that eventually reached over a half-million, the *Stars and Stripes* ended the war a hefty $700,000 in the black.

By 1918 the *Herald*'s circulation had shot up to an astonishing 350,000—requiring the printing facilities of several different plants around Paris—and the paper, apparently for the first time, was profitable. Bennett, however, did not live to savor his triumph fully nor see the war's end. On May 15, 1918, the *Herald* announced his death with a banner headline in a black-bordered issue. Never before had his name appeared in the paper he owned.

Two years later Bennett's executors sold his properties—the *New York Herald*, the Paris *Herald*, and the *New York Evening Telegram*—to Frank Munsey for $4 million, a figure effectively reduced when it was discovered that a million dollars of profit had accumulated in the Paris *Herald*'s bank account. But with the troops gone and the palmy wartime days over, the *Herald*'s circulation rapidly fell back to around ten thousand, and the paper knew lean times.

Just as rapidly, the situation swung around again. The postwar boom in America began the flow of expatriates and tourists to Europe, circulation and advertising picked up, and the *Herald*'s pages expanded from wartime paper restrictions. In 1924 ownership changed as well when Munsey sold the *New York Herald* and the Paris edition to the *New York Tribune*'s Reid family (Elisabeth Mills Reid and her son and daughter-in-law, Ogden and Helen Reid) for $5 million. In New York the sale created the estimable *Herald Tribune*. In Paris it ushered in what *Herald* staffers would look back upon as a rich period of economic success and editorial improvement.

STAFF STALWARTS. Before the war the paper had acquired two central figures of its postwar editorial staff. Eric Hawkins was eking out a living in Paris writing for British papers—among them Manchester's *Sunday Chronicle*, where he conducted a column called "Gossip of the Boulevards"—when the sinking of the *Lusitania* in 1915 brought the sudden need for more manpower on the *Herald*'s copy desk. Hawkins was immediately hired and set to work compiling a casualty list. Nearly a decade later, in 1924, he began his long run as the paper's managing editor.

While Hawkins gave the *Herald* a steady editorial hand, May Birkhead gave it readers. A dressmaking business in Missouri provided the twenty-six-year-old seamstress with funds for a transatlantic crossing in 1912 aboard the *Carpathia*. When the *Titanic* went down, the *Carpathia* was one of the ships that steamed to the rescue. *Herald* editors in New York scanned the passenger list, and one remembered that a May Birkhead had been featured in an earlier *Herald* story about small-town success.

Bennett himself radioed a message, beseeching the young woman for details of the sinking and the rescue. Birkhead had no newspaper experience but went to work interviewing survivors and having sketches made, sending what she could to the *Herald* by wireless. When the *Carpathia* returned to New York she had more material for the paper. Later, in Paris after her journey resumed, Bennett called her to his office, lauded her journalistic enterprise, and hired her as the Paris *Herald*'s society correspondent.

From the beginning the Commodore had insisted that names make news, especially those of the socially prominent. One of the *Herald*'s avidly read columns, "American Register," simply ran lists of those who had written their names in register books in the paper's business and advertising office on the Avenue de l'Opéra. (In *The Sun Also Rises*, Jake Barnes and a French girl, Georgette, take a taxi up the avenue and pass "the New York *Herald* bureau with the window full of clocks." When the girl asks what the clocks are for, Jake explains, "They show the hour all over America." "Don't kid me," Georgette says.) A second column, "Personal Intelligence," followed the trail of the international set. Conducted by Birkhead, working exclusively under Bennett and seldom seen in the *Herald* newsroom, the column—the name changed, none too accurately, to

"News of Americans in Europe"—became a circulation-building mix of information and gossip about European aristocrats and social climbers from across the Atlantic.

With America in the war Birkhead branched out, becoming an accredited correspondent who used a friendship with General Pershing for stories issuing from the high command. With the war's end she branched out again, adding news of the Paris fashion industry to her social reporting, with her work becoming a main ingredient of the *Herald*'s postwar success. The paper was probably bought more in hope of seeing one's name in her columns, Al Laney believed, than for any other reason—and frequently bought in bulk, allowing friends back home the hopefully awed delight of viewing the name in the company of other notables.

Birkhead's *Herald* days ended just as oddly as they had begun. During a leave of absence granted by the paper for a voyage back to America, she inexplicably wired stories about Queen Marie of Romania, aboard the same ship, to the *New York Times*, then followed up with reporting for the *Times* on the Queen's American tour as well as her return to Europe. Understandably angered, the *Herald* management left it to Eric Hawkins to inform Birkhead that her twelve-year run with the Paris paper was over.

RUE DU LOUVRE. The prewar staff Hawkins and Birkhead joined, made up mostly of Britons and the paper still printing some material in French, was little changed in the immediate postwar period. The paper continued to be put out from drafty editorial space in the building at 38 Rue du Louvre, cramped on a mezzanine above the composing and mailing rooms and with a wall of towering windows overlooking the abundance of Les Halles. Dominating the space was a massive table, built to Bennett's specifications, where a dozen deskmen could sit around the rim beneath dangling electric bulbs. In the U-shaped opening or slot in the center of the table and facing the windows, the slot man, night editor, or managing editor presided, his title changing with the years. A small room off to the side housed tickers of the paper's leased wires from London and New York that spun out the cryptic tapes expanded by the deskmen.

Most of the staff worked nights, arriving in late afternoon, going out for a leisurely dinner, and finishing between midnight and 2 a.m. A few men came in during the day, but until the mid-twenties there was little local reporting, or legwork, beyond covering arrivals on boat trains and at hotels together with the hometown events of the American colony. Joseph Freeman, who joined the paper in 1920 fresh from Columbia University and with ambition split between journalism and poetry, was one of the night men, working at the copy desk and writing by hand rather than typewriter. After hours he and friends, all *Herald* or *Tribune* staffers, led a "collective bohemian life. We finished work at two a.m., talked in cafés until dawn, slept till ten, breakfasted at the Rotonde, and spent afternoons seeing the sights, reading, writing, and above all talking talking talking—art, sex, psychoanalysis, the social revolution."

All in all, remarked Al Laney, it was "a placid sort of life" for the staff, with wages low but demands few other than "the rather pleasant though dull routine of unskinning and blowing up the few hundred words coming by cable each night." Meanwhile, he added, the paper limped along, "dull, stodgy, badly edited and offensive to the eye. It appeared to be more English than American and was."

THE GREAT EXILE. During his four-year reign as owner, Frank Munsey left the *Herald* largely in the hands of the director he had installed, Laurence Hills, with a central command to keep an eye on expenses. Hills did with a vengeance, with the result that staff changes were few and far between. Among the rare new hires, though, was a Harvard man and a former editor at the *New Republic* and the *Dial*, soon to be hailed—among other epithets—as the Great Exile of the expatriate period.

Harold Stearns's influential essay collection, *America and the Young Intellectual*, and his equally influential edited anthology, *Civilization in the United States*, were about to be published when in 1921 he heeded their call for abandoning a stifling America and boarded a Cunard liner for Europe. From Britain he moved on to Paris in the company of Sinclair Lewis, whose novel *Main Street* had just appeared to wide acclaim. "Whenever and wherever we could lay hands on a brandy or a whiskey, we did so," Stearns said of their Prohibition-free journey.

When an exhausted Lewis left the city after five days, Stearns retreated from a pricey Right Bank hotel to cheap lodgings in Rue Delambre in Montparnasse and settled into an agreeable life among, as he noted, mostly American "students, newspaper men, artists, or plain serious drinkers." Just before Christmas, his money gone, a providential letter came from the *Herald* saying a job was waiting for him after the holidays. Stearns assumed that a friend living in Paris, the American sculptor Jo Davidson, had put in a good word for him with Laurence Hills.

On the paper Stearns functioned as a reporter and then a deskman, combining the work with a weekly column for the *Baltimore Sun*, a regular "Our Paris Letter" for the glossy society magazine *Town & Country* (about which more in Chapter Six), and European literary scouting for the New York publisher Boni & Liveright. His principal job, desk work on the *Herald*, he found both satisfying and drearily routine. It meant the

> perpetual "re-write" of local stories, the obituaries of famous
> Americans . . . the petty personals and society gossip, the
> figuring out of the standings of the major baseball teams . . .
> the eternal "playing up" of prohibition farces and tragedies
> . . . trying to put some sense into the interviews with
> American big-wigs who came to Paris . . . the so-called book
> and play reviews which for the most part were mere publicity
> "puffs," and, finally, the local side of big "interpretative"

stories, which the highly paid New York correspondent of the paper in Paris brought to the office for cabling.

To keep his sanity, Stearns decided the demands of the job required he give himself a vacation every six months. But as his second Christmas in Paris neared, he took a longer departure, walking away for good. It was after a return to France following a brief trip to America that his long down-and-out Paris period began—and when a lifeline of sorts appeared in the form of a job as the Paris *Tribune*'s turf columnist.

In this unlikely position Stearns became notable, as he himself noted, for actually going to the Paris tracks, weather notwithstanding, while the *Herald*'s resident tout ventured out only on pleasant days, otherwise staying in town and studying the racing papers. His competitor, Stearns sniffed, had a high percentage of winners since he recommended only the consensus favorites. It was the safe way of making race selections since, as he wrote, "you will never make a fool of yourself—and hence seldom, either, will you get, or give, a thrill. It is suspiciously like life itself in that respect."

DON'T CHANGE ANYTHING. Another new hire stayed far longer and built a stronger, if stranger, reputation as a columnist of the sporting life. In 1921 William H. "Sparrow" Robertson, a tiny, wiry figure of sixty-four or thereabouts, appeared at the *Herald* with little more by way of experience than a few sports pieces in the *New York Sun*. Installed by Hills as sports editor, the paper's first staffer with the title, it was soon apparent that Sparrow Robertson had little knowledge of any sports beyond boxing and track. All in all, he was—in Eric Hawkins's choice phrase—a "fulsome flop." But Hills, through intuition or stubbornness, stuck with him, and Sparrow's time in the limelight came when he switched to a mixture of sport and gossip gleaned while meeting "old pals" on jaunty and seemingly unquenchable tours of "thirst emporiums," the concoction duly recorded in off-key language and enshrined in a daily column, "Sporting Gossip—by Sparrow Robertson." The accompanying photo presented a solemn Sparrow in a seldom-removed fedora.

There were well-intentioned attempts to convert Sparrow's copy into ordinary English until someone on the paper realized its zany charm was in its distortions and ordered that it be printed exactly as written. In practice what this amounted to was that *Herald* copy editors, faced with the column, were given a confounding instruction: "Don't change anything. Just make it readable." The happy result, according to a newsman on the rival *Tribune*, was that many *Herald* readers turned to the column first "to savor the mayhem it inflicted on the English language." Another *Tribuner* thought the mayhem was located in a prose style that resembled that of an eight-year-old child, and offered a recreation he insisted was not a caricature: "Last night P.M. met my old pal Joe Squgg. He was a famous foot runner. In Olympics 1924 did the 500 in under 12 minutes. Joe's in business now. So he's, you know, 'loaded.' He took me to vespers at Jeff Dickson's thirst emporium. With other dear old pals we went up the hill to Jacks."

Among the column's devoted readers was Eugene O'Neill, living in a French village while working on *Mourning Becomes Electra*, who said of Sparrow, "Why, he's the greatest writer in the world!" Ezra Pound's praise was confined to Sparrow's unique place on the *Herald*. "I haven't bought the Herald," he raged in a letter dashed off with Poundian spelling in 1935. "I will not by a rag that prints Lippmann/ it iks a nuissance not to have an american paper printed in Europe/ but one CAN, and more people ARE getting London papers. . . . At any rate, Sparrow is all they've got. . . and the paper stinks." Other readers pleaded with Hawkins, as managing editor, to rid the paper of Sparrow and his column—or at least, in the words of one, "Why don't someone in your outfit get this bird Sparrow lined up on his grammar?" All such complaints Sparrow blithely ignored. Hawkins recalled seeing him genuinely angry only when the composing room mistakenly placed on his sporting column the title of Walter Lippmann's political column, "Today and Tomorrow." "Who the hell's this guy Lippmann?" an outraged Sparrow demanded. "Where'd they get that *stuff*?"

BOOJ. Sparrow Robertson's opposite number was Vincent J. Bugeja. A learned, multilingual, British-educated Maltese, Bugeja—known among staffers as Booj—had studied to be a Jesuit priest but left, according to one account, rather than sign a statement saying the theory of evolution was false. He had no newspaper experience when he walked into the *Herald* in 1920 and asked for a job. "My dear fellow," he replied when Hawkins wondered how he expected to do the work, "I've *read* your newspaper."

Four times Hawkins turned him down before Bugeja wrangled an interview with the managing editor of the time, Gaston Archambault, who, equally skeptical, asked him to produce a writing sample. Bugeja showed him an article, printed in a Jesuit magazine, on non-Euclidian geometry. "It's not exactly the kind of thing we want," Archambault told him. "But I'll take a chance."

Among the many hats Bugeja wore during his *Herald* career, which lasted until the German occupation and resumed thereafter, was chief editorial writer. He produced as well news stories on a variety of heavyweight subjects, including science under the name B. J. Vincent. He also held the staff's admiration for—as Laney put it—his "political, photographic and amatory avocations on the side." Among recollected antics in the latter area was crashing the students annual Paris Quatz' Arts Ball while wearing only a pair of Bikini-style drawers—and getting thrown out for overdressing. Another was joining in an impromptu dance with Josephine Baker during the entertainer's seductive performance at an annual Anglo-American Press Association gala.

AMERICANIZATION. The Reids' purchase of the *Herald* in 1924 co-incided with the high-tide period of the American invasion of Paris, bringing healthy increases in advertising and circulation. Hills, with the title of editor and general manager, still was charged with keeping a tight hold on the purse strings but otherwise given a free hand with the once-again profitable paper. He was difficult to work under—temperamental, erratic, overly fretful about the competing papers—but the changes he oversaw were welcome. His mark on the paper, some staffers believed, now nearly matched that of the founder.

As Paris became more American, the *Herald* followed suit. While the paper was still in Munsey's hands, Hills had attempted to Americanize it in appearance and staff; standing in his way had been a Frenchman, Gaston Archambault, a Bennett holdover and the paper's strong-willed managing editor. When the adaptable Eric Hawkins replaced Archambault in 1924, the barrier was removed; able to work with Hills, they together set out to change the paper. The size was expanded to a regular eight pages that would soon become twelve to sixteen with additional rotogravure sections; syndicated features were added from the *New York Herald Tribune*; cable coverage was improved; and the paper was generally given a more American-style appearance.

The most important development was the addition of new staff members—"the beginning," thought Hawkins, "of a staff that made the Paris *Herald* an incubator for the most colorful, competent and sometimes crazy newspapermen that ever populated a city room." A large, lumbering, overwhelmingly earnest Oregonian, Ralph Waldo Barnes, brought the paper all three qualities.

When he joined the Paris staff in 1926, however, the first impression of Barnes was that he was a near-disaster as a newsman. He had graduated from Willamette University and had a master's degree in economics from Harvard, but his newspaper experience was nothing more than a short stint as a reporter on the *Brooklyn Daily Eagle* and an even shorter one as a deskman on the *New York Evening*

World. On *World* stationery Barnes had written Laurence Hills asking for a job on the *Herald*, and Hills, impressed by the connection with the New York paper, told him there might be something for him in Paris. Barnes then went to the *Herald Tribune*'s New York office for a job, reasoning that if he was going to work for the Paris paper he first needed a sense of the home paper. He worked just long enough to earn the transatlantic fare for himself and his wife.

Barnes hardly seemed cut out for newspaper work, let alone on a casual Paris-American paper. He was a labored writer, passionate and idealistic, given to expressions no more wicked than "Golly Moses!", inclined to pursue endless background research no matter how minor a story. Invariably overloaded with books and magazines he was studying, he brushed material from desks as he made awkward passage through the newsroom, leading to the nickname the "Ambulating Kiosk." In the composing room the name hung on him for his last-minute additions to stories was "Insert Barnes."

Barnes usually was kept to a seat at the copy desk. His first reporting assignment, an effort that ended in dogged Barnesian fashion, was coverage in August 1926 of Gertrude Ederle's swim across the English Channel. In a tugboat with other reporters, he trailed her crossing, grimly seasick. After Ederle landed, the tugboat captain refused to dock due to darkness, so Barnes leaped in water that turned out to be over his head. He sloshed his way ashore and in darkness searched fruitlessly for a farmhouse telephone to file his story, finally locating an old man with a motorboat willing to take him on another journey through seasickness to an available telephone.

LINDBERGH. Competent though his Ederle story was, Ralph Barnes, still considered a novice at reporting, was held in the office on the frantic night of Charles Lindbergh's Paris landing on May 21, 1927. Eric Hawkins assigned the paper's top reporter, Jack Pickering, to the story, with other reporters assisting him. In the mob scene at Le Bourget field that followed the arrival, Pickering reached the plane but Lindbergh immediately vanished into the exuberant mass of humanity before he could speak with him. Unable to reach a phone, Pickering worked his way back to the office through snarled traffic.

It was past midnight when he appeared, clothes torn and his mood disconsolate. "Christ, what a story!" he moaned to Hawkins. "I practically had my hands on him. Then, presto! He's gone. First guy to fly it, and not a single word from him. We're high and dry." The managing editor finally settled him down, positioned him at a typewriter, and Pickering banged out a story that would lead the morning paper.

The arrival story was one thing, interviewing the intrepid flyer remained another. The *New York Times* had purchased exclusive rights to Lindbergh's story, yet its men, like Pickering, had lost track of him in the airport melee. As disclosed later, French military pilots had rescued Lindbergh from the plane—aided, as Lindbergh revealed, by tugging his helmet on an American correspondent and crying "Here is Lindbergh," making the hapless figure the object of the mob's attention—and had seen him off on a car to the American embassy, where officials denied his presence to allow him time to sleep.

Enter Ralph Barnes. As the night's deadline loomed, the *Herald* about to give up on an interview, Barnes held out for more effort and requested taxi money for one last try. The editor on duty, Al Laney, too weary to resist, handed over a hundred francs. Barnes tried the American embassy, as had other reporters, but refused to believe the denials handed out. When he returned to the office for more money, it was decided to keep an emergency staff in the composing room until he came back a second time.

On his way to the embassy Barnes stopped at the Hôtel Continental and told reporters still gathered there he was going to demand permission to see Lindbergh. There was laughter at his presumption, but a delegation piled into taxis to accompany him.

The ambassador, Myron T. Herrick, met the reporters and admitted that Lindbergh was in the embassy but insisted he could not be disturbed until morning. At this point Lindbergh sent down word he was awake. Barnes led the stampede of a dozen or so reporters up the stairs to find the flyer in bathrobe and slippers and—with the consent of Carlisle MacDonald, the *New York Times* reporter present, who had little choice to do otherwise given the readied pencils around him—willing to answer a few questions.

"Write!" the news editor shouted when Barnes returned to the office with the story.

"I don't know what to say," Barnes pleaded. "Give me a chance to organize my notes. I can't think."

"Don't think. Write. Write what he said. Never mind the notes. Just knock it out like he said it. Hurry up. Get it on the paper."

Barnes did, but painfully, the sheets snatched from his typewriter paragraph by paragraph, the originals sent to the composing room and carbon copies, marked "Urgent *Tribune* New York," dashed by relays of cyclists to the cable office for transmission. Never before had Barnes written in rapid takes, unable to look back at what came before, half the story in type in the composing room and sent by cable to New York before he finished the final paragraph. Nonetheless, his six-hundred-word story, almost entirely a string of quotes from Lindbergh, was straightforward and compelling. It made the front page of the late edition of the *New York Herald Tribune*, though—as customary—under the byline of the paper's Paris bureau chief, Wilbur Forrest. In the Paris *Herald* the interview was prominently played next to the Lindbergh banner story but, in keeping with the paper's usual practice of the time, carried no byline.

Also kept closeted in an office down a corridor from the *Herald* newsroom on the night of the landing was Leland Stowe, Wilbur Forrest's young assistant in the *Herald Tribune*'s Paris bureau. After finishing Wesleyan University in 1921, the short, energetic Stowe had gone into newspaper work in Massachusetts as training for an intended career as a novelist, then shifted his interest to reporting for the *New York Herald* and was among the handful of staffers kept with the paper when it merged with the *Tribune*. In 1926 he won a place in Paris working under Forrest.

For the Lindbergh landing Forrest—an experienced hand who had come to France a decade earlier as manager of the United Press Paris office and later replaced Heywood Broun as the *New York Tribune*'s lone correspondent in the field during World War I—had cannily arranged with the Commercial Cable Company to hide a man on the second floor of a building overlooking the field, who was linked to the company's office by a private telephone line. A pre-written bulletin Forrest gave the company simply said Lindbergh had arrived safely, with the precise time left blank.

As the silver monoplane circled the floodlit field and came in for a landing, Forrest, viewing the scene himself from the second-floor vantage point, shouted to the cable man to release the bulletin with a time of arrival inserted. The result was the *Herald Tribune* in New York learned the transatlantic flight had succeeded before Lindbergh shut down the plane's engine—and before Forrest's competitors could locate telephones in mob-scene aftermath.

Back in the Rue de Louvre office, the *Herald Tribune* bureau shared with the Paris *Herald* the bits and pieces of information coming in, and Stowe cranked out a four-thousand-word story for transmission. When Forrest finally made it back to the office, he added a new lead and fresh details and sent the story to New York with his byline. In a memoir Forrest produced seven years later, *Behind the Front Page*, Stowe's work on the Lindbergh story received no mention. Barnes's interview with Lindbergh was reprinted in full, but Barnes was not named and the impression left that Forrest was the one who had written it.

By the time his memoir appeared, Forrest was working in the New York home office of the *Herald Tribune*, and Barnes and Stowe both had moved on to prominent careers as European correspondents. Barnes had become the first staff member of the Paris *Herald* promoted to the *Herald Tribune*'s foreign staff while Stowe had replaced Forrest as the Paris bureau chief and had named Barnes as his assistant.

BYRD VANISHES. A second major story of 1927 closely followed Lindbergh's arrival. Commander Richard E. Byrd's *America*, a multi-engine plane carrying Byrd and a crew of three, was scheduled to land at Le Bourget on the night of June 30, with Jack Pickering again the reporter on the spot for the *Herald*. Radio messages indicated Byrd had reached France and possibly flown over Paris, but there was no indication on the ground where, or if, he had landed.

When Pickering returned to the office empty-handed, the *Herald* went to press with a story under a banner headline reading BYRD VANISHED IN STORM SOMEWHERE NEAR PARIS. Early in the morning a report came in that Byrd had set the plane down on a beach in Normandy. Maps were produced to pinpoint the spot, and *Herald* men, Pickering with them, raced off on a stormy airplane flight from Le Bourget to Caen.

From Caen a taxi took the reporters to the beach area and a sighting of *America*, partly submerged by the tide. In the nearby home of a village mayor they found Byrd and the crew, freshly shaved and having breakfast. Like Lindbergh, Byrd had given exclusive rights to his story to the *New York Times*, but for the next two hours he spoke freely with the reporters—and entrusted Pickering with carrying his official military log of the flight to the naval attaché at the American embassy in Paris. The following morning the *Herald* carried a richly detailed account of Byrd's story together with his official report under his byline. When the Paris bureau of the *Times* complained, the home office of the *Herald Tribune* cabled Eric Hawkins a crisp reply: "Let the heathen rage."

TRAGEDY IN YAP. Don Donaldson joined the *Herald* the year before Ralph Barnes, and as an experienced deskman was put in charge of the copy desk. Later, presiding as well over evening makeup, he gave the paper a brighter, more contemporary look. Makeup—with an edition for the night trains to European cities and then a front page remade for Paris distribution—was considered enjoyable duty, and Donaldson and other nightside staffers would toy with front-page designs before having stories in hand to fill the arrangement.

Late one night, still without a story to go into the lead space under a three-column headline, Vincent Bugeja took a brief item from the French news agency Havas about a typhoon striking near the tiny Pacific island of Yap and raised it to high drama. TIDAL WAVE SWEEPS YAP; THOUSANDS FEARED LOST, the headline declared. The story ran a half-column and was followed by another half-column shirttail of background by Bugeja that learnedly began: "Practically unknown to anybody but the most specialized students of geography, the Island of Yap. . . ."

As it happened, the storm's devastation was more unknown than the island: no other paper in the world reported it. Although the following day the Paris *Tribune* delighted in pointing out that the storm was modest and had hardly touched Yap, the *Herald* remained unruffled. "The *Herald* just left Yap at the bottom of the Pacific," said Al Laney. "The boys did not seem to be much interested in a second-day angle to the story."

BURNETT AND FOLEY. Two other late-twenties newcomers, Whit Burnett and Martha Foley, brought the *Herald* seasoned skills. After Burnett, a Utah native who had published a pair of novelettes in *Smart Set*, was let go in 1927 by the *New York Times*, he went to Europe with a plan to write fiction full time, with Foley, his partner (later, in Vienna, she became his wife) and an equally capable newspaper hand from Boston who had worked on papers in San Francisco and Los Angeles and was now with the *New York Mirror*, joining him as soon as possible. When she did, with a leave of absence from the *Mirror*, she discovered Burnett had finished some stories he was unable to sell, and his money was gone. Foley took a letter of introduction to Jay Allen, a Paris correspondent of the *Chicago Tribune*, who suggested she try for a job at the *Herald*. They could give her only two weeks' work on a travel supplement, and with that finished she and Burnett went back to temporary jobs in America, saving for a Paris return.

With a nest egg of $500—enough, Foley calculated, to live comfortably in Paris for five months—she crossed the Atlantic on her own. Again she applied at the *Herald* and was taken on, as she put it, as a maid-of-all-tasks that included expanding cables, rewriting French papers, and local reporting, where she made a point of interviewing publishers who came to town in hopes they would publish her work in the future. She was also a quick and efficient copy editor—the "only girl in the history of the Paris *Herald*," said Al Laney, "who could sit down at a desk and hold up her end at reading copy." Women were rare at copy desks everywhere, as Foley well knew. "Sitting around the big table called a 'desk,'" she said of her time on American papers, "with mugs of coffee or spiked prohibition 'near beer,' making ribald comments as they edited the day's news, male copyreaders enjoyed a grand, uninhibited stag party."

Whit Burnett joined the *Herald* after Foley cabled him in New York about an opening. He rose rapidly from copy reader to day editor, but what Foley considered a sarcastic manner of speaking when handing out reporting assignments ("Much of his talk that antagonized people would not have seemed harsh if it had been softened with a smile") caused the staff to rebel, and Burnett was transferred to feature writing.

For the managing editor, Hawkins, Burnett was an able newsman but "a born rebel who saw most things with a jaundiced eye." No doubt Hawkins had in mind the Burnett-Foley *American*

Mercury article about the *Herald*, where he was lightly mocked as a "pleasant Britisher . . . somewhat baffled by the spectacle of American journalists"—and an example given of Hawkins changing in a column the Americanism "So's your old man!" to "Your father is also." Not so, Hawkins would maintain: the change was made by Don Donaldson on the copy desk as a bit of fun with one of the paper's columnists.

Burnett and Foley had troubled management in another way when they spearheaded a move to raise salaries on the paper—"the first editorial strike in history on an American newspaper," as Foley characterized it. Foley asked everyone on the staff for a list of ordinary day-to-day expenses, averaged the figures, and Laurence Hills was presented with a request for cost-of-living increases. The general manager's response was to search out American haunts in Paris for new employees. He also called Foley to his office and offered her a substantial raise. "What about the others?" she asked. "What do you care about them?" Hills replied. A strike deadline was set but was not necessary when the paper's printers voted not to cross a picket line. "Thanks to those wonderful printers," Foley recalled, "the first American newspaper editorial strike was won. The *Herald* could get plenty of barflies to scab, but where would they find French printers who knew English?"

Whether what took place amounted to a strike is questionable. In Al Laney's view, a strike was never a possibility given the number of available men and women in Paris eager to work on the *Herald*; when the petition was submitted, management simply made some salary adjustments. Laney makes no mention of a role by the French printers. In their *American Mercury* article, Burnett and Foley referred only to a "concerted demand" by the staff: "The *Herald* pays its people better than the other papers in Paris, although its present wages were not altogether a voluntary thing but resulted from something of a concerted demand on the part of the only staff which had remained put for more than four or five months."

THE CULTURE BEAT. After arriving in Paris on her own, Martha Foley had gone to Sylvia Beach's celebrated bookstore, Shakespeare and Company, to replace a copy of *Ulysses* she had given away and to buy the inaugural issue of *transition* with James Joyce's "Work in Progress." Later she became close to the journal's founder and his wife, Eugene and Maria Jolas, and did clerical work for *transition* before heading to her evening chores on the *Herald*. Through the Jolases she met Joyce, the connection limited to sitting with him among friends on a café terrace and hearing him remark about his "Work in Progress," on its way to becoming *Finnegans Wake*, that he planned "a mighty synthesis."

Al Laney believed other *Herald* staffers had more important ties to Joyce. Due to his failing eyesight, Sylvia Beach, the original publisher of *Ulysses*, typed much of his correspondence, and when overly busy farmed out work to *Herald* staffers whom she trusted to respect his privacy. The typists could have cashed in with articles for American magazines about Joyce's private life, though Laney notes that none did. Nor did they speak much about their work, and neither does he. Laney writes knowingly about Joyce in his history of the *Herald* ("Although he had a ready wit and talked volubly on occasion, neither he nor those in his presence, aside from members of his family, ever seemed quite at ease") but says nothing about typing for him himself.

Ezra Pound was a *Herald* link to literary Paris of a different sort. The poet directed a steady stream of contributions to the paper's Mailbag column, most—according to Martha Foley, who for a time was charged with censoring them—"laden with maledictions, obscene and scatological, upon persons or events reported in the paper, as well as upon the paper itself." When she came upon something that could be cleaned up, it appeared in the paper, often under such Poundian pseudonyms as E. Weight or Ezra Sterling. Most submissions went to the wastebasket. Pound remained, nonetheless, a thorn in the *Herald*'s side. In the 1931 inaugural issue of Samuel Putnam's

New Review, of which the poet was the associate editor, he lambasted the paper as a "daily insult . . . to every yankee in Europe." Among its litany of faults was that it was run by "englishmen all over eighty" and had no license to "prostitute the name of Tammany's fair city" on its masthead. There simply was no saving the paper: "Apart from its telegraphic service, the Herald ouight to go die."

On one occasion Foley's deskwork played a role in the rescue of another American poet. In a French newspaper she ran across a story about an Englishman arrested after a brawl with police outside the Café Sélect. The name was garbled and did not seem properly English. She passed the clipping to the day editor, and the reporter told to investigate, Eugene Rosetti, learned the culprit was Hart Crane.

Foley immediately phoned Rosetti and urged him to impress upon the police that Crane was a major American poet: "Tell them we love his poems so much that if they don't let him out of prison this minute not another single American tourist will ever come to France again!" The threat likely had little if any effect since Crane was released only after several days in La Santé prison, an appearance before a judge, a fine, and a promise to mend his drinking ways. In a *Herald* news story about the release, Whit Burnett reported that the poet left the prison in a haggard condition, clutching in his hand a piece of stale prison bread.

PHARAMOND'S. A bald, ponderous, red-faced Romanian who spoke English well and wrote it with difficulty, Eugene Rosetti was for some years the *Herald* reporter covering French politics after earlier work with the *Tribune*, where he wrote a regular editorial page column called "Little Tours of Paris." Laney considered him an enigma, in part because he was a professed royalist turned strident Communist, in other part because he usually brought in only "sensational misinformation" yet remained comfortably lodged on the staff. Where Rosetti was unquestionably valuable was as a guide to

Paris dining, leading eating excursions about the city and fastening on Pharamond's as a favored spot. Located on a hidden-away street near the paper's office and ordinarily frequented only by the French, it was the place where many staffers were introduced to the pleasures of the local cuisine—and to pointed orations from Rosetti about the misguided dining habits of Americans:

> Barbarians! You Americans are all barbarians! You should be civilized! Learn how to eat! Stop anesthetizing your palates with cocktails! Stop smoking at the table! Fill your mouths full and give all the taste buds a chance! Put your meat and vegetables on separate plates! Not all in a mess on one plate! Throw all your Coca-Cola in the ocean and learn to appreciate wine!

Whatever fellow workers thought of Rosetti as a reporter, Laney maintained they owed him a lasting debt for his gustatory guidance: "All around the world today, there are men who are ready . . . to run up a *salade sauce Albert* according to the recipe which Rosetti worked out with the headwaiter at Pharamond's. For this alone, Rosetti's memory will remain green."

THE MAN FROM *TRANSITION*. Within the *Herald* staff, the figure with closest ties to literary and artistic Paris was Elliot Paul. A published novelist, musician, and legendary carouser, Paul had been a versatile newsman and ambiguous influence on the Paris *Tribune* when he left in 1926 to join his newspaper colleague Eugene Jolas in starting *transition*. "I needed an editorial assistant," said Jolas,

> and had the names of several newspapermen then living in Paris under consideration. Elliot Paul seemed my best choice and I decided to invite him to join me. He gave enthusiastic acquiescence to the plan, which included a small salary that permitted him to quit the newspaper work entirely and devote himself exclusively to the task.

Paul stayed with *transition*, as Jolas's co-editor, through the journal's first twelve monthly issues, then, with publication occasional, shifted from contributing editor to advisory editor. The eighteenth issue in November 1929 announced that Paul and *transition* had parted company.

With his return to newspaper work Paul applied first at the *Tribune*, where the then managing editor, Ralph Jules Frantz, reluctantly turned him down. When Paul asked why, Frantz told him he was aware of his ability but was wary of his pied-piper effect on young members of his staff. "Paul at the time," said Frantz, "had boundless energy and could get by with a small amount of sleep, no matter how much he had drunk. But I feared my staff, not having the same stamina, would not be able to stand the pace, and that only too often I would find my men unable to work."

Paul's taste for nightlife was well known, but so was his skill as an able and inventive deskman. Quickly hired by the *Herald*, one of his tasks was conducting the Mailbag, where letters he wrote himself stoked many prolonged reader controversies. Other inventions were inspired by the French newspapers. One such, drawn from frequent crimes-of-passion stories about Parisian women shooting husbands and lovers, led to Paul writing an imaginary interview with a Montmartre promoter who ran a shooting gallery with life-sized men as targets, allowing wronged women to hone their gun skills. The interview was widely translated and reprinted in the French press—and soon thereafter a French entrepreneur opened just such a shooting gallery.

Paul also edited what he called a "semi-cultural page" for the paper's Sunday edition and, "in order to have a few features that would not cost Mrs. Ogden Reid any of the vast sums of money she seemed to be planning to take with her, after death," wrote for it a weekly article on French painters from Poussin to—an adopted Frenchman—Picasso. Picasso gave him a pen-and-ink drawing for reproduction with the article, but when Paul saw the proof he found that "our alleged 'art' department" had decided the drawing was lacking and someone had retouched it. Paul had the drawing restored and another print made, then "kept a proof of the 'corrected' drawing for Picasso, who treasures it to this day."

LEFT BANK NOTES. As a novelist and former *transition* editor also reputed to understand the work of both Joyce and Gertrude Stein, Paul's presence on the paper drew the *Herald* staff closer to the cultural interests of Left Bank expatriates. Such as it was, however, the closeness failed to rub off on management and was not seriously reflected in the paper's pages. "Modern books, art and music . . . can be dismissed, as the *Herald* dismisses them, in a few lines," Burnett and Foley caustically observed in their *American Mercury* article. "Its Book Page, in comparison with the supplement of its New York *Herald-Tribune* stepmother, is what a railroad station book cart on the Continent is to Brentano's."

A modest effort in at least reporting on Left Bank literary and artistic matters was made by Arthur Moss and his wife of the time, Florence Gilliam, later to become a mainstay on the Paris *Tribune* as a theater critic. Moss's "Around the Town" column developed into a regular *Herald* feature and his "Around the Riviera" a periodic one, while Gilliam turned out columns called "Round the Studios" and "With Latin Quarter Folk."

Although Gilliam's columns of the mid-twenties had the rare distinction of occasional signatures at the end with her name or initials, they were, like Moss's culture columns, mostly a grab bag of gossip and news items. Typical was the opening of a "With Latin Quarter Folk" column on January 11, 1925: "Harold Loeb, former editor of the 'Broom,' published on the Continent, is going back to America for a brief visit. He has a book soon to be off the press, which will figure among the important spring publications of Boni and Liveright." Or the close of a column on October 5, 1926: "Theodore Dreiser, who left Paris last week, was guest of honor at several delightful parties. Madame Llona and Mrs. Lewisohn are to

be congratulated for the tact and discretion with which they entertained, without betraying his presence to the world at large." Another culture column of the period, "Soliloquies on the Left Bank"
(or, now and then, "Soliloquies from Left Bank"), turned out by
R.A.—presumably staff member Roscoe Ashworth—was more distinctive in its whimsical chronicling of across-the-river affairs.

In the latter half of the twenties the *Herald*'s attention to cultural
matters picked up. The Monday edition carried short reviews of
English and French books, and on Sunday there was a page of
lengthy reviews, some written by staff members. Among the re-
viewers was Willis Steell, a dignified, white-haired former Broad-
way playwright who toiled on the paper while his daughter studied
in Paris for an opera career. Possessed of what Laney called "a bubbling sense of humor and a delightfully half-cynical outlook on
everything," Steell brought both qualities to another of his tasks,
editing the Mailbag. In 1928 came a column reporting on current
magazine fare, "Looking Over the Magazines," written by Wilfred
Barber and others. Mixed in were Don Donaldson's lengthy narra-
tives of Parisian life under the heading "Little Stories of Real Life
in Paris" and regular columns on theater, cinema, art, and music.
The latter two were conducted by Frenchmen—art by Georges Bal
and music by Louis Schneider—both producing their copy in
crabbed French script requiring labored translation in the newsroom.

The music critic—given to writing in purple ink on small slips
of paper and composing his critical pieces before concerts took
place—posed an additional problem. Musicians (as well as artists
and authors) routinely paid for favorable reviews in French newspapers, and, working for a Paris-American paper that could help
American performers build a reputation abroad, Schneider was in
position to expect greater compensation. When Martha Foley
learned the Irish tenor John McCormack had paid him $250 for
praise in the *Herald*, she was outraged enough to complain to Eric
Hawkins and threaten to go to the paper's owners if he took no ac-

tion. It was a sticky matter for management in that Schneider, as a French citizen, was entitled by law to a separation bonus if fired, one substantial enough to affect the paper's budget. (In his string of complaints about the *Herald* in the *New Review*, Ezra Pound had included "the stinginess of the [paper's] owner in not bribing Schneider to get off the paper.") Wolfe Kaufman of the paper's staff finally suggested a crafty solution: Schneider would continue turning out music criticism but none of his work would be printed, with Elliot Paul covering musical events and writing critical pieces the *Herald* actually published.

Still, the paper's cultural coverage continued to compare badly with the *Tribune's* greater interest and livelier manner. With few exceptions, admits Laney, the *Tribune* gave a better picture of what he calls the "Young Intellectual movement" since it had "much more space for such doings and a steadier stream of Young Intellectuals in its employ." The tribute, however, comes with a downside, Laney adding that the "Young Intellectual was likely to be an indifferently trained newspaperman and unable to fit easily into the rather dull routine of making a newspaper." The *Herald*, with fewer such in its supply, was in effect fortunate, having more men who could "bring themselves to knocking out a bit of orthodox, unadvanced prose for the *Herald* at a few hundred francs a week."

FAREWELLS. During the late twenties the *Herald* had its largest and most professional staff, and with the addition of the United Press to its Associated Press and Havas news services, together with expanded cable coverage from New York and London, the deskmen and a handful of local reporters were putting out an improved paper. Sudden needs for breaks from office routine remained common, however—and a matter of mystery to Eric Hawkins until he learned they were hasty visits to a neighborhood bordello where girls wore only bow ribbons. Lasting departures were frequent as well. One staffer left a note on his typewriter when he left: "If I don't come back, you can look for me in the Seine." When next seen, some weeks later, he was in New York.

Now and then sudden good fortune sparked the leave-taking. Charles Wertenbaker, who wrote short stories while on the copy desk and sent them to popular magazines back home, departed when a letter came telling him of a sale to the *Saturday Evening Post*. At once he put on his hat, waved a check at his deskmates, and announced, "So long, slaves."

John Weld's farewell was equally triumphant. He had been a cub reporter on the *New York American* when he and a friend left for France with plans to write novels and become foreign correspondents. They reached Paris just after Lindbergh's landing and were taken on by the International News Service as reporters, covering the hero's every move, the jobs lasting until his return to New York. After a period of novel-writing in a pension on the English Channel, Weld, out of money, was hired by the *Herald* in 1928.

His fellow workers struck him as a bizarre assortment of "expatriates, wanderers, iconoclasts, romantics." Chief among the latter was Elliot Paul. Short and stout, with a Van Dyke beard and sparse hair artfully combed across his head, he was hardly an imposing figure, yet he had been married (at this point) three times and, as a published novelist and founding editor of *transition*, possessed what Weld considered a major talent together with an admirable weakness for aspiring writers. He took to visiting Paul's living quarters in the Hôtel du Caveau in Rue de la Huchette, there to play bridge, admire the view of Notre Dame cathedral and barges moving on the Seine, and indulge in Paul's generosity with food and drink.

Through Paul, Weld met Henry Miller, whom he came to like but who seemed, at age thirty-nine, too old to succeed as a writer. He also became one of the *Herald* men typing letters for Joyce. Joyce preached the need for literary persistence, and Weld's persistence paid off when a novel, his second, was accepted for publication. The agent's letter, read in the *Herald* office, also informed him he had a contract with Columbia Pictures for writing an original film scenario at a salary of $200 a week.

A stunned Weld managed to shout, "Hey, listen to this," and read aloud the letter. Some staffers assumed it was an April Fool's joke. In Eric Hawkins's office Weld received congratulations, the managing editor adding, "I must say I'm not all that surprised. I've seen a number of people leave this office on their way up the ladder." He was thinking, Weld guessed, of such former *Herald* men as Ralph Barnes, Reggie Coggeshall, Ed Skinner, Jack Pickering, Dean Jennings, Wolfe Kaufman.

Weld stayed on a week while the *Herald* found a replacement. Before leaving Paris he said goodbye to Joyce, joking that he might adapt *Ulysses* to the screen. A final evening of bar crawling with El- liot Paul, Tom Cope, and George Rehm of the *Herald* staff began at midnight at Harry's New York Bar, wound down in the early morn- ing with onion soup and fresh bread in Les Halles, and ended with Weld in Notre Dame cathedral praying he might someday return to Paris.

For those left behind, the paper might exhibit improvement but newsroom life retained its familiar placid and pleasant pace. Ken- neth Stewart, a deskman in 1928 and 1929 who also for a time wrote a monthly Paris theater column for the *New York Sun*, recalled the typical round of work:

> On a normal evening at the *Herald* the nightside would
> straggle in at about eight o'clock, well wined and dined, to
> take over from the day staff, which had leisurely collected the
> tourist registrations at the Right Bank hotels, recorded the
> comings and goings from the Riviera, interviewed arrivals on
> boat trains, listened to the talks on international amity at the
> Anglo-American and Franco-American luncheons. Richard,
> the French copyboy with the old man's face, would grin at us
> as we came in and mutter something about "les américains
> fous." After a few preliminaries, we would drift out again to

the corner bistro for coffee or a liqueur, come back to deskeletonize the cables which Roland Kilbon had filed from New York, translate a few odds and ends of politics and crime from the Paris papers.

After the paper went to press the staff would repair to M. François's bistro, a *Herald* hangout, or cross the river to Montparnasse and while away the rest of the night on the terraces of cafés, "all the while piling up saucers and eavesdropping on conversation sounding more like Hemingway than Hemingway himself." As often as not Elliot Paul would appear and, for those sufficiently able, lead excursions into the Paris of Parisians that were "memorable in toto if not in detail, for by the time he got his giddy guests as far as his beloved Hôtel du Caveau they had no mind for minutiae."

RUE DE BERRI. The Americanization effort of 1924 was one watershed point for the interwar *Herald*, the move to new quarters in December 1930 another. The imposing nine-story building at 21 Rue de Berri, designed in the form of an H from an overhead view and located just off the elegant Champs-Elysées on the former property of the American Church, was state-of-the-art in its editorial and printing facilities. There were numerous settling-in difficulties, but in retrospect they would seem minor irritants compared—just as the move took place—to the economic storm crossing the Atlantic and the political upheaval brewing in Europe.

Looking back, some old hands insisted the new building marked the end of the *Herald*'s best days, and just before the move a number of important staffers had left the paper, among them Wilfred Barber and Lee Dickson, who went to the rival *Tribune*, and Ralph Barnes, who was assigned to the *New York Herald Tribune*'s Rome bureau. But competent men were also joining the paper. Elliot Paul and Ned Calmer had come over from the *Tribune*, with Calmer's terms of employment—as Eric Hawkins informed him later—a two-week trial period, a salary of eight hundred francs a week, two weeks' vacation after one year, and work on either the day or night shift depending on the paper's needs. William L. Shirer, his career with the *Chicago Tribune*'s foreign service brusquely cut short, had reappeared in Paris and joined the *Herald* as a copy reader and reporter. Just ahead was the arrival of Eric Sevareid.

Unforeseen in the move to Rue de Berri was the difficulty the new location posed for the staff in finding convenient places to drink. The "nearest approach to a quenchplace of thirst," noted Burnett and Foley in the *American Mercury*, was now an

> elaborate *terrasse café* on the fashionable Champs-Elysées at which ladies in long dresses sit beneath colored parasols and sip tea. . . . It is hard to imagine the staff of the *Herald* dropping off here on the search for a sip of the old nectar which . . . made working on the *Herald* something of the adventure which, to all right-thinking Americans, working on the *Herald* ought to be.

In Al Laney's view, the real problem with the location was that nearly all drinking spots in the area closed by 3 a.m., as cafés in Les Halles never had. A solution of sorts came about when the owners of the nearby Onyx Bar—known to all as Monsieur and Madame Onyx—simply shifted the *Herald* crowd into a back room after the mandated closing time, providing food and drink while the police thoughtfully looked the other way.

ALCOHOLIC DREAM. The need for a ready "quenchplace of thirst" where one could sip the "old nectar" were kindly circumlocutions, if *Time* magazine was to be believed. In a 1939 Press section article about *"Le New York"*—with an accompanying photo of a dapper Laurence Hills looking owlish behind dark-rimmed glasses—it wasted no words: "The *Herald* of the 1920s was a newspaperman's alcoholic dream." Laney considerably expanded the time frame: "Irresponsibility due to excessive indulgence in alcoholic beverages had, for forty years, been one of the Paris Herald's chief problems." Eric Hawkins insisted that "mostly our staff men controlled their drinking until the presses rolled" while at the same time pointing a finger at the effects of red wine during working hours: "I found that American newspapermen who could handle a bottle of bourbon with ease were frequently pole-axed by a couple of glasses of red wine with their dinner. They would return to the news desk in mid-evening, sit down to a typewriter or a piece of copy and promptly fall asleep." In the *American Mercury*, Burnett and Foley remarked in passing that during the paper's Rue du Louvre period the office had been commonly warmed in winter with *grogs américains*, and in summer beer was kept on the desks—or was until the managing editor protested it might give visitors a wrong impression of the paper, whereupon the beer was kept under the desks.

The age itself, of course, was one of the hard-drinking journalist, on duty and off, and the age continued beyond the profligate interwar years. Into the immediate post–World War II period beer and bookies were still part of the accepted atmosphere of the city room of the august *New York Times*, as were brass spitoons, wastepaper-basket fires, and ongoing card games. If on the one hand Paris fueled temptation with the supply, cheapness, and cultural acceptance of drink, on the other it elevated it to a higher order of living—or so some *Herald* staffers wished to believe. "We drank quite a bit," allowed Kenneth Stewart, "but we also learned how to drink. We often substituted apéritifs for cocktails, and discovered the civilized uses of wines. The Frenchmen we met taught those of us accustomed to bathtub gin how to sharpen our sense of taste instead of deadening it." Harold Stearns would raise the same banner of proper imbibing: "There was no longer any point in being uncivilized about drinking—when all the fine wines of France were at your disposal all of the time."

In any case, what and how much staffers drank after hours was their business while what they consumed on duty was the *Herald*'s, at least in theory. With the move to Rue de Berri a ruling came down that anyone, sober to begin with, who got drunk during working hours would be fired. The rule was more or less observed until, more than a year after the shift to the new building, Elliot Paul broke it in a forthright manner.

His writing in the paper about art pleased one reader enough to send a check to a nephew on the *Herald* staff with instructions to take Paul to dine at a fine restaurant. When the invitation from the nephew came, Paul was at work. He promptly went to see Laurence Hills, cited the drunkenness rule, and set out his intentions: "I came to work at ten this morning cold sober. It is now noon. It is my intention, sir, to go out at this moment and get good and tight. I wish to save you the trouble of firing me. I fire myself. Good day to you, sir, and goodbye."

Returning to the office some years later, Paul is said to have gone directly to the clothes rack and searched about. Then he shouted, "Where is my hat, goddamit? I left it right here." He had been gone so long that no one on the paper's day staff remembered seeing him before.

WET OBLIVION. If the new building lacked location for the drinking crowd, its modern heating system presumably eased the misery of Paris winters—the season that for many newsmen formed the acid test of expatriate life. Burnett and Foley weighed in at length on winter's rigors:

> It is in the Winter, those dreary rainy days of Winter
> unknown to the summer tourists, the Winter of flu and
> firelessness, of rows with concierges, of electric heaters which
> blow out their fuses, of gas heaters which blow out the staff,

of woolen underwear and the total lack of sun, that the *Herald*
staff burrows in and gloomily settles down. . . . The man
responsible for the furnace waits until the real onslaught of
Winter and then, without previous examination, has it fired to
the fullest and the cussed thing explodes. Then begin
negotiations which last for months, and the staff upstairs
works in its overcoats, the office boy is rushed to the *bistrots*,
and the office is warmed from the inside out—*rums chauds* and
grogs américains. It doesn't matter. Only the old stand-bys, the
Winter time colony, read the paper. It is all understandable. A
Paris Winter is a wet oblivion.

Evidence suggests the passage may have come from Burnett's typewriter rather than Foley's since his youth in the dry climes of Utah
had left him particularly vulnerable to the dripping season, or so for
a time he believed.

Burnett made many visits to the American Hospital in Neuilly
with a variety of complaints, all caused—so he assumed—by the
"big rain." As a member of the working press he was well treated by
the hospital staff, given a private room for a few francs, and minis-
tered to by American nurses. "A few such pleasant days," he happily
noted, "and practically any reporter was soon up and about, and
usually dating up the nurses." After several such hospital stays,
spring near, he chanced to read his hospital record that had been
left—presumably by accident—on a nearby table. After each of his
complaints a physician had written *phobia, phobia, phobia*. Armed
with his new medical knowledge, Burnett took a vacation from the
Herald, traveled to the French Pyrenees, basked in the sun.

HARD TIMES. Ample space within the paper's new building was
available to rent out for what house ads declared "Europe's Most
Modern Offices" in a Paris "skyscraper," but aside from the parent
Herald Tribune's Paris bureau and the Scripps-Howard newspaper

chain's European bureau there were few depression-era takers. Costs of maintaining the building fell short of rental income, and there was little outside printing work to produce income and fully utilize the new plant facilities. At the same time the *Herald*'s circulation was plummeting from 39,000 in 1929 to less than 10,000 in 1934.

As the decade wore on and the depression eased, the flow of American tourists picked up, and the *Herald* eagerly took notice. When 500 passengers from the *Champlain* arrived on a boat train at Gare St. Lazare in the spring of 1936, the paper declared it a "deluge." When 550 Americans came shortly thereafter for a wine tour of France, it printed each of their names. The Paris International Exposition opening in May 1937—the *Herald*'s fiftieth year—attracted a genuine deluge, yet summer travelers came and went while the paper's main constituency, the permanent Paris-American colony, was decidedly thinning out under the cloud of war. A story in the paper on May 5, 1937, reported the French census had found only 8,253 American residents in the city. At the same time the *Herald* was giving dense coverage to the exposition, Ralph Barnes speculated in a page-one dispatch that the German military would be ready for war by 1940—and, inside the paper, display ads promoted Pan American's twice-weekly Clipper service from Lisbon to New York, a major route of escape from war-torn Europe in the period just ahead.

Faced with a steady flow of red ink, Laurence Hills cut staff and reduced salaries to the point where even he worried they might be too low for employees to get by. He resisted when New York suggested scaling back the paper from eight pages to six, but took such humbling measures as asking the French government for a delay in tax payments and approaching the French news agency Havas and the *Petit Parisien* newspaper about a takeover of the *Herald*. Nothing helped, or helped enough, and the paper's existence through the period depended on regular infusions of money from the New York home office.

P.A.C. A bright spot in the otherwise dreary depression was the emergence of an uncommon writing career by a highly uncommon Paris-American. A letter to the editor on March 18, 1933, sweetly praised "that delightful—or should I say 'deleteful'?—institution, the Mailbag!" while acknowledging the thrill of seeing "our initials in print therein!" The initials, P.A.C., were those of Pauline Avery Crawford, whose contributions to the Mailbag developed into a feature as familiar to loyal readers as Sparrow Robertson's column— and equally an ingredient of the *Herald*'s snug, small-town appeal. The most prolific and enduring of a core of Mailbag writers in verse, Crawford's specialty was the topical poem, light or serious and in varied forms, in response to *Herald* news items, Mailbag contributions, or simply the shifting seasons. Christmas brought forth

> Hark!—the herald angels clamor—
> Step inside for gifts of glamour!
> Peace on earth! let business thrive!
> Give her Chanel Number 5!

While her verse made her a modest celebrity in Paris-American social circles, in print Crawford inspired attacks as well as tributes, the former vigorously answered in kind and carried on in Mailbag exchanges that went on for days. A writer named Chandler ended an assault with

> Your dithyrambs cause me to laugh, O
> You latter-day daughter of Sappho;
> Your lyrical stencil
> Suggests a dull pencil;
> Your meters are wavery
> Paulina Avery.

To which Crawford retaliated with the opening lines

> Wake! For a Bard would scatter into flight
> The prattlings of us Poets overnight—

And in the Mailbag's homely columns, Lo,
A man named Chandler wants to start a Fight.

Raised in Colorado and educated at Goucher College in Baltimore, Crawford came to Paris in 1926 as the dutiful wife of a husband on sabbatical from a teaching position at Lafayette College in Pennsylvania. After they returned home her life swiftly swirled into tragedy when her husband committed suicide following an affair with a faculty member's wife. With two young sons and no longer able to endure a small-town college community, Crawford returned to Paris, whereupon she was afflicted with a crippling disease that resulted, following botched treatment during a two-year period in the American Hospital in Neuilly, in the amputation of a leg.

Fitted with a prosthesis, Crawford resumed her Paris life in a ground-floor apartment off the Boulevard Raspail and worked at poetry while waiting out a slow-moving case of medical malpractice finally settled in 1935. In the same year she published her only book, a collection of poems drawn from her tortuous medical experience, called *Sonnets from a Hospital*. She was too impatient, she maintained, to wait for her poetry to appear in magazines or books, preferring the immediate satisfaction of newspaper publication. For its part, the *Herald* apparently printed nearly all her contributions—or did until, toward the end of the thirties, her increasingly political verse clashed with the paper's conservative editorial positions.

Although Crawford lived on the Left Bank, took pleasure in the café life of Montparnasse, and pursued interests in literature, theater, and art, nothing of the new and experimental currents of the time found their way into her verse. She was wholly comfortable writing in settled forms and having her work in the commonplace pages of the *Herald*. Her audience, the only one she sought, was the established American colony of the Right Bank. She had, nonetheless, firm views about political developments of the day and expressed them in sharply worded verse that brought equally intense response from readers. With the Spanish Civil War she stoutly defended the

Republican cause, and against the threat of Nazi Germany railed against isolationists and appeasers. When war with Germany finally came she rushed off a defiant limerick:

A bluffer grown bigger and bigger
By pulling his lies with such vigor
Grew suddenly littler
When poor Mr. Hitler
Had nothing to pull but his trigger.

TAKEOVER. Despite the troubled economic climate of the thirties, the Reids in New York struck a deal late in 1934 with the *Chicago Tribune* to buy its Paris edition. The immediate benefit to the *Herald* was slight—a small increase in subscribers and newsstand sales together with an equally small increase in advertising and advertising rates. The *Herald* also gained a few able staff members from the Paris *Tribune*, though an unexpected consequence would appear later when, the city's pool of available newsmen reduced, the *Herald* was forced to scramble to fill vacant positions.

In a two-column, page-one boxed story on October 31, 1934, the *Herald* announced that the takeover would begin on December 1, with the merged papers published by the *Herald* and carrying the titles of both "for an indefinite period." Another page-one story on December 1 made clear that only the titles of the two papers were combined and went on to welcome new readers with a generic promise to "make them feel at home in an American newspaper atmosphere." As for its former rival, the *Tribune* could comfort itself with retiring honorably from the field after seventeen years of "meritorious existence." Inside, the *Herald* reprinted a boxed story from the previous day's *Tribune* in which the paper bowed out with a stiff upper lip by wishing the survivor success and prosperity.

Nine months after the takeover, the *Herald* rid itself of the Gothic lettering of the *Chicago Daily Tribune* from beneath its name and began bearing the title and typograpical look of the parent *New York Herald Tribune*, while among Paris-Americans it was still known as the Paris *Herald* and among Parisians as *Le New York*. But neither a new name and address nor a lack of competition could slow the paper's precipitous depression-era slide. Laney is blunt: "Its prestige was largely gone; it was losing money rapidly and making some compromises with honor. It was no better off with its neighborly rival out of the way."

LAURENCE HILLS. The "compromises with honor" had to do with the operation of the paper under Laurence Hills. Stricken with cancer, the general manager was making erratic decisions, recalling for some the Bennett days of rule by whim. Spencer Bull, a veteran newsman who had bounced back and forth among Paris-American papers, was abruptly hired as day editor when Hills ran into him in a bar after a weekly luncheon of the Anglo-American Press Association and Bull caught the general manager's interest by casually holding forth on what was wrong with the *Herald*. When Bull appeared in the newsroom in his new position, the staff was stunned. "The gray little man who was so bent as to be almost deformed," as Laney described him, had over the years established a well-earned reputation for irresponsibility that reached a dubious peak with a fanciful and libelous story about the Prince of Wales written while a deskman on the *Tribune*.

Another of Hills's impetuous moves turned out well. About the same time Bull came on board, he hired a young deskman named Frank Kelley. The copy desk was down to a couple of men and help was needed; the problem was that Kelley was a graduate of the Columbia University School of Journalism, an immediate disqualification in the eyes of most newsmen of the time, and had no practical experience. His one merit for the staff was that at Columbia he had taken a journalism course from their former colleague Kenneth Stewart. For Hills, Kelley's overriding appeal was that, while on a

European tour after his graduation, he had dated Hills's daughter in Paris. Put to work, he survived a rocky initiation, and in time his skills were such that he was shifted to London as a Paris *Herald* correspondent. Eventually Kelley was elevated to the *Herald Tribune*'s foreign staff and became, in Al Laney's estimation, the Paris *Herald*'s best contribution to the home paper after Ralph Barnes.

Personnel decisions were minor irritants compared with Hills's willful blindness to the likelihood of war in Europe. He resisted dire warnings coming from the *Herald Tribune*'s informed bureau chiefs, confident that war could not possibly come—or in denial over what war would do to the Paris paper's revenues—and gave the regimes of Hitler and Mussolini favorable editorial treatment in a futile effort to hold on to advertising from German and Italian sources.

For the correspondents, Hills was a lightning rod for another reason. Late in 1937, management in New York had given him the added duty of director of all the *Herald Tribune*'s European operations, replacing in the position John Elliott, the Paris bureau chief who in the twenties had worked on the Paris *Herald*. Hills was charged with reorganizing the paper's European coverage in an effort to cut costs, which he swiftly did by informing bureau chiefs they were no longer to produce the same sort of special-dispatch coverage as the *New York Times* and were to rely on wire services for routine material. Their work, as Hills wrote in a directive, was narrowed to "dispatches that in a sense seem exclusive in news, as well as presentation. This means short stories, as well as long. Crisp cables of human interest or humorous type cables are greatly appreciated. Big beats in Europe in these days are not very likely."

Predictably, correspondents were outraged at abandoning head-to-head competition with the *Times* in favor of humor and human-interest pieces at a time when they believed big beats in Europe *were* likely. The economy-first measures were not loosened until, late in 1938, the former European correspondent Dorothy Thompson—who had joined the *Herald Tribune* in 1936 and whose "On the Record" column appeared regularly in the Paris *Herald* along with

Walter Lippmann's "Today and Tomorrow"—wrote Helen Reid that "when Larry Hills was put in charge of the foreign service, practically every American journalist was appalled." And added: "I have many old friends there . . . and they tell me that the Paris *Herald Tribune* is playing the fascist game from start to finish. Inasmuch as this is certainly not the policy of the *Herald Tribune*, I feel that you ought to do something about it."

The Reids did. Summoned to New York, Hills was told to cover European fascism without bias in the *Herald*'s news columns and that henceforth all political editorials would come from the home office. The Paris paper was allowed to comment only on noncontroversial matters. Eric Hawkins, running the paper in Hills's absence, professed pleasure with the ruling, though he insisted that in its news columns—where bylined reports by such top *Herald Tribune* correspondents as Joseph Barnes, Ralph Barnes, John Elliott, Frank Kelley, and Walter B. Kerr regularly appeared—the Paris *Herald* was fully and properly covering the move to war.

FEATURE WRITER. Not long after Hills rejoined the *Herald* in the spring of 1939, Eric Sevareid departed, the beginning of a journey that would recast him from a Paris-American newspaperman to a household name in American broadcasting. A graduate of the University of Minnesota and a dedicated journalist whose early model was the swashbuckling Richard Harding Davis, Sevareid had caught on with the paper two years earlier after he was summarily fired by the *Minneapolis Journal* for a story in which he confused the American Legion with the Veterans of Foreign Wars. A bus delivered Sevareid and his wife to New York, a cargo ship to Europe. England was their first stop, where Sevareid, eager to make a name for himself as a freelance writer, wrote penny-a-word articles for the University of Minnesota's student newspaper and chanced to meet a striking, dark-eyed American five years his senior, Edward R. Murrow.

When he moved on to Paris, Sevareid felt at once a liberating freedom from both American and British taboos, certain that in France "nobody really cared a damn what you did, how you dressed, or what you said." He and his wife dropped plans for a European bicycle tour, settled into the Hôtel Sélect where rooms cost fifty cents a day, began taking French classes.

When he joined the *Herald* in December 1937—walking in and applying just as a staffer was walking out for good—his immediate superior was the day editor, B. J. Kospoth, who had come over after a long tenure on the Paris *Tribune*. To Sevareid, Kospoth was a "complete misanthrope who loved but three things—his riding horse, the legend of Napoleon, and Adolf Hitler." New on the staff, Sevareid was on the receiving end of bullying treatment from the editor as well as an unwelcome earful of his views; both continued until Sevareid threatened blows and Kospoth "subsided into baleful silence."

With the chief editorial writer, Vincent Bugeja, Sevareid fared better. Among the learned staffer's varied interests was nudism. One bitter March day he took Sevareid to a nudist camp on an island in the Seine, ripped off his clothes, and dove into the freezing river, thereafter leaping up and down on the grass and slapping his hairy chest. The camp, located near Villennes-sur-Seine, was a frequent source of *Herald* stories bursting with ornate prose. One such raised the issue of how nudists cope with winter: "What, the question is, does a nature colony addict do when the rain comes down, when the wintry blasts from the boreal north nip at the birds' tails and blast the last leaf on the tree?" The answer was they put up a tent community and christened it "Physiolopolis."

As a feature writer (and eventually following Kospoth as day editor), Sevareid wandered the city for stories that caught his interest, then competed for space and bylines with an energetic feature-writing colleague, Rosamond Cole. Among his interests were the actor Charles Laughton's lengthy Parisian eating trail; a dazzling show of English painting opening in the Louvre; "Jumping Joe"

Savoldi, a former star football player at Notre Dame now on an international wrestling tour; a self-named "Vagabond Co-Ed" from the University of Wisconsin making her way about the world with stunts that included blowing cigarette smoke bombs; a parade along the Champs-Elysées of what the story's headline called the "Mighty French War Machine," an ironic display given events that would shortly unfold. Now and then Sevareid got a prominent by-line for straight news, as when he reported on General Pershing visiting Paris and joined other staff members Robert Sage, Rosamond Cole, and Edwin Hartrich in covering the Paris visit in July 1938 of Britain's King George VI and Queen Elizabeth.

When Sevareid interviewed Gertrude Stein, her libretto for a new version of the opera *Faust* was just finished and she read him portions of it, nearly shouting—as he wrote in the *Herald*—"with laughter when she spoke a particularly good line." She also had finished a children's book and had launched into a novel about "publicity saints," a modern replacement for the religious variety. She considered Charles Lindbergh "publicity saint No. 1," reported Sevareid, in that there was about him "a certain mystical something" even though "he does nothing and says nothing and nobody is affected by him in any way whatsoever." The Duchess of Windsor was a similar figure, and Stein acknowledged that she herself was a publicity saint, "but of a minor order."

Later, in a memoir that included his Paris days, Sevareid recalled that the interview had been widely reprinted, to Stein's considerable delight. Withheld from the interview, he added, were her political views. She had told him that Hitler was not dangerous because he was a German romanticist who wanted glory but could never endure "the blood and fighting involved in getting it." Mussolini, on the other hand, *was* dangerous—an Italian realist who would stop at nothing. "Like most artists," Sevareid concluded, "she thought in terms of the human individual and was quite lost when she considered people in groups. She could not think politically at all."

In December 1938 Sevareid and his wife crossed the Rhine by train for a close-up view of the Third Reich. From this vantage point, the *Herald*, when they picked up copies, seemed maddeningly remote with stories about continuing appeals for peace and lengthy discussions of Hitler's motives. To Sevareid it was clear the German leaders were riding a motorcycle downhill, and there was no way of halting the headlong rush to war.

CRIME AND PUNISHMENT. Back in Paris, Sevareid turned from impending war to covering a sensational murder trial. Jean De Koven, a young American dancer visiting Paris, was strangled to death for the change in her purse by a handsome, magnetic German named Eugene Weidmann. When captured, Weidmann confessed that he and three accomplices had murdered a total of six people, all for money. Parisians together with an array of international journalists crammed a Versailles courtroom for his three-week trial.

For days on end in March 1939 Sevareid chronicled the trial in the *Herald*, his long accounts, usually bylined and played on page one, appearing alongside reports from Rome about a new pope, Pius XII, and the latest stories from Franco's Spain and Hitler's Germany. Weidmann struck Sevareid as a primitive figure who took lives without qualm yet a man of high intelligence who was fluent in languages and read philosophy in his prison cell. Women in the courtroom were mesmerized by the killer's charm, and Sevareid concluded he was a finer actor than any of the assembled lawyers.

"Eugene Weidmann died yesterday with his eyes tightly closed," Sevareid began a riveting page-one story on June 18. "He shut them instinctively as he caught sight of the guillotine's hanging knife when he stepped from Saint Peter Prison in Versailles at 4:30 a.m.—in bright daylight—but otherwise he did not flinch." He went on in exact, scene-setting detail to portray an event that, from the moment Weidmann emerged from the prison doors and was pushed "against the polished wood of the machine," lasted just ten seconds.

Years later Sevareid marveled still at the speed and efficiency of the execution, the guillotine seeming "the least horrible formal death one could possibly imagine." Standing only a few feet distant, he had seen neither Weidmann's severed head nor his body. He had heard, though, the "savage, bloodcurdling scream like an animal pack's" that arose from the witnessing crowd as the condemned man was rushed to the knife—a detail he had delicately withheld from the newspaper account.

Sevareid's response to the nature of execution by guillotine mirrored almost exactly that, seventeen years earlier, of Webb Miller to the death of Henri Désiré Landru, the infamous "bluebeard" murderer of women. A veteran war correspondent now chief of the Paris bureau of United Press, Miller covered the trial in the same courtroom where Weidmann would be convicted. At the execution on February 25, 1922, he stood fifteen feet from the guillotine—an execution, which after Landru emerged from prison, took twenty-six seconds. "Despite the peculiarly horrible features of execution by guillotine," wrote Miller later, "I found the shock to my nervous system less severe than that caused by watching executions by hanging." On the drive back into Paris, however, a young embassy official accompanying him, looking ill and with shaking hands, was affected enough to keep sipping cognac. The bottle was finished before the city was reached.

DEATH IN SPAIN. In Spain war had already come, and Sevareid lost a close friend from the *Herald* staff when James Lardner, the second of Ring Lardner's four sons, was killed at age twenty-four, among the last American volunteers to die in battle. "All you guys will have to meet this thing somewhere pretty soon," Lardner had said when he left the paper to fight for the Republican cause. "I just decided I'd like to meet it in Spain." On August 11, 1938, the *Herald* reported that Lardner had been hit by shrapnel during a bombing raid on the Ebro Front. After hospitalization he returned to action. On October 12 the paper reported his death.

After attending Harvard, Jim Lardner had joined the *Herald Tribune* in New York before moving on to the Paris *Herald*. The city was a joy, but the paper struck him as a depressing "chamberof-commercistic sheet." His lone moment in the sun came when he was assigned, together with Sonia Tomara of the *Herald Tribune*'s foreign staff, to cover the wedding of the Duke of Windsor and Wallis Simpson. During May and June 1937 he spent two weeks in Tours, his daily accounts usually appearing on page one and usually bylined, and after the wedding in the nearby Château de Candé on June 3 his two-column story led the paper.

Restless with the *Herald* and eager to write about the Spanish war, Lardner managed to get accreditation as a correspondent for a Copenhagen newspaper, for the International News Service, and, through Laurence Hills, for the *New York Herald Tribune*. From Paris he set out by train for Barcelona in the company of a pair of celebrity journalists off to cover the war, Ernest Hemingway and Vincent Sheean. Due to the vast success of his 1935 book *Personal History*, Sheean—who also had been hired by the *Herald Tribune* for war coverage—was nearly as famous as the famed novelist. During the spring and summer of 1938 Sheean's copyrighted stories from Spain appeared frequently on the Paris *Herald*'s front page—with headlines that played up the onetime Paris-American journalist's name value: "Vincent Sheean Sees Loyalists Hang On Though Pushed to the Sea"; "Vincent Sheean Tells of Loyalist Retreat in Censored Dispatch"; "Vincent Sheean Is Under Fire as Fascist Planes Raid Puigcerda."

Sometime after he arrived in Spain, Lardner made up his mind to join in the fighting. Hemingway and Sheean tried to dissuade him, but the only issue for Lardner was how to go about enlisting. Despite weak eyes he was finally accepted due to the propaganda value of having Ring's son on the Republican side, though it was understood that he would be kept behind the lines and out of danger. Nonetheless he eventually found his way into the International Brigade and saw intense fighting before his death on a scouting patrol. His body was never recovered.

ROMANCE. Another former *Herald* man, Brandish Johnson, Jr., who during Lardner's period with the paper wrote a people-and-places column called "The European Stroller" and did some drama criticism, died in the Spanish war while working for *Newsweek* magazine. According to a *Herald* report, a shell hit a car he was traveling in with two other correspondents, killing all three. Reading of his death—and seeing an accompanying photo of three flag-draped coffins—Francelia McWilliams immediately applied at the *Herald* as a drama critic.

She had come to Europe after losing an American job and was now desperate for money while living on credit at the British-American YWCA. At the *Herald* she informed Eric Hawkins she was an assistant drama critic of the *Washington Evening Star* presently traveling in France—and produced the single review she had written for the paper when a drunken boyfriend had been unable to write it himself. By coincidence, replied Hawkins, the *Herald* recently had lost its drama critic and agreed to take her on, offering 250 francs a week for one or two stories with a byline, 500 without a byline. McWilliams went for anonymity.

Her first story was a film review, and in the editorial office she passed it to a staff member seated in the slot of the copy desk. Jerome Butler gave the review a quick read—and immediately realized McWilliams was short on newspaper experience. He also realized she needed a job. He would edit the review, he told her, if she would come to the restaurant where he dined each night before starting work. "Watch what I do," he added, "and maybe you'll learn. This will just be between us, all right?"

There was more between them than the review, as it turned out, and in 1939 McWilliams and Butler were married. They remained in Paris until early June 1940 when Butler, a veteran of World War I, concluded that the dust cloud hanging over the city had been stirred up by the advancing German army. From Bordeaux the couple departed France on the liner *Washington*, and when the ship was stopped by a German submarine they were forced into lifeboats until it was determined the vessel belonged to a neutral nation.

ON THE RADIO. With his bylined stories in the *Herald*, Eric Sevareid had gained a following with readers in Paris and beyond. Edward R. Murrow in London was among them, and in the summer of 1939 he phoned Sevareid with the offer of a job reporting for CBS radio. "I don't know very much about your experience," said Murrow. "But I like the way you write and I like your ideas." Murrow's fledging European news group included only William L. Shirer and Thomas Grandin in addition to himself, but he believed it had a future. "There won't be pressure on you to provide scoops or anything sensational," he told Sevareid. "Just provide the honest news, and when there isn't any news, why, just say so. I have an idea people might like that."

Sevareid at the time was working days at the *Herald* and nights at the Paris bureau of the United Press, not untypical double duty for hard-strapped Paris-American newsmen. He found his wire-service colleagues able but working under unrelenting pressure to put fresh material on the wire and update the leads of running stories. From New York each week came reports measuring their success against other wire services in getting their stories placed in subscribing papers. "It was like two or three competing merchants," Sevareid decided, "each watching the others like a hawk and putting gaudier and gaudier displays in his window to attract passing customers."

When the New York head of the UP visited Paris and offered an attractive position with the service, Sevareid debated with himself. War was coming and he wanted to report it back home, but could he work under the agency system? The debate was still ongoing when the call came from Murrow.

Sevareid agreed to make what he thought was a private test broadcast for executives in New York, then learned shortly before going on the air that his words would be carried live over the entire CBS system. He hastily rewrote his planned remarks on the Weidmann execution and managed to carry it off, New York responding that the material was good but his delivery bad. "That's all right," Murrow reassured him. "I'll fix it. Quit your other jobs anyway and don't worry about it." Sevareid was uncertain but cast his lot with Murrow. The $250-a-month salary that came with the job, princely by Paris-American newspaper standards, was surely a factor.

GUERRE TOTALE. Before the defining event of the German invasion of Poland on September 1, 1939, Laurence Hills had already reversed his personal views and was defying the home office by running page-one editorials in the *Herald* signed with his initials and calling for French resistance and American involvement in the coming conflict. In the paper the morning following the invasion, Eric Hawkins used the paper's largest type to blare the news: WAR BROKE OUT IN EUROPE YESTERDAY AT ABOUT DAWN. A third of a column on the page was left blank, the first war-period work of a censor. Inside, the shipping and weather reports were likewise blanked out, and "The Pariscope"—an editorial-page column of casual jottings that after a time was signed "Oliver Optic," the name of a popular writer in the days of Horatio Alger—closed with a strange assertion of the newspaper truth-telling to come:

> Newspaper men are notoriously prone to write their memoirs
> for an unsuspecting public. But this time it's going to be
> different. We are going about, pencil and pad in hand, and
> whenever a colleague makes a *bon mot* we scribble it down.
> Thus, in the final version, we will be accurately recording the

symptoms, the jitters, the comments and the mélange of this
incredible world we, newspaper men, seem to create. Boys
and girls, when we are ready to let fly, it's hold your hats and
file your libel suits.

The paper of September 4 announced that France and Britain
had declared war on Germany, yet what immediately followed were
months of the eerie calm of the *drôle de guerre*, the phony war.
Shrunk by government order from eight pages to four, and with
frequent white spaces revealing the censor's hand, the *Herald* was
down to 6,500 in circulation—a surprisingly strong figure,
nonetheless, given the situation—and advertising had virtually vanished. With Hills's health worsening, Hawkins was now running the
paper while also serving as the elected president of the Anglo-
American Press Association.

In the *Herald*'s office foreign correspondents streamed through,
searching for a war that seemed not to exist. Americans had been
advised to leave for home, but few on the paper's staff had elected
to go. "It is strange how little outward impression a declaration of
war creates," noted Harold Ettlinger in his diary. For some years
with the Paris *Tribune* and now a Paris correspondent for the Associated Press, Ettlinger occupied himself during the tranquil days
with private gas-mask practice in his living quarters. "There is no
sensation whatever. Truth may be stranger than fiction, but it seems
to lack drama at crucial moments. Much is going on, but we cannot
see it."

While the front page of the *Herald* was thick with military stories by correspondents Frank Kelley, John Elliott, Walter B. Kerr,
and Ralph Barnes, the inside pages carried on as if hardly anything
had changed. Sparrow Robertson's column made its daily appearance, though now with a single-column head, "Sporting Gossip,"
and without Sparrow's rakish photo. Audrey Ames's "On the
Screen" column and E. C. Foster's "Music in Paris" still appeared;
Pauline Avery Crawford's verses continued to grace the Mailbag.

The "News of Americans in Europe" column reported on travelers as if Paris were as favored a destination as ever ("Mr. John Armstrong, who came from New York and is making a long stay in Paris, has chosen the Lancaster as his headquarters"), and obituaries announced the passing of the notable, among them—in the paper of September 26—the dashing war correspondent Floyd Gibbons, said to have reported every major conflict of the past quarter-century.

When Germany swept into the Low Countries in May 1940 the phony war was abruptly over, the invasion route to Paris now wide open, and Americans and others rapidly abandoned the city. A. J. Liebling, in Paris as *The New Yorker*'s wartime replacement for Janet Flanner, wrote of the swiftness with which "the war became *de facto*," catching by surprise the correspondents who, like himself, had remained encamped in the city. The few among them who had forecast catastrophe—"the prophets of doom"—had been proven right, but through the months of uneventful waiting "it had required effort or a built-in neurosis."

The *Herald* of May 11, reporting the German *blitzkrieg*, carried a page-one editorial by Hills, one that seemed addressed to himself as much as readers: "It is useless to blind one's self to the deadly dramatic import of yesterday's developments. The 'guerre totale' has commenced." The United States, Hills concluded, must decide quickly on a course of action. Three days later, in the Mailbag of May 14, Pauline Avery Crawford made her decision:

> Sing a song of sick pacts,
> > A pocket full of lies,
> War and twenty blackmails
> > Baked by the spies;
> When the war was opened
> > The spies began their heils
> Until a Yankee Eagle flew
> > Across three thousand miles.

By late May the paper was down to two pages—a front page of war news and an editorial page with an occasional Sparrow Robertson column. In an editorial on May 20, Hills held out hope that eighty-four-year-old Marshal Pétain, a hero of World War I, might yet rally the military to a defense of France and Paris. The hope was seriously weakened when, on June 3, the city was bombed for the first time in a concentrated attack of planes flying at twenty thousand feet, with their main target the vast Citroën works on the Quai de Javel.

Eric Sevareid, having lunch in a Left Bank café, heard the planes arrive with what seemed the roar of an approaching thunderstorm, and that night, in his CBS broadcast, he reported forty deaths, two hundred casualties, and the miraculous escape of the American ambassador. William Bullitt had been in the Air Ministry building when a bomb came through the roof, landing six feet from him but failing to explode. Bullitt fled the building, leaving his hat and gloves behind. That night the bomb went off, obliterating among other things the hat and gloves.

A. J. Liebling's location at the time of the bombing was the bar of the Hôtel Lotti. Afterward he took a taxi to a neighborhood that had been hit, seeing six-story apartment buildings that had been "shaved down to the first floor, as if by the diagonal sweep of a giant razor." Yet already women were clearing broken glass from sidewalks—and the terrace of a café in the bombed area, "twenty minutes after the all-clear, was doing a record business with clients who wanted to '*discuter le coup*.'"

On June 10 the *Herald* published a single sheet, put out by Eric Hawkins, Robert Sage, B. J. Kospoth, and a few others still with the paper, with the lead story by John Elliott, chief of the *Herald Tribune* bureau, reporting that the German advance on the city appeared to have reached its terminal point. Trucks were available for delivery of the edition only within Paris.

Earlier, on June 7, a cable from Ogden Reid in New York to Hills in Paris had decided the question of the *Herald*'s role under occupation: DO NOT BELIEVE HUNS WILL REACH PARIS THIS CENTURY BUT IF THEY SHOULD YOU AND MRS. HILLS SHOULD BE ELSEWHERE STOP WE WILL NOT PRINT PROPAGANDA AND UNDER INVASION COULD NOT PRINT NEWSPAPER STOP THINK EMPLOYEES THEIR FAMILIES SHOULD BE EVACUATED TO FRENCH LOCALITIES THEIR CHOICE OUR EXPENSE UNDER YOUR DIRECTION WHENEVER THEY DESIRE LEAVE BEST WISHES. The cable proved well timed, if not prophetic, for four days later, June 11, Paris was formally abandoned to the Germans as an open city—a government decision, as historians would note, that preserved the city from further attack while devastating what remained of French morale.

On June 12, 1940, with German troops in the suburbs, the *Herald* put out its final wartime edition—a single, censored sheet bearing a cruelly hopeful headline over a report by Walter B. Kerr: "Great Battle for Paris at Crucial Stage." The sheet's reverse side was blank except for a few small ads—one, surreal in context, by a woman seeking a position as a lady's maid, another a cinema notice announcing "Talkies in English"—and the paper's masthead. No delivery trucks were available now, and the final edition appeared on no newsstands.

Two days later German troops entered the undefended city.

CHAPTER TWO

World's Zaniest Newspaper

To any shrewd American reader, the
Tribune *was his comic morning cocktail. . . .*
—HAROLD STEARNS,
The Street I Know

LE SHEE-KAH-GO. "I Never Knew Hemingway," Waverley Root called an early chapter of his memoir of seven years on the *Chicago Tribune*'s Paris edition, distancing himself from fellow interwar Paris-Americans who invariably maintained they did. In fact, Root knew Hemingway but Hemingway never knew him. One reason the two failed to fully connect was that when Root arrived in Paris in 1927 Hemingway's time in the city was winding down—and beyond this Hemingway's only involvement with the Paris *Tribune*, then as earlier, was as a regular reader and frequent subject of its Left Bank columns and news stories.

Scott Fitzgerald, on the other hand, made sudden nighttime forays to the newspaper's editorial office. During one, he took over the slot of the copy desk and drunkenly announced, "Come on, boys. Let's get out the god-damned paper." After the difficult evening— Fitzgerald singing, insisting others join him, and ripping up news copy—staff members piled him into a taxi and, several bar stops later, delivered him to his apartment. "Scott, you bastard!" Zelda shouted from an upper window. "You're drunk again!" During another, Fitzgerald arrived at the office with his wife, announced he had just visited a nearby brothel, and added, "Grand place, you fellows ought to go there and see what life is really like."

But a lengthy list of remembered and half-remembered Paris-Americans of literary or journalistic note were once, like Waverley Root, in *Tribune* harness: Henry Miller, Harold Stearns, Elliot Paul, James Thurber, William L. Shirer, Eugene Jolas, Vincent Sheean, Virgil Geddes, Wambly Bald, Ned Calmer, Robert Sage, Lawrence Blochman, Bravig Imbs. Here they labored with a core group of more or less committed and capable journalists to produce a paper that Shirer pronounced, with an ironic salute to the *Chicago Tribune*'s self-styled eminence as the World's Greatest Newspaper, "the world's zaniest newspaper, a crazy journal without peer."

Shirer had in mind the paper's reputation as the leader among Paris-American dailies as a madcap place to work. Harold Stearns recalled his *Tribune* days in a similar frolicking, out of *The Front Page* spirit: "Though I didn't at the time fully realize it, working on the *Tribune* had been a one-way ticket to the Never-Never-Land of male irresponsibility, absurdity, and entertainment, of which all men in their hearts forever dream—and so seldom ever reach." The *Tribune*, however, had more than newsroom high jinks to recommend it. The paper was livelier and exhibited more personal character than the dominant *Herald*, and, during the years the two were head-to-head morning competitors, generally matched it in news content, appearance, and the effort, never notable on either paper, put into local reporting.

During the middle twenties the *Tribune* likewise equaled the *Herald* in boasts of overall superiority, with daily page-one house ads claiming it was read "by more Americans than any European daily newspaper published on the Continent. All statements of other newspapers to the contrary are false." Where the paper unquestionably bested the *Herald* was in attention to Parisian intellectual and cultural life. If the *Herald* was the hometown paper of the established Right Bank American colony, the *Tribune* filled the same role for the shifting throng of Left Bank expatriates. It was, as Shirer said with only modest exaggeration, a paper "mostly written and almost entirely read by the bohemians of Montparnasse."

OUT OF THE LOCAL ROOM. While today the Paris *Tribune* is scarcely more than a footnote in journalism history—even in thick accounts of the parent paper such as Lloyd Wendt's *Chicago Tribune: The Rise of a Great American Newspaper* it gets only a passing nod—in literary history it occupies a small but significant niche. Eugene Jolas is recalled as the founder in 1927, with Elliot Paul as his co-editor, of *transition*, the literary journal Malcolm Cowley pronounced "the boldest and bulkiest of the expatriate magazines." Over the next decade *transition*—edited in its early days from a tiny fourth-floor room of a hotel at 40 Rue Febert—printed an impressive amount of innovative new writing, including James Joyce's "Work in Progress" together with stories and poems by, among Americans, Gertrude Stein, Hart Crane, Allen Tate, Archibald MacLeish, Kay Boyle, Ernest Hemingway, and William Carlos Williams.

Samuel Putnam, the Paris-American editor, translator, and biographer of Rabelais, held that "it was *transition* that really awakened the broader circles of American intelligentsia to the fact that something was going on in Europe and among our expatriates." In news items and culture columns the *Tribune* vigorously promoted the journal, as in a 1927 report about the attention it was getting from American critics: "Continuing its sensational sweep, *transition*, the new magazine edited in Paris by Eugene Jolas and Elliot Paul, is making a profound impression in the literary circles of America, according to word received from there."

Staff members were frequent contributors, and the scholarly Robert Sage—who appeared with Jolas, Paul, Virgil Geddes, and Bravig Imbs in the initial issue—eventually became the third member of the editing team. In 1929 Sage, a University of Michigan graduate who had worked on the *Detroit Times* before coming to Paris, co-edited with Jolas *transition stories*, a collection dedicated to Paul and containing work by *Tribune* staffer Emily Holmes Coleman along with Jolas, Paul, and Sage himself. To some, the link between the paper and the journal was so close that *transition* seemed virtually an extension of the *Tribune's* book page and its arts-dominated Sunday magazine. "This most advanced of reviews," observed Putnam, "may thus be said to have come out of the local room."

When Jolas ended publication in 1930, temporarily as it happened, B. J. Kospoth, then the *Tribune's* art critic, wrote a glowing obituary pointing out that "an unusual feature about *transition* is the fact that it was conceived and executed by newspapermen. It was a real newspapermen's venture." Kospoth concluded by quoting approvingly Jolas's remark that in many respects *transition* was "an offshoot of *The Tribune*." The link between the *Tribune*, especially its Sunday magazine, and *transition* can be overstated—the one a newspaper supplement with a decided slant toward literary and cultural matters, the other a journal of original fiction, poetry, and criticism. The connection, as Kospoth rightly characterized it, was that *Tribune* newspapermen created, maintained, and wrote for the journal.

The connection reveals the extent and range of literary-cultural interest among *Tribune* staffers—interest possibly greater than that of any collection of newsmen on a paper of small circulation and limited life span. Kay Boyle maintained that "many who wrote on a regular basis for the Paris Tribune were among the most prolific of the avant-garde writers" of the time—the "many" and "prolific" excessive, yet it is true that several *Tribune* staffers appeared in *transition* and they were indeed swept along by advanced currents in literary work. As well as a showcase for their work, involvement with the journal gave *Tribuners* the stimulating sense that, from the distance of expatriate Paris, they had—as Robert Sage cautiously observed in an open letter to Eugene Jolas when *transition* was closing down—made "american literature . . . a little different just as all literature has been a little different since the publication of *Ulysses*."

TENT MATE OF THE ARMY. The Paris *Tribune* had its origin in the *Chicago Tribune*'s Army Edition, launched in Paris with patriotic pride on July 4, 1917, and directed to the American Expeditionary Forces that had joined the European war. Before he turned fervent isolationist, the war was a foreign involvement that Colonel Robert R. McCormick, the *Chicago Tribune*'s editor and publisher, both applauded and—hence his military title—took part in. He pledged that any profits from his wartime Paris operation—and despite hefty cable tolls he expected some from a newsstand price of two cents, later raised to four, plus advertising revenue from mail-order houses offering clothing and boots in short supply in the war zone—would go to the military.

The four-page tabloid saw itself as a daily letter from home for the troops, as a page-one story announced in the first issue, written and edited by men who had eagerly come over from the parent paper in Chicago. Switching metaphors, the paper proclaimed that "we have become a tent mate of the army. Whenever troops were called to France the call fell on equally responsive ears in the office of The Chicago *Tribune*. . . . We are here with the vanguard of the army."

Directed by Joseph Pierson, a stateside employee who had come up with the idea of a Paris-based paper, the Army Edition brought with it such familiar features of the home paper as John T. McCutcheon's drawings, the editorial-page column "A Line O'Type or Two," and "The Gumps" comic strip. On August 11 the paper announced a forthcoming feature, "How Peggy Came to Paris," by Peggy Hull, a war correspondent in Paris representing the *El Paso Morning Times* and a syndicate of Western papers. A large photo on page two of the young and attractive Peggy accompanied a breezy self-interview in which she concluded, "Well, if you don't like my stuff, don't read it."

On August 14 the series began, bylined "Peggy" and billed as "the story of a girl's adventures on land and sea on her way to see General Pershing and the American Army in France." Lively and laced with dialogue, the long articles continued daily through August 18 when Peggy finally met with Pershing. The series was followed with a help column in which soldiers wrote Peggy about Paris shopping problems—Christmas gifts for home folks and the like—and she responded in the paper. Later, a friendship in Paris between Peggy Hull and Colonel McCormick's wife resulted in McCormick asking the reporter to contribute articles to the Army Edition on life in the military camps as seen from a woman's point of view. Later still, in November 1918, Hull joined an American expeditionary force in Siberia with an official correspondent's pass, the first issued to a woman by the War Department.

Equally offbeat work began appearing in the paper on August 20 when Ring Lardner brought his popular "In the Wake of the News" column to Paris, telling George Seldes, briefly the Army Edition's managing editor, that "the Colonel sent me to France to write the comic side of the World War." His arrival was announced in Lardnerian verse:

> Although preliminary dope
> Had driven me trés frantic,
> I didn't see no periscope
> While crossing the Atlantic.

But on the whole neither Paris nor the war brought out the best in Lardner, and less than a month after arriving he steamed home to cover the World Series. The ending of his final Paris column on September 16 was a tourist's shopworn complaint about a city gratefully left behind: "Au revoir, and I hope next time I see you, you will have some of the modern conveniences such as drinking water and soap."

During his French stay Lardner also turned out "Reporter's Diary" pieces for *Collier's* magazine, work later collected in a book

with the straightforward title *My Four Weeks in France*. In his reporter's guise, Lardner left Paris and traveled to an American camp
and the British front, yet his dim view of French ways remained unchanged. "The train leaves at seven to-morrow morning," he wrote
about his departure for London, "and between now and then I have
only to pack and to settle with the hotel. The former chore will be
easy, for I possess just half as much personal property as when I
came. Parisian laundries have commandeered the rest."

SPITTING IN THE *HERALD*'S EYE. Two months after it first appeared,
the Army Edition expanded from a tabloid to a full-sized publication that ordinarily was only a single sheet printed on both sides but
with a larger news hole and more space for money-making ads for
woolen underwear, trench coats, and portable bathtubs. Profits
were modest, but with the war's end in 1919 McCormick was able
to redeem his pledge to the military by issuing General Pershing a
check for 106,902 francs and 82 centimes—by one accounting,
something over $2,000.

But what seemed an ending was a beginning. The Army Edition
was seamlessly continued as the European Edition of *The Chicago
Daily Tribune and the Daily News, New York*, the paper's official title
(with the masthead listing as editors and publishers both Mc-
Cormick and his cousin Joseph Patterson, chief of the *Daily News*),
while among staff members and readers it was commonly known as
the Paris *Tribune* or the Paris Editon or *Chicatrib*, its cable designa-
tion, and among Parisians as Le Shee-kah-go. Joseph Pierson was
unceremoniously dumped by McCormick as director of the new
paper and Floyd Gibbons, the *Chicago Tribune*'s ace war correspondent, placed in charge both of the Paris paper and the *Chicago Tribune*'s newly formed foreign news service.

McCormick's explanation for carrying on with a Paris paper was
set out some three years later in a boxed page-one Paris *Tribune* editorial on January 28, 1923, the date marking the return home of the

last troops in Europe of the American Expeditionary Forces. Head-lined "We Remain in France," the editorial linked the paper with the wartime Army Edition but stressed new contents ("world news, po-litical, scientific and economic news, the doings of society, literary, dramatic and music reviews") and a new role "*as the remaining link of communication, in both directions*, between the old world and the new." The emphasis was McCormick's, who added: "Experience shows that it is not easy for peoples separated by leagues of water and en-grossed in their separate problems to understand each other. Misun-derstandings will arise. It is our mission to minimize these and, by truthful publicity, to work for friendship and comity."

Others thought, less nobly, that McCormick was simply envious of the Paris *Herald*'s prestige and wanted to show Europeans that New York was not the only important American city by providing them in the *Tribune* with what William L. Shirer called "a red-blooded American newspaper to interpret America's attitude toward Europe." Waverley Root wondered if McCormick kept publishing only "to spit in the *Herald*'s eye," a paper the editor-publisher con-sidered directed to the pampered Americans of the Right Bank.

Ever the businessman, McCormick was also mindful of turning a profit with the new paper. By January 1922 the Paris *Tribune* had edged into the black, and the following year he boldly forecast profit, barring another war, in the range of $50,000 to $100,000. The surplus would remain with the Paris paper—as his *Tribune* ed-itorial outlined the future—to "improve the service to our readers, to establish pensions, sick benefits, home buying funds, and annual bonuses to employees; eventually, we hope to build a Paris home for our enterprise not unworthy of this Center of Art." As it turned out, the *Tribune*, always in the *Herald*'s business shadow, rarely if ever made money of any amount, nor did the generous employee bene-fits or a fitting building of the paper's own ever materialize.

Whatever the full explanation for its continuing life, the seven-column, usually eight-page daily *Tribune* developed into a familiar fea-ture of expatriate life through the twenties and on to the paper's abrupt demise in 1934. How it managed its relatively long, seventeen-year life in competition with the established and steady *Herald* remained to many an ongoing mystery. While it had a heavily Left Bank–Montparnasse readership, the *Tribune*'s editorial office (after a move from earlier quarters at 420 Rue St. Honoré) was located on the Right Bank, on the edge of Montmartre, in rented, rear-entrance, fourth-floor space at 5 Rue Lamartine of the labyrinthine building of a French daily, *Le Petit Journal*, which the paper also depended on for its printing and distribution. While its Paris workers were a restless collection of drifters, literary hopefuls, and able professionals, its Chicago chief was an impetuous autocrat who seemed wholly unlikely to maintain an essentially unprofitable and often unruly European edition of a Midwestern newspaper.

In the view of some staff members, the Paris *Tribune* survived as long as it did because McCormick gave little attention to what the paper actually printed. "Had McCormick read its columns, or understood them," said William L. Shirer, "he either would have suffered a stroke of apoplexy or killed the paper immediately—perhaps both." An outside observer, A. J. Liebling, who tried and failed to catch on with the rival *Herald* while a casual student at the Sorbonne in 1926–1927, took the position that McCormick, aware of the incongruity of the *Chicago Tribune* maintaining a foreign affiliate, "satisfied his conscience by keeping the Paris by-blow on the stingiest footing possible," a parsimony aided by the fact that many of his employees were stranded expatriates "who came cheap, because they were always in oversupply while prohibition lasted." Waverley Root bypassed speculation about McCormick's conscience but thought the paper's poor salaries had the welcome effect of insulating it from his dictates. Staff members had little to lose in quitting their jobs, and once their names were known in the confined world of Paris-American newspaper journalism it was easy to find other work. The overall result, Root concluded, was that the staff was "left alone to create our own Paris *Chicago Tribune*, a paper decidedly not cast in the image of the Chicago *Chicago Tribune*."

Staffers could not, however, duck McCormick's periodic European inspection tours and employee dinners. At one dinner of some thirty workers gathered about a large table, the paper's sports editor, Hérol Egan, took a chair beside McCormick and began a conversation about the failings of the American military high command in World War I. A Texan renowned on the paper for reluctant work habits, Egan had served in the war and considered himself an expert on the subject. Unfortunately, so did McCormick, who during the war had, as Major McCormick, commanded the American artillery attack on the village of Cantigny. When Egan said in a voice heard by all, "And the worst thing, Colonel, the very worst thing that happened in our army was when our artillery shelled its own infantry at Cantigny," McCormick rose from the table, announced "That man has spoiled my evening," and stalked out. "Never fire that man," he later ordered, "and never give him a raise." Over the years only the first part of the command was followed since Egan was considered a boon companion on the paper. "His likeability," said Root, "was the coin by which he compensated for his frequent incompetence."

THE COLONIAL MOLD. With the exception of its spirited attention to Left Bank intellectual and cultural concerns, the Paris *Tribune*'s day-to-day fare gave its Chicago master little cause for alarm. In their 1931 *American Mercury* article about the Paris *Herald*, Whit Burnett and Martha Foley said that paper, "like all colonial papers, is a front page of news backed up by several pages of rewrite and reprint." The *Tribune* was cast in the same colonial mold. Its front page came from costly cable dispatches sent from New York, where the *Chicago Tribune* maintained a correspondent, and expanded in the Paris office to a few sentences or a column. When A. J. Liebling knew the paper in the late twenties, the expanded cables, so he maintained, largely "consisted—apart from the inevitable sports results—of cheap shootings in Chicago, Jimmy Walker's didos in New York, and the grim, persistent efforts of the press to read humorous profundity into Calvin Coolidge's dim silence." Cable material was augmented with reports from the *Chicago Tribune*'s foreign news service correspondents around the world, the material transmitted over a leased wire from London, and with news rewritten or reprinted from the Paris, London, and New York papers together with mailed features, editorials, comics, and cartoons from the parent paper.

As with the *Herald*, local stories derived largely from boat trains and the hotels, civic organizations, and the diplomatic run. Stories with an interest to Chicago together with important diplomatic developments and nearly everything having to do with French politics were handled by correspondents of the *Chicago Tribune*'s Paris bureau, housed in the same Rue Lamartine quarters, with carbons of their stories turned over to the Paris paper and printed with credit to the foreign news service.

The local American colony had replicated the civic organizations found at home, and *Tribune* reporters—ordinarily no more than three or four—joined their *Herald* counterparts for droning speeches and ritual celebrations at the Chamber of Commerce, Rotary, American Legion, American Club, and the like. Shipping lines and hotels supplied lists of arriving Americans, but legwork was required in tracking notable figures from the boat trains at Gare St. Lazare to plush hotels on the Right Bank and arranging interviews. In Elliot Paul's 1930 novel *The Amazon*, the narrator, a foreign correspondent who has worked for a time for a Paris-American newspaper, tells of his dislike for "routine reporting, especially in Paris where it means a continual round of interviews with fatuous business men, opera singers, moving picture directors, big-game hunters, and various visitors from America who can afford first-class railway carriages and expensive hotels."

Stories turned up by the paper's day staff together with cable material and clippings from the French press were left impaled on a newsroom spike as raw material for the night staff putting the paper together. A great oval table was the room's centerpiece, with the semicircular slot on one side occupied by the city editor during the day and the news editor at night, the men arranged along its rim used both for rewrite and as copy editors. The room's corners housed desks of the managing editor, sports editor, and financial editor, with the society editor's desk outside the room on the other side of a corridor, where there were also a few stray desks and typewriters for reporters. Outfitted with French keyboards, the typewriters proved hazardous for some staffers who, slipping into American keyboard style as they banged away, found—as James Thurber put it—that "everything turned out in commas and parentheses and other punctuation marks."

SOCIETY BEAT. Like the *Herald*, the *Tribune* maintained a centrally located business office, this at 5 Rue Scribe, where tourists could register, with their names appearing the following day in the paper's closely watched "Arrivals" column. News notes in the daily "The Social World" column were on the order of "Mr. and Mrs. Frederick G. Garrison, of Chicago, after an extended stay in Bilbao, have arrived in Paris, for a short visit. They are staying at the Hotel Continental." For the truly notable there were lengthy staff-written profiles in the "Who's Who Abroad" column, with politicians, business tycoons, and cultural leaders typically the featured figures. On occasion, notable foreign correspondents of the *Chicago Tribune* made the space—among them, Sigrid Schultz, a rare woman correspondent in Europe who had followed George Seldes as chief of the Berlin bureau, and Larry Rue, who held the enviable position of a roving correspondent and had a book soon to appear, one that—as his profile limply noted—would reveal his "many thrilling experiences."

The inner life of local society was retailed in "Today in Society," the daily column written for several years by May Birkhead and appearing generally at the head of the second column on page one, the space personally ordained by Colonel McCormick. Once when

Waverley Root was making up the page, the column was shifted a few inches down and then jumped to an inside page. That issue of his Paris paper apparently came to McCormick's attention, for the next day Root received a cable from the editor-publisher instructing him never again to shift the column from its privileged position.

Society editors tended to come and go on Paris-American papers. Considered unskilled workers since most news was phoned into them and they were seldom glimpsed in the editorial office, they were poorly paid and easily replaced. Birkhead was an exception, hired by McCormick after her long tenure on the *Herald* in the hope her prestige would draw more Right Bank readership; fittingly, she was said to send her copy to the *Tribune*'s office each night in a chauffeured limousine. However it arrived, Root thought her work one of the few areas in which the *Tribune* gained a news rather than cultural edge on the *Herald*: "She had been on close terms with its [society's] members since birth, and knew about all the skeletons in all the closets, although she was discreet enough never to mention them. Since she was always the first to be informed of impending events in high society, anyone who wanted to be up-to-date had to read the Tribune."

DON'T MAKE IT TOO LONG. When local news stories turned up with interest beyond Paris, the *Tribune*'s betters on the foreign staff usually took over and the paper was left with running their carbons. With Lindbergh's arrival at Le Bourget field in 1927, questions of interest were overwhelmed and both staffs had on their hands the major news story of the twenties. Oddly, the *Tribune*'s then managing editor, Bernhard Ragner, failed to see it as such even though the preceding day the paper had run a page-one story announcing "Lindbergh Winging Way Over Sea Toward Paris" and a sidebar adding "Paris Prepares Great Reception for 'Flying Fool.'" On the night of the landing Ragner assigned the main story to Ralph Jules Frantz, at the time the paper's young city editor, with William L.

Shirer helping out. There would be only one wrap-up account, the pair were told.

When Shirer made it from Le Bourget through the minefield of congestion before Frantz, Ragner told him, "I guess it's your story. But don't make it too long." Frantz appeared a short time later and begged to write a follow-up account. The managing editor held his ground: "One story is all I want." Frantz countered with a request to at least go to the office of the Commercial Cable Company, where he knew the *Chicago Tribune's* bureau chief, Henry ("Hank") Wales, was writing accounts to transmit to Chicago, and bring back carbons of his story. "Go if you want," Ragner shrugged, "but we won't be able to use it."

When Frantz returned with Wales's material the paper's pages were locked up for the night. Meanwhile the bureau chief had cabled his account to Chicago, where it appeared under his byline as the page-one lead with an accompanying Lindbergh interview. Wales left the impression that, in both cases, he was the only reporter present. In the lead story Lindbergh's first words after leaving the cockpit were "Am I in Paris?"—with Wales's answering "'You're here,' I told him, as the mob jabbered in French, which was not in the least understood by the bewildered American." "I showed him news flashes already sent to America," Wales wrote when Lindbergh said he wanted to send his mother a telegram, "to tell his mother of his safe arrival."

In the sidebar interview, Lindbergh spending the night in the American ambassador's residence, Wales wrote that "he received me in the bedroom in his pajamas, sitting on the bed, when I arrived to deliver his mother's telegram of congratulations," and went on to record the airman's laconic account of the flight. In fact, Wales's assistant, Jay Allen, had been the sole *Chicago Tribune* representative among the several reporters present at the impromptu bedroom interview. Nonetheless Wales's page-one work was handsomely rewarded the following day with a cable from Chicago: CONGRATULATIONS YOUR LINDBERGH EXCLUSIVE STOP MAILING FIVE HUNDRED BONUS. MCCORMICK.

In the Paris *Tribune*, Shirer's Lindbergh story led page one under a modest two-column headline and attribution to the "Tribune Press Service." The opening was appropriately dramatic: "Dropping with the grace of a bird out of the darkened sky, Captain Charles Lindbergh whom they called a Flying Fool back home swooped down on Le Bourget field at 10:22 o'clock. . . . " Brief page-one stories added that the paper had been besieged that night by phone calls seeking news about Lindbergh and that, as a headline had it, "Paris Enthusiasm Knows No Bounds."

Through the following days the paper was jammed with Lindbergh stories, with the lead page-one accounts carbons of Hank Wales's work for Chicago. When Lindbergh flew from Paris for frenzied receptions in Brussels and London, Wales reported the flights from an accompanying airplane. Only when Lindbergh left for home on an American naval ship departing from Cherbourg was the bureau chief's hold on the story broken, with Jay Allen, referring familiarly to the flyer as "Charlie Lindbergh," credited with the report.

RESIDENT INTELLECTUAL. Where the *Tribune* escaped both the colonial mold and the narrow Midwestern reputation of the parent paper for a distinctive presence of its own was mainly in the work of its in-house columnists and critics together with broad news reporting of the Parisian cultural scene. Among the columnists, Alex Small stood out. A *cum laude* Harvard graduate who in World War I had joined the French ambulance corps before transferring to the American infantry, Small arrived at the *Tribune* in the summer of 1925 after a period of college teaching and settled in for the duration of the paper's life as its prominent page-one columnist and resident intellectual.

At first a junior member of what was then a three-man reporting staff, he was given the "donkey work" of meeting and seeing off the boat trains. "Any office boy could have done this job if he had his wits about him," he recalled, "but neither I nor my colleagues had crossed the Atlantic to keep our wits about us":

> Still I did get all but the most crassly impossible names of the tourists spelled right. This was highly important as a source of revenue to the company. It was amazing how many people would buy 10, 20, 50, or even 100 copies of Le Shee-kah-go to send back to the folks in Tulsa just because their names had appeared in a ship's list.

Elevated to a columnist, Small's usually twice-a-week "Of Fleeting Things"—dense, wide-ranging, acerbic—was often at odds with the pieties and platitudes of expatriate life as well as much of the century's conventional wisdom. A pet subject drawing his testy commentary was the "ultra-precious artistic and literary activity" of the time, with the work of the Left Bank's grand deity, James Joyce, a continuing case in point. "Mr. Joyce has deliberately chosen to break the ordinary social contract between author and reader," Small argued in a weighty column on April 10, 1927, ostensibly about the new, experimental writing appearing in *transition*. "This fundamental concept of the old esthetic code being neglected, Mr. Joyce can have no complaint if intelligence (the intelligence that brings order out of chaos) condemns his writing as nonsense."

Among lighter matters that caught Small's passing interest were the end of Prohibition in America, the fortieth anniversary of Guy de Maupassant's death, the French passion for boating, and the traditional cafés of Paris under assault by a new cosmopolitanism sweeping the city. For expatriates, likely oblivious to the café crisis, he defined in a column on January 12, 1929, the café's essential qualities as

> . . . marble-topped tables, a rococo whatnot in two or three stories for the bottles, and a red-nosed and pot-bellied

proprietor in shirt sleeves and collarless. The customers
should be steady ones; they are called in French *piliers de café*,
exactly as Anglo-Saxons refer to "pillars of the church." . . . In
it cocktails are unknown and Americans are still regarded,
without sympathy and without hostility, as simply *étrangers*
who live at home in mountain-high houses. . . . The café is
not an object of beauty; its lay-out and furniture are testimony
to the superb bad taste of its owner and the indifference of his
customers.

To his *Tribune* colleague Edmond Taylor, Small had the severe
appearance of a Savonarola, with a bald patch on the roof of his
head suggesting a monk's tonsure. As for his column, Taylor was
impressed by its learning, wit, and range of subjects; few things in
the paper matched it "either in brilliance of style or in irrelevance
to the mainstream of twentieth-century life." Small's annual autumn column, he added, tied to falling leaves on the Avenue Foch
and enriched with "bleak insights dredged from the depths of a seasonal hangover," was a perennial masterpiece. To another colleague,
Carol Weld, Small as a columnist was an "erudite placer of one
word after another until totaling a thousand."

Some on the paper, however, dismissed Small's work as too
pedantic and obscure for a newspaper and the man himself as self-
important and overbearing. "Possessing a certain baggage of Latin
and Greek," grumbled Bravig Imbs, ". . . he belonged to that group
of cultivated men who think it smart to be hard boiled." Waverley
Root offered the curt observation that in conversation Small was
most alert to the sound of his own voice. But for fellow Harvard
man Harold Stearns (who said he suggested the name of Small's
column—a title Somerset Maugham had not used for *Of Human
Bondage*) it was Small's work alone that mattered—work far too
good for the *Tribune* as well as a "wastrel Paris audience that to a
melancholy extent had no deeper or keener intellectual interest
than has anybody trying to recover from a hang-over."

A SLIGHTLY ALCOHOLIC GHOST. Wambly Bald's "La Vie de Bohème (As Lived on the Left Bank)" column, a weekly scattershot collection of Left Bank reporting, gossip, barbs, and publicity blurbs, was finely attuned to the paper's audience, wastrel or otherwise. After finishing the University of Chicago, the improbably named Bald had roamed the country with periods of itinerant journalism until 1929 when, working as a seaman out of New Orleans, he shipped off to Paris. A plan to stay a few weeks changed after he savored the sweet life of Montparnasse. Learning that a *Tribune* proofreader had returned to America, he applied for the job and was hired.

Bald refused when Ralph Jules Frantz, now the *Tribune*'s managing editor, tried to promote him to the regular editorial staff, but under Frantz's prodding he was persuaded to begin the column. It ran regularly from October 1929 to July 1933 and was among the paper's most closely followed features. Samuel Putnam, whose *New Review* often drew Bald's notice, pictured the baffling working method of the "Montparnasse chronicler" as "wandering in and out of the Quarter like a slightly alcoholic ghost, seeing nothing, hearing nothing, and telling all." Bald's quirky writing style, added Putnam, was located "somewhere in between *Gentlemen Prefer Blondes* and *The New Yorker*, with a dash now and again of James Joyce or the Surrealists."

Usually Bald leaped right in with his columns, as in one on January 19, 1932:

What does the Left Bank think about?

The *avant-garde*, the poets, the hermits—what do they think about? Why do they forsake the ordinary? It's the inner eye.

The inner eye goads them on; it forces their dreams with promises of extra-terrestrial booty. It makes victims of the guys on the Left Bank. New ideas are the coin of the Quarter, bright tokens beyond value. Bob Brown has a new idea. He played with it for 15 years, and now it pops without ceremony.

Brown's slow-to-develop idea, Bald went on to explain, was a reading machine with words printed in tiny type on a spool of tape and
read through a magnifying glass. Brown hoped the machine would
accelerate reading, but—as Bald noted—"if only he could speed up
the human brain, the machine would be a wow, but it is not that
modern."

Montparnasse and its inhabitants provided no lack of material,
but at times Bald backed into a column before hitting his stride. On
June 23, 1931, for instance:

> Someone in the next apartment is playing the Victrola and the
> music is tickling my fancy. That music and this weather have
> given me thoughts, and when I get thoughts, I smoke many
> cigarettes. I have already smoked half a package but still can
> think of nothing significant. However—to plunge into
> problems.

The problems turned out to be questions about the current health
of expatriate Paris, with Bald inviting reader answers:

> Has Bohemia folded? Is the Dôme just a café? Has the "lost
> generation" found itself? Is it true that mediocrity has
> whitewashed the Carrefour? If so, does it make any
> difference? All replies, if accompanied by a stamped envelope,
> will be considered.

Other *Tribune* columns of note were the literary musings of Elliot Paul in "From A Litterateur's Notebook" and Eugene Jolas in
"Rambles Through Literary Paris." Louis Atlas in "Most Anything
Can Happen" offered relaxed, amusing glimpses of Left Bank life.
(Ordinarily printed with a headline beneath the title, the column
stimulated creativity on the copy desk. A column about loud radio
music from an apartment above irritating a French tax inspector at
work below bore a headline reading "Tars and Tripes Forever Men-
ace Fiscal Conjuring.") Brief treatments of the same cultural land-
scape appeared in "Latin Quarter Notes," written by Paul

Shinkman, Alex Small, Edmond Taylor, and other staff members; in "What the Writers Are Doing" by Harold Ettlinger; and in the Montparnasse news items of "Montparno," the catchall identity of several staff writers. Long, informed critical reviews came from Waverley Root on books, B. J. Kospoth on painting, Florence Gilliam on theater, and Irving Schwerké on music.

Like Alex Small, Kospoth and Schwerké had long *Tribune* tenures and developed wide pro and con followings for their work. Schwerké, for example, a trained musician from Appleton, Wisconsin, wrote his first review for the paper in 1921 and stayed to the end in 1934. In addition to his *Tribune* work he was Paris correspondent for music journals, organized musical events, produced a number of books, and in 1951 was awarded the French Legion of Honor. Gilliam, who also wrote for several publications as well as the *Tribune*, likewise arrived in 1921, remained in France for two decades, wrote a book about the country, returned after the war to live in the Hôtel de Crillon in Paris as its unofficial hostess, and received the Legion of Honor.

In the *Tribune*'s news space the cultural icons James Joyce and Gertrude Stein were ongoing subjects, and readers were kept duly informed of such literary minutiae as Scott Fitzgerald's use of the Riviera as a setting for a new novel under way. Maxwell Bodenheim's departure from Paris for Greenwich Village was worth a lighthearted interview (beneath a headline reading "Lure of Greenwich Village too Strong for Maxwell Bodenheim; Back He Goes"), as was the Paris arrival of the popular novelist Arthur Roche, who confided that he might have set a record by having four serial novels running simultaneously in four American magazines. Paris visits of Booth Tarkington, Sinclair Lewis, and Theodore Dreiser produced stories on the state of American letters and the virtues and vices of expatriate life. The suicides of the poet Hart Crane and the painter Lawrence Murphy were reported at length, as was the death by natural causes of the American dancer Maurice Mouvet. Notice was taken of the divorce decree granted by a Paris court to Hadley

Hemingway and the marriage of Kay Boyle to the American writer and painter Laurence Vail, the former husband of Peggy Guggenheim. The expatriate writer Carl Van Vechten's popular new novel *The Tatooed Countess* came in for extended analysis in an editorial, drawing praise and criticism. "It's a grand novel," the paper decided about the playful story of a mature, Europeanized woman's return to her provincial Iowa town. "The title itself is a knockout, and the thesis is of high comedy, but also it is Greenwich Village again looking at American life through the keyhole."

SUNDAY SUPPLEMENT. The *Tribune*'s attention to the culture beat gained high prominence with the introduction in 1924 of a Sunday magazine section, a four-column, twelve-page tabloid fronted with a fine etching. Edited by Roscoe Ashworth, the first issue on February 17 defined itself as a weekly periodical treating literary and artistic matters that fell beyond the scope of a daily newspaper—a combination, as it was put, of an American-style Sunday supplement and an English weekly review—and announced it would accept and pay for unsolicited contributions.

The issue's centerpiece was the first of a dozen "Literary Causeries" by Ford Madox Ford, this on the subject of "The Young American Writers" with an accompanying photograph of Ford with James Joyce, Ezra Pound, and the American lawyer John Quinn, a financial backer of Ford's *transatlantic review*. Among the issue's other features was the column "Reviews and Reflections" by Louis Gay, the pen name of Lewis Galantière; an appreciation of Igor Stravinsky by the modernist composer George Antheil; and—a curiosity—an article entirely in French.

In subsequent issues Ford's "Causeries" ranged across French writers, Bill Bird's Paris-based Three Mountains Press, and the Dadaist movement. A London Letter was added to the magazine along with an occasional short story. Critical articles came largely from *Tribune* staff members—among them Lawrence Blochman, B. J. Kospoth, Florence Gilliam, Irving Schwerké, and Bernhard Ragner—and there were outside contributions from Paris *Herald* writers Vincent Bugeja (on Kant) and Arthur Moss (on clowns). An unsigned literary odds-and-ends column, "Bookworm's Brevities," appeared each week, as did staffer Lansing Warren's Lardner-inspired "Dear Pard" column of letters home by an immigrant bartender ("In France yuh don't have to hunt out a high class expensive bar to get Good Stuff . . . it's there on sale at the Corner Bistrot. And the bistrot, lemme say, is the Bulwark uv the Nation. There's no place like it in America and never was").

In late May the magazine expanded briefly to sixteen pages and, Ford's "Causeries" concluded, Eugene Jolas inaugurated a central literary column called "Through Paris Bookland," later changed to "Rambles Through Literary Paris." David Darrah, who had followed Floyd Gibbons as the *Tribune*'s managing editor, suggested the column, and at first Jolas hesitated about following in the British writer's commanding footsteps. When Darrah persisted, Jolas launched in, viewing himself as applying "American reporting methods to the creative and aesthetic issues of the day. I considered myself primarily a reportorial observer and recorder of the ideological currents in post-war Paris." Contacts made through the column with both expatriate and European writers and artists would serve him well when he began *transition*, a journal he would think of as "a kind of higher journalism" in which he reported on new European intellectual movements and introduced Europeans to new English-language writers.

In the November 16 issue B. J. Kospoth produced a long, admiring commentary on Jolas's poetry in which he pointed to the poet's use of newspaper experience in his verse. "The drama of the modern newspaper," wrote Kospoth, "has never before been told in prose or verse untainted by sentimentalism." In the same issue, in a "Rambles" column otherwise given over to European writers, Jolas penned an open letter to Hemingway, praising him as "destined to create a new literature on the American continent" but taking folksy issue with two poems appearing in the German journal *Der Querschnitt*: "We ain't able to follow you there. . . . We simply give up. . . . We believe you're on the wrong track. . . . Please give us another 'My Old Man' and let it go at that."

Learned articles and reviews still appeared in future issues but so did the comic strips "The Gumps" and "Smitty," and the front page featured such light fare as Lansing Warren's "Some of the Ways to Spoil Vacations." The magazine now had the look of a typical American Sunday supplement more than a British weekly review. By late 1924 it had fallen off to eight pages, and by 1925 was gone altogether, with Jolas's "Rambles" column and Warren's "Dear Pard" surviving in the newspaper's regular Sunday edition.

FLUENT IN FRENCH. The *Tribune*'s pay was notoriously poor—$12 to $15 a week, in francs, for proofreaders and ordinary editorial staff, less than the *Herald* paid and far less than the dollars earned by the *Chicago Tribune*'s elite foreign correspondents. The money was enough, barely, to live on in Paris—"enough," calculated Morrill Cody, "for a small hotel room and food and an occasional drink at the Sélect or one of the other popular cafés in the neighborhood— though for married staffers with families outside Grub Street work was usually a necessity." Given the paltry pay there was frequent staff turnover, with periods, as one staffer noted, when the editorial office "was like the terrace of a café—men came and went so fast. Hello, and so long." A lack of new recruits, however, was never a problem.

After two years at Dartmouth, Bravig Imbs arrived in Paris in 1925 with ambition as a poet, little money, and no newspaper experience. He applied at the *Tribune* as a skilled reporter from Chicago who was fluent in French and was immediately put to work on the rim of the copy desk. "I don't know a word of French. Help! Help!" he was soon begging in a typed note to the figure beside him when given French clippings to translate. "Slip the cuttings under the table," came back a message from Geoffrey Fraser. "I'll slip them back with the translations."

Soon thereafter Imbs was fired by the paper, though later re-hired in the advertising department and as a proofreader. In Fraser, a rare Englishman on the staff, he had made a useful friend. In 1926 Fraser found a printer and acted as publisher for Imbs's first book of poetry, *Eden: Exit This Way*. He also drew Imbs's attention to Elliot Paul.

WRITING MENTOR. After service in a signal corps unit in France in World War I, Paul in 1925 had reappeared in Paris with newspaper experience in Boston and three autobiographical novels in a modernist mode to his credit: *Indelible: A Story of Life, Love and Music in Five Movements*; *Impromptu: A Novel in Four Movements*; *Imperturbe: A Novel of Peace Without Victory*. Hired by the *Tribune* as a proofreader, he found himself "struggling with copy which had been written by either drunken or illiterate American exiles and set up by French compositors who confused English with Canadian French." While proofreaders in America were members of the printers union, on Paris-American papers they were considered editorial department employees yet housed in a basement area among the clanking Linotype machines. Despite their link with the workers above, Imbs was aware of "an invisible but very real barrier" between the men around the copy desk and the handful of eye-shaded figures laboring below, leaving him "a little dashed to think that a man I had pictured penning his books in some distinguished library was working at a lowly trade, much lower than mine."

Because of rapid turnover among proofreaders, jobs were easy to get, or thought to be. When the Canadian writer John Glassco learned that his monthly allowance in Paris had been cut in half by his father, a friend suggested that "perhaps one of us should get some kind of work. I'll go to the *Chicago Tribune* and see if they need a proofreader." They did not. "In the evening," Glassco recalled, "we decided to go to the counter of the Dôme and drink until things looked rosier." Once hired for the lowly trade, Elliot Paul soon rose to the rewrite desk, establishing himself as a versatile deskman with a rarefied sense of humor. Along with others on the staff, he was adept at nursing one-sentence cable dispatches into a half-column or more of fanciful copy. Under his hand a cable about a missing star pitcher for the bearded House of David baseball team turning up in Kokomo, Indiana, became a convoluted tale in which the pitcher's beard was entangled in a wringer while working in a local laundry, thus exposing his true identity and returning him to teammates.

Unwisely placed for a time in charge of the paper on Sundays, the managing editor's night off, Paul would arrive at the office early, clip the most readable stories from the London Sunday papers, paste them to copy paper, compose headlines, and ship the material off to the composing room. When the staff appeared for work he would inform them that, the paper filled, they could have the night off. A night off was a night drinking, and Paul led the way on Parisian prowls that left many ruined for the following day's work.

Paul was a staff guide in another sense—as the paper's resident literary figure and dispatcher of advice to younger colleagues. For Bravig Imbs, who took a room in Paul's hotel to be close to him, he aided in the writing of Imbs's first novel, *The Professor's Wife*, and reviewed an earlier book of poetry in the *Tribune*, where he observed that Imbs "is a resident of Paris, works at various disagreeable occupations in order to remain here." When Imbs ran into a roadblock with his writing, Paul's remedy was daily diligence:

> Set yourself the task of writing a certain number of pages each
> day; let nothing deter you from the task, be it headache or
> mood or despair. You will find that the days that were the
> hardest will show the best writing; you will be amazed at the
> speed the manuscript increases, and eventually you will

produce such a quantity that you will be enabled to destroy
pages and pages without any feeling of loss. The seven books
I like the best are the seven I wrote and threw into the stove.

On another occasion, Imbs disenchanted with a finished novel, Paul
lectured on the use of personal experience in fiction:

> The first step is autobiographical writing. The writer, of
> course, gets disgusted with that, but generally not so quickly
> as you have. You will probably experience a reaction and will
> try to write in a "detached" manner. That won't do either
> because it is impossible to be detached from one's own
> experience, even in a historical novel. Then you may try to
> impersonate a character who tells the story from his point of
> view. That is better, but it is not direct enough. Also it may
> lead you into purple patches and those you must avoid at any
> cost. Phrases may be beautiful but their beauty is never of the
> highest quality. Remember that if one sentence is better than
> another, throw the latter away. You must learn to write
> directly what you feel—and there is nothing more difficult.

Another recipient of Paul's literary outreach was Virgil Geddes,
the *Tribune*'s financial editor—the glorified title of the staff member who assembled stock-market figures. The numbers job was
ideal, Geddes believed, since it left his mind free to work on plays
and poems, and during his years on the paper from 1924 to 1928 he
wrote five plays and three volumes of poetry. Paul published his poems in *transition* and wrote a preface for his first book, *Forty Poems*,
published in Paris in 1926. When Geddes's five-act play *The Frog*
was performed in Boston in 1927, the *Tribune* reported its "emphatic success." Likely from the hand of Paul, the news story went
on to note that the play had been written the previous summer "at
leisure moments spent in the tranquil atmosphere of the *bistrot*
called, paradoxically, *l'Hôtel du Caveau de la Terreur*, in the rue de la
Huchette. . . . One humid day, Miss Katharine Huntington, one of

the directors of the Boston Stage Society, walked into the *Caveau* with Elliot Paul, a habitué. She met Geddes, and, later, carried away with her 'The Frog.'"

Service of a different sort was provided for the painter Grant Wood. After William L. Shirer took him to an exhibition at the Galerie Carmine of works by his Iowa friend, Paul joined Shirer in passing the hat in the *Tribune* office to boost the painter's career. Unknown to Wood, who was trying to catch on in the Impressionist style, Paul then wrote up advance accounts of the exhibition and mailed them to prominent critics along with a few hundred francs in each envelope, the usual manner of creating goodwill in French critical circles. Favorable notices followed.

In his "From a Litterateur's Notebook" column Paul took up the cause of modernist writers in general and Gertrude Stein in particular. The Sunday paper with stories of Lindbergh's landing also carried the second of a long, detailed, and sympathetic four-part assessment of Stein's work. For Paul, in her latest work she was interested in the arrangement, sound, and effect of words rather than their definition—interested, as he phrased it, with "mature experiments" in "narrative without explanation, in description with cataloguing, and in the creation of abstract patterns which may be enjoyed as music, architecture or sculpture is enjoyed."

In *The Autobiography of Alice B. Toklas*, Stein credited Paul with "the first seriously popular estimation of her work" while "at the same time he was turning the young journalists and proof-readers [on the *Tribune*] into writers. He started Bravig Imbs on his first book, *The Professor's Wife*, by stopping him suddenly in his talk and saying, you begin there." Paul returned the compliment by dedicating to Stein his 1930 novel *The Amazon* in which during World War I an imposing woman forms a female signal corps unit.

The novel was published by Horace Liveright, the firm that the same year put out *The Governor of Massachusetts*, a novel drawing on Paul's days as a Boston newspaper reporter. The story goes that when Liveright returned the manuscript of the novel with a request to cut sixteen thousand words, Paul for several weeks made no response, then returned the manuscript without changes and was told it was now acceptable.

One in the stream of recollections of Paul's exploits, the story fits with his view of literary revision: he had no time for it. "When you write rapidly," he maintained, "you write in your own style. There is no good in trying for style by rewriting, by torturing sentences. You knock the life out of it, and probably out of your ideas." (At least in one instance, Paul's disdain for revision failed to extend to changes from an editor's hand. He credited Saxe Commins, the Random House editor of his 1941 memoir *The Last Time I Saw Paris*, with an "amazing job," and added: "I feel that I should name you as co-author of the book.") Along the same line, Paul dismissed note taking in literary work: "Your memory retains what is useful to you. When you make notes you remember only the notes. And when you start writing, the notes aren't enough; most of what you saw and heard has disappeared."

James Thurber, hired by the *Tribune* in the same period as Paul, conducted a running argument with him about the value of rewriting. Paul clung to his position that a writer should leave work just as it rolls from the typewriter. One day he came to the newspaper office and said a sixty-thousand-word manuscript had been stolen and he had no carbons or notes. Everyone was horrified, save for Paul. "But it didn't bother him at all," marveled Thurber. "He'd just get to the typewriter and bat away again."

POET IN THREE LANGUAGES. Eugene Jolas, born in New Jersey and a self-described "neo-American," had worked as a reporter for the *Daily News* in New York and other papers before reuniting in 1923 with family members who had returned from America to the German town of Forbach in Lorraine. Here he read books and wrote lyric poetry in French, German, and English, unable to settle on one language. When an attempt at writing and selling newspaper feature stories in Germany failed to yield enough income, he applied to American papers in Paris and in 1924 joined the *Tribune*.

Jolas rose quickly from the copy desk to reporting to city editor. In 1926 he briefly left Paris for New York, where he was married and planned to stay. But after another move—to New Orleans where he considered taking over the faltering literary magazine *Double Dealer*—he returned to Paris and the *Tribune*. The debut of *transition* followed in 1927. After shutting down the journal in 1930, Jolas resumed publication in 1932; in all, he published twenty-seven issues in Paris from 1927 to 1938, with three edited in New York in the period 1936–1937.

"Magazine journalism and *avant-gardisme* were beginning to pall," he explained about his eventual removal to New York, "and I longed to return to straight reporting." With the *Herald* the only American newspaper operating in Paris in the late thirties, he thought his job chances better in New York, and in time found work as a staff correspondent writing American stories in French for the news service Havas. His boss, Percy Winner, had worked in Paris for both the *Herald* and the *Tribune* and was now the chief Havas correspondent for North America. In the same office, translating European news into English, were Sam Dashiell, formerly a *Philadelphia Public Ledger* correspondent in Paris, and Leon Edel, the future biographer of Henry James. The bilingual Edel had worked on newspapers in Montreal and at the beginning of the thirties studied at the Sorbonne, a period in which he described himself as also "a junior hanger-on of the expatriates in Montparnasse."

WRITE A COLUMN ON THAT. Lanky, bespectacled James Thurber was a newspaperman in Columbus, Ohio, when in 1921 he hatched an ambitious plan for freelance article writing and fiction writing in France. It was 1925 before he arrived, and when neither articles nor fiction in a Normandy farmhouse went well, he applied to the *Tribune* after being turned away by the *Herald*. "I got thirty men ahead of you who want jobs," he was told by David Darrah, who then asked: "What are you, by the way, a poet, or a painter, or a novelist?" When Thurber said he was a newspaper-man with five years' experience who knew how to get the news and write it and put a headline on it, he was told to come to work the next night.

Thurber's stay with the *Tribune* was no more than a year but enough to establish him as a newsroom legend. He had a particular genius for inventing parody news features—"mainly," he claimed, "for the enjoyment of the other slaves." One happened to escape the copy desk and was set in type before it was caught and tossed out. In Thurber's merry recollection the story involved robbery, rape, gambling, and sex—matters that, as calculated by Bernhard Ragner, would have cost the paper billions in libel if it had appeared. "Some of us," said Thurber, "still dream about that libel suit that was never filed."

He was equally adept at supplying on demand column fillers of a sentence or two. One well-remembered item, with a Washington dateline, read: "'A man who does not pray is not a praying man,' President Coolidge today told the annual convention of the Protestant Churches of America." It was a matter of pride that he "got away with a dozen or more phonies which were printed." Yet another specialty was padding out cable dispatches: "We got only fifty words of cable each night and the city editor would take sentences out of this cable and pass them around the desk to Bill Shirer, Elliot Paul, and me, saying, 'Write a column on that.' I shall always remember two sentences he handed me. One of them was, 'Christy Mathewson died tonight at Saranac.' The other said simply, 'Admiral Richard E. Byrd flew to the North Pole and back in seventeen and a half hours.'"

Late in 1925 Thurber followed Lawrence Blochman (later a successful mystery writer, translator of French literature, and, in 1956, editor—suitably for a former Paris-American journalist—of *Here's How!*, an around-the-world bar guide produced by New York's Overseas Press Club) as assistant editor of the *Tribune*'s Riviera supplement, published in Nice during the winter high season. A short-lived innovation of the paper, the supplement made its appearance in 1923 as a single sheet printed on both sides and enclosed with a day-old copy of the Paris paper delivered to Nice by train. Publication ran from December to April, with the sheet essentially a gathering of predictable columns: Latest Arrivals, Riviera Personals, Notes on Riviera Society, The Nice Races, Riviera Amusement Programs.

When it reappeared for a second season, the supplement had grown into a four-page tabloid appearing seven days a week and carrying a front page of general news. Page two featured names from the "Riviera Social World," page three events "Along the Riviera," page four "Riviera Sporting News" together with stock quotations. There were now some locally written articles, among them a profile of Frank Harris of *My Life and Loves* notoriety, living and writing in Nice at age seventy, and a weekly series on music by Henry Russell, a former opera producer living in Monte Carlo. For the final edition on April 7 the supplement editor, Thomas Van Dycke, wrapped up the season with a leisurely chronicle that began: "The *Tribune* correspondent ruefully folds up his Remington typewriter, stretches his arms, puffs at his pipe and reads the timetable."

In Nice—with a welcome three-dollar raise in pay to fifteen a week—Thurber found his editing task not unlike work on his college daily, the *Ohio State Lantern*, some years before. "Editing these pages," he said, "was something like playing a cross-eyed left-handed woman tennis player. You never know where anything is coming from, and everything takes a queer bounce. My only achievements on these papers consisted of little feats of technical ingenuity." One such on the Riviera supplement was taking lengthy cuttings from the French Bureau of Tourism and simply dropping them into the paper when he was short of copy. Another, when he was lacking three or four columns of material, was to increase the type size of the entire paper. "This may have been," Thurber thought, "the only 10-point issue of a paper ever got out, I don't know."

Another diverting feat was the invention of eccentric guests who had just arrived in Nice, the copy turned over to his wife in her role as the supplement's society editor. Said Thurber: "I made up dozens of items for her, when she ran short, about mythical lords and ladies, commodores, and generals, and villas and yachts." One item read: "Lieutenant General and Mrs. Pendleton Gray Winslow have arrived at their villa, Heart's Desire, on Cap d'Antibes, bringing with them their prize Burmese monkey, Thibault."

INVENTING THE NEWS. While inventions of a similar sort were commonplace in the *Tribune*'s Paris office, obvious fabrications or straightforward mistakes apparently brought little response from readers. Elliot Paul said the only way the *Tribune* was certain it *had* readers was when errors appeared in the baseball scores or in stock quotations, since "a slip in either of those departments brought showers of protests, in person, by phone, by letter, or telegram." Virgil Geddes recalled that shortly after Paul had become a *Tribune* proofreader he changed "Greatest" to "Worst" in the masthead, with the result that for several days the paper went to press as "The World's Worst Newspaper," and no one seemed to notice.

An invention with heroic status among *Tribuners* involved the reporter Spencer Bull. During a Paris visit in the early twenties by the Prince of Wales—later King Edward VIII and then Duke of Windsor—the British embassy issued handouts on his busy and grimly routine activities. After Bull picked up one for the final day, he stopped at a café for drinks before moving to the office to turn the handout into a news story. When he came to an item about the prince reviewing a troop of British Boy Scouts of Paris, boredom, drink, or simply creativity overtook him and he enhanced the hand-out with a scene of his own:

> Stopping before one manly youth the Prince inquired: "What is your name, my lad?"
>
> "None of your goddamned business, sir," the youngster replied. At that, the Prince snatched a riding crop from his equerry and beat the boy's brains out.

The story passed through copy editors and proofreaders and appeared in the paper under a two-column headline: "Prince of Wales Bashes Boy's Brains Out with Bludgeon." The resulting scandal, as Harold Stearns noted, was awful but temporary. The prince accepted the paper's apology and declined to sue, but with strings attached. The *Tribune* was required to reimburse the British embassy for copies of the paper it had snapped up on Paris news-stands and signed a pledge that future stories about the royals would be cleared with the embassy. As for Bull, he was fired—though it was said he was later kept well supplied with free drinks and meals by admirers of the man who had accused the Prince of Wales of murder.

When William L. Shirer joined the *Tribune* some two years later, Bull's prank was still making the rounds of the copy desk. When Waverley Root arrived, he also heard about it, including an account from Bull himself, but it still seemed too outlandish to be-lieve. By looking into the back files of the French paper *Le Temps*, Root learned the period of the prince's Paris visit and the exact day he reviewed the Boy Scouts. He then examined the *Tribune*'s bound volumes of all its Paris issues. The paper for the day in question was missing.

Spencer Bull's first Paris news job had been with the *Herald* in 1919, and over the years he had bounced back and forth among the American papers, with numerous storied deeds clinging to him. Among them, thoroughly discounted by most, was that during

World War I he had performed secret work for American intelligence. When he died in 1935 and a service was held in Neuilly, former colleagues were astonished to find his casket draped in the Stars and Stripes and a military honor guard present.

The *Tribune*'s long-running sports columnist, Hérol Egan, was renowned for another reason. His column, "The Once Over," was a necessity since the *Herald* had one, though it was accepted that Sparrow Robertson had an insurmountable edge in bad writing and wide readership. A further disadvantage was that, unlike Robertson, Egan found it painfully difficult each evening to produce his column. Long periods were spent before a typewriter fiddling with his pipe, after which he would abruptly vanish from the office, leaving a sheet of paper in the typewriter with only the title of his column and the byline: "By Hérol Egan." Brought back from a nearby bar, he would resume tending his pipe before vanishing again, the sheet of paper in the typewriter now reading:

By Hérol Egan

The

One night, the column delayed as usual, Waverley Root wrote it for him by chronicling Egan's nightly ritual of starts, stops, and disappearances, beginning with "8:07 Egan sits down at his typewriter." The sports editor was troubled when he read the column in page proofs, wondering how the crowd would take it in Harry's New York Bar, where he ordinarily repaired after the paper was out. When someone there said, "Egan, this is the best damned column you ever wrote," he smiled with evident relief and replied, "Yeah, I didn't have anything particularly interesting to write about tonight, so I thought a little joking wouldn't hurt."

ANARCHS AT HEART. Putting the most favorable face on them, the *Tribune*'s newsroom pranks were part of a deliberate campaign to separate the paper from the *Herald*. While the rival paper was considered careful and conservative, the *Tribune* viewed itself as bold and liberal. The staff made an effort to "'jazz up' our reports," said Eugene Jolas, "often growing lurid and sensational over the leads, applying the tabloid technique. We invented our own grotesque cable stories as fillers, and played gaily with nerve-demoralizing headlines. But we also tried especially to emphasize the new intellectual and aesthetic developments in Paris, and whenever possible, to scoop the *Herald* with unusual stories and interviews." He added that "we were all anarchs at heart, and the disorder that reigned in the editorial rooms was an exact reflection of our state of mind."

A joyfully retold story among staffers, one revealing the paper's intended disorder, involved Hérol Egan, just back from a trip to Spain, explaining in a column about crowd behavior at a bullfight. A good matador, wrote Egan, might be awarded by the crowd's acclaim one ear or two, but if he was superb he could get both ears "and a piece of tail." On the *Tribune* the story slipped easily into print. On the watchful *Herald* it presumably never would have left the copy desk.

Harold Ettlinger thought many *Tribuners* imagined themselves following in the noble tradition of the old *New York World* in producing a paper that was liberal and daring—and one in calculated opposition to its reactionary parent in Chicago. He relished the "chronic indigestion" that would develop if its back-home superiors "troubled to read carefully the columns of their Paris edition from day to day." While the Chicago paper was solidly Republican, "the Paris paper did what it could to favor the Democrats"—knowing all the while that what it said "was of little consequence in American national affairs, but it felt good nevertheless to be so independent."

KIRBY'S CHAIR. The antics of staffers like Spencer Bull and Hérol Egan were comic, at least in the retelling. Madison Kirby's were, in the end, tragic. An athlete at Stanford in younger days, Kirby liked to show he had not lost his conditioning by leaping sidewalk garbage cans during after-hours bar crawls. Possibly he was demonstrating it again, or simply his sobriety since he had the night off, when he appeared in the *Tribune* office and undertook a window-walking feat, successfully performed many times before, of going out one of the French windows of the newsroom, inching along a narrow ledge, and coming in a second window.

This time he lost his balance, fell, and died in a hospital of his injuries. Waverley Root, who witnessed Kirby's fall, managed to write a story about the death and then telephone it to the *Herald*. "This was not," he remarked later, "the sort of news on which we wanted to have a scoop."

In New York, a man planning on joining the *Tribune* was particularly touched by Kirby's death. Sterling Noel had been on the receiving end of letters from Kirby urging him to come to Paris for a possible job on the paper. For $50 a friend could provide him with a ticket on a French-bound freighter, and since at the moment his net worth was $78 Noel decided to go. Just before he left news came of Kirby's death. Noel was devastated but went through with his travel plans. When he reached Paris he found the *Tribune*'s managing editor waiting for him, and his first night in the city he was put to work on the copy desk. The chair he occupied had been Kirby's.

NEW MAN ON THE DESK. One night, working on the copy desk in Paris rewriting French papers, James Thurber discovered that the earnest young man in the chair beside him, puffing a pipe and anxiously consulting a French-English dictionary, was a fellow Midwesterner. Twenty-one and fresh from Iowa's Coe College, William L. Shirer had taken a cattle boat and borrowed $200 for a European tour he expected to last two months. In Paris, his money running out yet reluctant to leave, he tried for a newspaper job, expecting little since his experience was meager and he had only a smattering of college French.

Eric Hawkins at the *Herald* took his name but held out no hope. Neither did David Darrah at the *Tribune*. On his final night Shirer and a friend went out on the town with their last francs; when they returned to their room in the early hours there was a letter under the door from Darrah asking Shirer to call at the paper. The next evening, after a short interview, he had a job. The reason, Shirer suspected, was that as a child he had lived in Chicago and the paper felt a need to have some staff members with ties to the city.

Thurber introduced the new man to others around the desk: Elliot Paul ("He's the only one of us writers who's got himself published"); Eugene Jolas ("He's our poet—in three languages, German, French, American. Sometimes he gets them mixed up"); an Irishman whose name Shirer failed to catch who claimed his novels were banned in Ireland. Sitting at a desk off to the side was Virgil Geddes ("Our other poet").

"Harold Stearns," Thurber whispered when a shabby, unshaven fellow appeared in the newsroom and chatted with the sports editor, Hérol Egan, about horse racing.

"Not *the* Harold Stearns."

"*The*," said Thurber.

The man who had conceived and edited *Civilization in the United States*, with its implied call for the young to abandon what Stearns in the preface called the emotional and aesthetic wasteland of American life, was one of Shirer's intellectual heroes. Viewing him in person was disillusioning. Over the next years in Paris Shirer would see Stearns often, usually outfitted in a soiled raincoat and weathered felt hat, usually drunk in a Montparnasse bar. He had about him the inscrutable look of a "silent Buddha, and people would say cruelly: 'There lies civilization in the United States.'" (Waverley Root held a minority view about Stearns's drinking. While Stearns had a "natural talent" for it, Root could never recall seeing him drunk: "His usual tipple was beer, and he was capable of spending all his waking hours screwed into his chair at the Sélect or the Rotonde as the saucers rose before him, with no visible change in his state except that it became more and more difficult to be sure that he was awake.")

That first night on the copy desk Shirer had an easy time of it, with Bernhard Ragner handling the slot and passing him simple stories to edit and headline along with brief items of French rewrite. When he finished work around one in the morning, Shirer fell in with Thurber, Elliot Paul, and Eugene Jolas for the long stroll from Rue Lamartine to the Latin Quarter. There were bar stops on the route through Les Halles before settling into an Alsatian brasserie near the Sorbonne for beer, sauerkraut, and sausage. It was after three o'clock when Shirer arrived back at his room and reviewed his day: "The first evening on the *Trib* had been wonderful. I felt confident I could stay on, and that meant staying on in Paris. I could hardly wait to get back to work the next evening."

PETER PICKEM. One evening while Samuel Putnam and his wife were touring the Left Bank with a literary and motion picture agent named Florence, they encountered Harold Stearns in a café looking the way he had to Shirer—"the next thing to a tramp."

"Harold Stearns!" exclaimed the agent. "Oh, yes, I've heard of him. I've read about him. . . . But what does he *do*?"

"He covers the races for the *Chicago Tribune*," replied Putnam.

"Bu-u-t . . . I thought you said he was an intellectual, a great intellectual. What—"

A parade of drinks followed, with the agent eventually telling Stearns she could make a best-selling author out of him: "You think I can't do it? You just leave it to little Florence. You write that book for me, that's all—" Stearns listened, reported Putnam, with amusement and wonder.

As early as 1924 Eugene Jolas had announced in his "Rambles Through Literary Paris" column that Stearns was writing a sweeping exposé of the Left Bank's American poseurs, a work that had Jolas's hearty approval. Hemingway approved as well since, as he remarked, Stearns certainly knew the subject from the inside. Never written, the exposé maintained a fabled existence in the expatriate community—and Stearns his reputation as a nonwriting writer whose creative life was confined to bar-stool talk. "Sure, I'm a writer," he insists as the character Wiltshire Tobin in Kay Boyle's 1938 novel *Monday Night*. "Sure, that's what I am. Only the trouble is I've never got around to writing."

What Stearns actually wrote in Paris was for newspapers and magazines, with his "Peter Pickem" column for the *Tribune*—his "technical racing reporting," as he embellished it—one of his sustained efforts along with his "Our Paris Letter" for *Town & Country* magazine. Stearns was out of money after he left the *Herald*, and Alex Small came up with an idea of how he might find a place on the *Tribune*. Hérol Egan, said Small, was too lazy to cover the tracks himself and would welcome help. If Stearns kept his salary demand low—Small suggested $20 a month at the start and whatever could be arranged as an expense account—Bernhard Ragner might be persuaded to put him on the payroll. Once he got to know the horses, added Small, Stearns might win some money at the races himself. Ragner went along with the idea—Egan pleaded his cause, Stearns assumed, for the reason Small anticipated—and in the summer of 1926 Stearns became "Peter Pickem," the name created in earlier days for the paper's turf expert of the moment.

Ordinarily Stearns's work got under way in late afternoon after his return from Auteuil or Longchamp or Saint-Cloud. Along the way he bought a copy of *Paris-Sport*, an evening racing paper that carried the day's results and prices together with full information on the next day at the tracks. (In a magazine article Stearns explained that the paper's inclusive name, *Paris-Sport*, was appropriate because in France "if you call a man a 'sportsman,' you still mean that he is a devotee of the track and the ponies.") Over a drink in a bar near the *Tribune* he studied the publication and made his selections for the morning paper, sometimes accepting the turf writer's, sometimes coming up with picks of his own. Then it was off to the office and writing the column while eyeing the clock so he finished by eight, the time when the night staff straggled in and typewriters were in demand. Dinner followed, often with *Tribuners* finishing up the day shift, then a walk to cafés and drink and talk until the early morning hours.

The racing columns were utilitarian, and Stearns produced them in perfunctory and generally impersonal fashion. A column on June 3, 1927, was typical—and near-comic in its indecision:

> For the feature of the day Peter Pickem has a curious idea on Ratissoire . . . to win this. After all, it is a handicap, and in all good handicaps any one ought to win, provided he has luck. Ratissoire is not a lucky horse ordinarily, but perhaps his day has come. Almost any of the other entries can give him a tussle—again it is a matter of luck.

Stearns's added work for the *Tribune* in "Left Bank Notes" was of the same order—often drawing on such standby subjects as Mont-parnasse's decline under tourism or its seasonal variations. The day before the Peter Pickem column above, Stearns waxed warmly— though with racetrack luck still a looming factor—about the Parisian mood on enchanted late-spring nights: "It is easier to be happy in Paris, probably, than anywhere else in this modern ma-chine world: with a little luck, it is easiest of all in Montparnasse, when—as now—it is in its old and best temper of good-humour, tolerance, and 'laissez-faire.'"

In 1930 Stearns left the *Tribune* to become the track tout of the Paris edition of the *London Daily Mail*, writing now—as he said— as the "dignified 'Lutetius' of London" rather than the "rather flippant 'Peter Pickem' of Chicago." His life on the *Tribune* had been satisfying enough, and he was not eager to leave it. After his final column in May he imagined a last-minute cable arriving from Colonel McCormick: WHATEVER DAILY MAIL OFFERS WILL OUTBID THEM STOP STAY WITH THE PAPER ENDALL. The cable never came, and Stearns's exit from the *Tribune* was saluted by the staff with a flow of drink and twitting remarks about "going over to the 'Limies.'"

Work on the *Daily Mail* was marginally more demanding than the *Tribune*, but the main change Stearns found was in the habits of staff members, who frequented different bars and lived generally respectable lives. The latter came as a relief after his *Tribune* days, yet only for a time. Despite some question about an American writing about horses among British newsmen who assumed their own innate knowledge of the subject, Stearns's column was—in his own view—well received. This was so despite the *Daily Mail*'s practice of picking for each race an "outside" possibility as well as first and second-place choices, an added task that Lutetius ably handled thanks to a good run of luck.

Illness, with terrifying periods of blindness, caused Stearns to end his connection with the *Daily Mail* after a year. For a time he moved in with the *Tribune*'s Alex Small, and when his health worsened he entered the American Hospital in Neuilly, where doctors diagnosed infected teeth and extracted them. He tried catching on again with the *Tribune*, but someone else was writing the turf column as double duty and there were no other openings. As for the *Herald* and the *Daily Mail*, he assumed he had burned his bridges with both papers. He ran into Hemingway, back in Paris after publication of *A Farewell to Arms*, who paid to get Stearns's typewriter out of pawn and suggested markets for freelance articles but had no leads for regular news jobs. Finally Stearns realized he had little choice but to return home. At the end of January 1932, age forty-four and after a decade in France, he left on a freighter from Le Havre, his passage paid by friends and the American Aid Society of Paris.

In his "La Vie de Bohème" column, Wambly Bald tried to strike an optimistic note about the departure. He hoped the figure he called a "cerebral solitary who lived pleasantly in a passive world" would, his teeth gone and health presumably improved, manage to "alter his view point and make him forget the appeal of great resignation."

"The deans of the Quarter," added Bald, "have not lost faith in one of the most promising young men of America."

THE ALCOHOLIC WAVE. As a casualty of alcohol, Harold Stearns had ample company on the *Tribune*. Ralph Jules Frantz, a veteran staff member who joined the paper in 1925 and from 1929 to 1934 was its capable and well-liked managing editor, acknowledged the paper "had a fairly liberal attitude toward drinking," a wry understatement at best. (Frantz was typically tactful when it came to addressing staff problems. He once sent Ned Calmer a two-page letter about the "unpleasant business" of two overdue books at the American Library. The director had complained to the *Tribune* since library cards, which ordinarily required a 100-franc deposit, were free because of employment with the paper. Frantz pointed out that the fine for the books was 113 francs and another 12 francs for sending notices Calmer had not responded to—and gently mentioned that it might be possible to withhold the money from Calmer's pay. He went on to outline various strategies Calmer might use to reduce the fine, among them telling the library director his wife had been ill and he had been under heavy expense, and ended on a cheerful note by congratulating the reporter on a "swell story" he had recently written from Nice and adding he was looking forward to having him back on the local staff.) Stearns himself was in awe of the office's "alcoholic wave" that, at its height, could make the appearance of the paper seem miraculous. On any given day, he maintained, *Tribune* editors could assume a fixed proportion of the staff would be useless due to drink—half "because it was not there, and the other half because it *was*."

Elliot Paul typically ended twice-weekly accordion lessons from a Frenchman with a number of refreshments, after which his music mentor "staggered eastward toward the Panthéon and I sashayed westward . . . to the *Chicago Tribune* office, where another drunken re-write man, more or less, made no difference at all." Joseph

Freeman, who at the beginning of the twenties had come over from the *Herald* and would later become editor of the *New Masses*, claimed that on the paper's night shift conversation flowed and "so did the *rum chaud*. The copy boy's exclusive job was to bring up from the canteen below beer, wine, cognac and anything else the messieurs on the desk ordered." On hot summer evenings cold beer also materialized by other means—in foaming buckets along a rope strung to a bistro that shared a courtyard with the Rue Lamartine building. Colonel McCormick, after a surprise visit to the newsroom, banished beer mugs from the rim of the copy desk—with the consequence, said Alex Small, "that every night at least half the staff . . . came on deck loaded to the extent of their meager pocketbooks. Rarely could these joyous ones be persuaded to go sleep it off out in the convenience. They had to help by yapping and scrambling the copy of those who worked."

Waverley Root, on the other hand, was inclined to downplay the alcoholic wave as a hindrance in getting out the paper. To reach the newsroom from the street, he pointed out, staffers had to climb five flights of stairs—a daunting obstacle that ordinarily caused those arriving drunk to retreat to nearby drinking places. "If you could get up the stairs," Root held, "you were sober enough not to be a nuisance." With a newsman's inbred low regard for the business side of the paper, Root insisted that Jack Hummel—the *Tribune*'s top business figure and in effect its publisher during Root's time with the paper, though the title was reserved for Colonel McCormick—was the only one he knew who regularly came to work in the morning drunk.

NIGHTLY SYMPOSIA. Edmond Taylor took the position that "the most prized intoxicant" of Left Bankers in the interwar years was not alcohol, not even sex, but talk. "Every famous café," he observed, "had a resident philosopher—the larger establishments usually had several rival ones—whose nightly symposia were attended by coteries of faithful disciples." Harold Stearns, Alex Small, Elliot Paul, Eugene Jolas, Henry Miller—all were impressive figures, with Stearns a uniquely taciturn sort who regularly held forth at favored haunts and maintained, said Taylor, "a slightly blurred imprint of the traditional European intellectual café life upon American expatriate society."

Taylor traveled among the various café talkers, but Alex Small was his favorite. The columnist's conversational manner was authoritative and even more embroidered than his prose—"an indefinable blend of Samuel Johnson, Brooks Adams, Rabelais, and Zenophon, with traces of Thomas Hardy and perhaps Ambrose Bierce." One night *Tribune* staffers arranged an oratorical contest in Gillotte's café between Small and Elliot Paul, a colleague who—as Harold Ettlinger noted—was equally inclined to assume the "central position in all after-work café sitting." Paul's conversational style differed from Small's overpowering approach but was slyly effective. He would set out his views on a subject at hand for some five to ten minutes, then lean back and allow another to have his say; when he resumed speaking he would pick up from where he left off, giving no indication he had heard anything said in between. "After two or three exchanges like that," said Ettlinger, "his opponent was likely to be too disconcerted to continue. It is not easy to argue when one's words appear to be completely ignored."

On the evening of the match, after having his say on a matter of contention, Paul leaned back and peered at the ceiling as Small began a response. As Ettlinger recounted the contest, Small went on for five, ten, fifteen minutes—and kept holding the floor, leaving Paul with nothing to do "but sneer, for it was beneath his dignity to interrupt." After an hour passed Paul pushed away from his table and left the café. Small took no notice of his leaving and, said Ettlinger, "would probably still be talking had not the rest of us stood up in turn and suggested a pub crawl across the left bank." Thereafter Paul and Small tended to avoid each other's company, and "there remained an area of low pressure about their typewriters on the copy desk."

BALANCE WHEEL. Café talkers like Elliot Paul and Alex Small enlivened after-hours life for *Tribune* staffers, but when it came to the daily grind of getting out the paper Waverley Root was a crucial mainstay. After undergraduate years at Tufts University and a period in Greenwich Village writing reviews and, as he put it, *New Yorker* short stories before *The New Yorker* was there to publish them, he had set off for Paris with a tin suitcase and typewriter in the spring of 1927. He was without definite plans until the bill for his hotel room came due. He was hired at the *Tribune* under the assumption he had worked for the *New York World*. In the paper he had published short reviews and he bore a letter of reference from Herbert Bayard Swope, the *World*'s eminent editor, but his actual newspaper experience had been on the Tufts student paper.

Taken on at $15 a week, Root worked under the *Tribune*'s day editor, B. J. Kospoth, a well-turned-out figure in his fifties who, as Root found, was "faithful to his theory that he should try to reach the office in time to go out for lunch." On Root's first day on the job Kospoth took the new man with him—to size him up, Root guessed, in the event that, as a former big-city newsman, he might be an office threat. Since they never again shared a meal, he assumed Kospoth determined he was not.

Root soon distinguished himself as a capable reporter and deskman, and in 1928 he was promoted to the *Chicago Tribune*'s foreign news service and sent to London. He worked effectively under the bureau chief, John Steele, but London seemed drab and dull after Paris and two years later he was back with the *Tribune* as news editor, the number-two man in the editorial command, a position he found happily rewarding and one he held until the paper folded. To his colleague Harold Ettlinger, Root—known to all as Wave—seemed an "almost incongruous mixture of the intellectual and the

The Paris *Herald* newsroom in Rue de Berri, Vincent Bugeja at the typewriter, Eric Hawkins standing in the rear. (*International Herald Tribune*).

Al Laney, a steady deskman on the Paris *Herald* and the paper's lively historian. (*New York Herald Tribune*)

Ernest Hemingway in the courtyard of his Paris apartment in 1924, about to leave newspaper work for the literary life. (Special Collections and Archives, Knox College)

John Weld, one of the Paris *Herald* staffers handling typing chores for James Joyce. (Sketch by Jeremy Blatchley from *Young Man in Paris*, Academy Chicago)

Martha Foley and Whit Burnett, key Paris *Herald* staffers, later sharp critics of the paper. (Princeton University Library)

Paris *Herald* staffers look on as Laurence Hills makes his first transatlantic phone call, Eric Hawkins leaning behind, Leland Stowe on the other phone. (*International Herald Tribune*)

Colonel Robert R. McCormick in 1919 with his ace World War I reporter Floyd Gibbons, first director of the postwar Paris *Tribune*. (*Chicago Tribune*)

Wambly Bald's photo appeared with his final "La Vie de Bohème" column in the Paris *Tribune* in 1933. (*Chicago Tribune*)

Eric Sevareid, whose feature stories in the Paris *Herald* caught the attention of Edward R. Murrow in London. (Velva, N.D., School and Public Library)

A sketch of Eugene Jolas accompanied a review of his poetry in the Paris *Tribune*'s Sunday magazine in 1924. (*Chicago Tribune*)

Discouraged by a book he was writing, Elliot Paul said he tossed the manuscript out his window, watched pages float down the Seine. (Sketch by Jeremy Blatchley from *Young Man in Paris*, Academy Chicago)

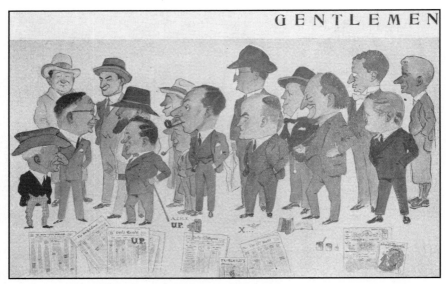

GENTLEMEN

"Gentlemen of the Press," a drawing in *The Boulevardier* magazine in 1929 by the artist Pandl, included among Paris-American newsmen a diminished Sparrow Robertson far left, Laurence Hills beside him, Jed Kiley in knickers, Harold Stearns in long raincoat. (New York Public Library, Astor, Lenox, and Tilden Foundations)

Correspondent and book publisher Bill Bird inscribed his photo to Sylvia Beach of Shakespeare and Company. (Princeton University Library)

Paul Scott Mowrer began as Paris correspondent for the *Chicago Daily News* before World War I and stayed on into the thirties. (Chicago Historical Society)

OF THE PRESS

Brassaï's sketch of Henry Miller in Wambly Bald's *Tribune* column brought the writer to Paris attention. (*Chicago Tribune*)

Vincent Sheean's popular 1935 memoir *Personal History* gave correspondents an enlarged conception of their role as reporters. (Port Washington, N.Y., Public Library)

Edmond Taylor rose from the staff of the Paris *Tribune* to become chief of the *Chicago Tribune*'s Paris bureau. (*Chicago Tribune*)

William L. Shirer, circa 1930, as Vienna correspondent of the *Chicago Tribune*. (George T. Henry College Archives, Coe College)

Like the Paris *Herald*, the *Tribune* maintained a public reading room and information office, this on Rue Scribe. (*Chicago Tribune*)

Colonel McCormick holds aloft the *Tribune*'s French office boy at a 1921 assembly of the local paper's staffers and European correspondents at the Paris Ritz. (*Chicago Tribune*)

Dorothy Thompson at the start of her career as a European correspondent. (Library of Congress)

Janet Flanner and Solita Solano on Crete in 1921, beginning their lengthy expatriate life together. (Library of Congress)

Chicago-born Sigrid Schultz became chief of the *Chicago Tribune*'s Berlin bureau in 1926, a post held until World War II. (*Chicago Tribune*)

Elliot Paul, author, as he
appeared in the late 1940s.
(Foto-Schell)

The CBS radio team of Thomas Grandin, William L. Shirer, and Edward R. Murrow at
Le Bourget airport in Paris, 1938.

Ned Calmer in 1934, the year
his first novel was published.

practical." He wrote with knowledge and wit about books, music, wine, and food, yet in the day-to-day operation of the paper he was "a balance wheel on the night desk. He could always get a paper out in time of crisis as long as there were one or two of the less picturesque members of the staff, like myself, on hand to help."

As news editor Root improved the operation of the paper by doing away with the copy desk spike on which the day staff impaled material. In theory, rewrite men on the night staff took the top story from the spike, rewrote it, and moved on to the next item on top; in practice, men searched through the stack for stories of interest or those easily revamped, with the result that some important or difficult material never left the spike. Root's innovation was to pass out stories individually to men he thought could handle them, check the results as they came back to him, then mark them for size and type of headline and direct them to copy readers.

At the same time he ran the night copy desk, Root wrote often and well for the paper in news accounts, book reviews, and lengthy pieces of cultural commentary for the Sunday edition. The commentaries could be learned and opinionated or simply amusing. Among the former he championed Theodore Dreiser over Sinclair Lewis, defended the American mind against critics at home and abroad, and vented his irritation with showy literary wordplay. Language, he maintained in a favorable review of Kay Boyle's novel *Year Before Last*, should always be employed as "a tool, a means of expression, and not an end in itself." In an amusing vein was "Americana," a lengthy piece about the varieties of unpleasant American types encountered in Paris: drunken tourists, schoolteachers on summer larks, political patriots, flamboyant artists. Most off-putting of all were the insular permanent residents who associated only with other Americans and looked upon "the native inhabitants of the country in which they have so strangely come to rest as foreigners." On the whole, Root nonetheless concluded, the Paris-American colony had circulating within it more pleasant and intelligent figures than any American city save New York.

During his time as the paper's news editor, Root's typical work-day began at three in the afternoon by going through French morn-ing and afternoon newspapers for stories to rewrite both for the *Tribune* and the Danish paper *Politiken*, for which he moonlighted as a Paris correspondent. About seven o'clock, stories written and edited, he phoned Copenhagen and dictated copy for translation into Danish. After an evening meal he returned to the office for his nightly stint in the slot of the copy desk while at the same time con-ferring with the managing editor about the use of reports coming in by wire and cable. When the managing editor left about eleven o'clock for the composing room to make up pages, Root stayed in touch over a house phone for late-breaking stories. At one o'clock, the workday over if he was not scheduled for the paper's "dog watch" until two, he was free to begin his Paris nightlife.

IN-AND-OUT STARS. Amid the alcoholic wave, nightly symposia, lit-erary endeavors, and other staff preoccupations, the paper was kept on a reasonably even keel through Root's efforts and a handful of other seasoned, relatively sober, long-serving staff members—"the few pros on the staff," as Frantz described them. They carried out their duties, however, in the erratic company of a revolving-door group of "in-and-out stars," as Harold Stearns called them, who kept shifting among the American dailies or dropped from sight en-tirely. In the front rank of the crowded parade of in-and-outers was Elliot Paul, as he would be again when he switched to the *Herald*. Elevated from a *Tribune* proofreader to the editorial staff, Paul would work steadily on the copy desk for weeks, then suddenly disappear—his departures, some assumed, coinciding with the ar-rival of royalty checks from his published novels. When he re-turned, the paper usually had a spot for him.

Not so Henry Miller. After he vanished for ten days from his job as a proofreader, Frantz concluded he had returned to America without notice and hired a replacement. When Miller reappeared, ready for work, Frantz told him—"regretfully," since Miller had shown himself a competent worker and genial companion—the position was filled. Miller took the news like a "good sport."

Later, Miller rejoined the *Tribune* with an upstairs job of assistant finance editor. After a short time the job fell through, ostensibly because Miller had been refused a French work permit. When Miller complained of injustice—other Americans on the paper lacked permits—Frantz let him return to his favored work of proofreading, though after a short time Miller quit. Frantz would recall about Miller's period with the paper that since half the staff "considered themselves budding geniuses of one sort or another—writer, painter, opera singer, Casanova or what have you, Henry didn't make as much impression on the rest of us as he might have on others in a different milieu."

LEGITIMATE CHILD OF MONTPARNASSE. Both Miller's *Tribune* jobs came about through the aid of Alfred Perlès, an Austrian who had appeared in Paris after World War I and supported himself with newspaper work, including time as a *Tribune* proofreader, while writing a novel in French. He had first met Miller in 1928 during a visit Miller and his wife made to Paris. When Miller returned in March 1930, nearly penniless but determined to make his way as a writer while his wife remained in New York, Perlès befriended him with meals and lodging.

"At the time I was working on the Paris edition of the *Chicago Tribune*," said Perlès, "and could afford to indulge in an occasional fit of generosity." He also farmed out Miller's Paris sketches as features for the *Tribune*'s Sunday edition, with the work, since the paper generally favored staff contributions, appearing under his name and others. According to Perlès, Miller gathered material "on long walks, preferably in the slummier parts of the city. . . . Notebook in hand, he would jot down a few notes, colours, impressions and incidents, which he later worked into minor masterpieces which, I must say, deserved a better vehicle than the *Chicago Tribune*."

In a letter in 1931, Miller gleefully announced he had "just sold about 350 francs' worth of writing to the paper. Printed a Lulu by me yesterday, called 'Paris in *Ut Mineur*.' Nobody knows who the author is. The great anonymous art of the 13th century." On March 8, 1931, the article appeared in the paper under Perlès's name. In Miller's account of his freelance work in *Tropic of Cancer*, the steamy autobiographical novel published in Paris in 1934, his *Tribune* articles were something less than the minor masterpieces Perlès believed:

> Now and then Carl [Perlès] came along with a job for me, travel articles which he hated to do himself. They only paid fifty francs a piece, but they were easy to do because I had only to consult the back issues and revamp the old articles. People only read these things when they were sitting on a toilet or killing time in a waiting room. The principal thing was to keep the adjectives well furbished—the rest was a matter of dates and statistics.

Shortly after his Paris arrival Miller had begun with the *Tribune* as a $12-a-week proofreader (the pay, he figured, about double what he needed to live in the city), working the night shift reading stock figures. It was bottom-level work in every way, but he gave it full attention. One evening while he was working as the paper's news editor, Edmond Taylor, who considered Miller the "head guru of the proofreaders' bench," debated with him about a point of style in some late copy while the clock ticked toward deadline. Miller, he acknowledged, had been technically correct.

In letters written while *Tropic of Cancer* was under way, Miller credited the basement toil among the Linotype machines with transforming his itinerant, hand-to-mouth Paris existence: "It forms the very core of my life, shapes it, directs it, permeates all my activities, my thoughts, etc." Even if offered promotion to the newsroom above, he insisted he would stay where he was, savoring the fetid air, the clatter of the machinery, the French compositors who seemed like figures out of a French novel: "I prefer this slavery. The very atmosphere of the place has gotten into my blood. I miss it on my night off." But at the same time he savored downstairs life, there was also anticipation that, work finished, he would "sneak up to the editorial room and knock off a few lines while the front-page men play cards. You understand, there is a little feeling between us down in the basement and the fellows upstairs who write the news. We don't belong. Tant pis!"

Along with the agreeable basement slavery were pleasurable walks to Gillotte's for evening meals before work began, beer at the bar of the Trois Portes during breaks, early-morning strolls after work back to hotels on the Left Bank in the company of fellow proofreaders Perlès and Wambly Bald. Now and then he accompanied Louis Atlas—a *Tribune* upstairs man who, according to Miller, was shunned by Perlès and Bald because he talked too much—and shared his hotel room for the night. Atlas, who read Proust in the original, played Brahms for Miller when he awoke and showed him clippings of articles he had written for the paper. "Some of these things ought to be preserved," he maintained. "Don't you think it's a shame for these things to be buried in newspaper files?"

The nights with Atlas did not appear in *Tropic of Cancer*, but Miller's *Tribune* proofreading days and his after-hours revels with his newspaper comrades Perlès and Bald would have a central place in the novel. Called Van Norden in the novel (with Perlès as Fred), Bald would also become one of Miller's most vividly rendered—and, from Bald's pained point of view, ill-treated—characters. (For more on Bald in the novel and the novel as a whole, see Chapter Seven.) It was Bald who had brought Miller to Paris attention in his "La Vie de Bohème" column on October 14, 1931—accompanied by a caricature of the scruffy subject at a table outside the Dôme by the Hungarian photographer Brassaï. As a joke, Brassaï said later, he added a champagne bottle in a bucket and put a champagne glass in the penniless subject's hand. In Bald's agreeable portrayal Miller was a vagabond novelist seen to by friends, a "legitimate child of Montparnasse, the salt of the Quarter. He represents its classic color that has not faded since Murger and other optimists. A good word is *esprit*." The column ended with Bald joining Miller's band of caring friends: "'What you need is food,' I said, reaching in my pocket. 'I'm your friend, too. Get yourself some food,' I said, and handed him a franc."

Perlès claimed Miller returned the favorable mention by dashing off some of Bald's columns for him—columns, according to Perlès, Bald found it misery to write: "No one reading his slight, trashy, not unhumorous column, could guess the agonies he went through in producing it." Miller, on the other hand, "could do this sort of thing with his left hand, as it were, in the twinkle of an eye. Whereupon Wambly would take him out, buy him a meal, and tell him what a wonderful writer he—Wambly Bald—was."

For his part, Miller in a letter noted in passing that for Bald's final column in the *Tribune* he had "knocked out for him" some of it "because he was empty and at his wit's end." "Don't mention this to anyone—just between ourselves," Miller added parenthetically. Ralph Jules Frantz believed otherwise—that Bald wrote the columns himself and worked hard on them. Whatever the case, ghostwritten columns were not unknown on the paper. In 1929 Kay Boyle signed on as assistant to the *Chicago Tribune–New York Daily News* fashion correspondent Bettina Bedwell and for $100 a month wrote twice-weekly columns that appeared in the Paris *Tribune* under Bedwell's name. (Later, Boyle collaborated with Bedwell, married to the American painter Abraham Rattner, on a thriller novel with a Paris setting—Bedwell plotting and outlining, Boyle writing—for a fee of $250 and 50 percent of royalties. Published in London in 1937 as *Yellow Dusk*, the book bore only Bedwell's name.)

HÔTEL DE LISBONNE. The area most *Tribuners* made their way to after working hours was the warren of cheap hotels in the narrow, winding streets off the Boulevard St. Michel. Here the Hôtel de Lisbonne at the corner of Rue Monsieur-le-Prince and Rue de Vaugirard was a favorite spot. Its rooms opened off long corridors lit by bare bulbs of minimal candlepower, with some of the rooms overlooking an interior courtyard of garbage cans and trash casually tossed from windows. Oddly for Paris of the time, the building had central heating, and within rooms there were washbowls and running water, with the heated variety emerging for a half-hour on Sundays. For bathing it was necessary to cross the street to a bathhouse providing tubs, soap and towels, and a measure of warmed water.

Occupied mainly by expatriate Americans, the Lisbonne's most compelling feature for *Tribune* residents was a $10-a-month rate together with the convenience, since so many of the staff lived there, of borrowing clothes, money, and female companions. "We had long bull sessions in each other's rooms," said William L. Shirer, "read and criticized each other's writing, argued over books and most everything else, planned joint adventures for the afternoon or evening, and advised and consoled those who threatened to fall apart from drink, frustration or unrequited love." Even after promotion to the *Chicago Tribune*'s foreign news service, able to afford better and often away from Paris on assignments, Shirer paid his rent to be assured of keeping a room in the Lisbonne.

Waverley Root chose different Left Bank quarters—a two-room, sixth-floor studio walkup in Rue de l'Ancienne Comédie, a street once housing Balzac. The studio lacked the humble refinements of the Lisbonne—lighting came from a gas lamp, heat from a potbellied stove—but it overlooked the rooftops of Paris and had the Eiffel Tower and Notre Dame cathedral as backdrops. Here Root lived in "unbroken enchantment," with days beginning before light when he left the *Tribune* and regardless of the weather walked home a mile and a half on a route that took him through the noisy bustle of Les Halles, a deep and timeless quiet when he crossed the

Seine, the student gaiety of the Latin Quarter, and at last into the ancient quiet of his own area:

> On this last stage, almost every building I passed was rooted deep in history. At this hour, I had the old streets to myself and they led me finally to the equally old street on which I lived. I mounted the six flights to my studio and, if I were lucky, saw, through the great window, Venus, the last star to pale before the rising sun.

GILLOTTE'S. While lodging was cheap if basic, food was cheap and often—under the guidance of staff connoisseurs—spectacularly good. Following World War II Root fashioned a major reputation as a food writer with, among other books, his original and erudite 1958 work *The Food of France*, which ordered the country by the type of fat—butter, oil, lard—used in regional cooking. During his *Tribune* days, however, Root bowed to Elliot Paul as the paper's official gourmet, leading the way to eating spots turned up on Paris excursions and organizing the staff's private feasts. Eric Hawkins of the *Herald* thought in discovering unique restaurants Paul was blessed "with a kind of extrasensory perception, like a pig rooting out truffles at the foot of an oak." Among his special finds was the Chicago-Texas Inn near the Eiffel Tower. Run by a former Pullman porter, the eatery specialized in a breakfast of corned beef hash and griddle cakes following an eye-opener of private-stock whiskey.

The dank, dark cellars of Paul's Hôtel du Caveau provided the setting for great staff binges—starting in the early morning hours after work was finished so all could attend—of roasted pig or lamb and fine wines, with Paul in the course of the evening strumming a guitar and leading in song. "It was the one place in Paris," said Shirer of the vaulted former dungeon, "where we could make as much foolish noise as we were capable of without disturbing neighbors or attracting the attention of the police. . . . Toward 6 or 7 a.m. we would finally have enough, pick ourselves up as best we could, and stagger home."

For ordinary dining the preferred spot was the Le Rendezvous du Petit Journal, which Root linked with the Hôtel de Lisbonne in that "neither was afraid of an overlay of good healthy dirt," though the restaurant had an advantage in that "we frequented it mostly at night, and since the lighting was dim, the dirt didn't show much." Known to all by the name of the owner, Gillotte's was a tiny place across the street from the rear entrance to the paper's offices that served as a virtual clubhouse for staffers as well as the dining location for nearly everyone working on the night side. In the paper's news columns the establishment made at least one appearance—as the setting for an interview with Maxwell Bodenheim—as "the famous old *bistrot* of Mon. Gillotte on the Rue Lamartine."

In addition to location and the fact it was open twenty-three hours a day (the missing hour devoted, ostensibly, to cleaning) and served adequate food—"it did not look like a temple of gastronomy," Root remarked, "and was not, but we ate quite well there even though the place's appearance suggested that this was an accident"— Gillotte's appeal was easy credit that allowed eating on the cuff until the fortnightly paydays. Bill settling was a ritual affair, Papa Gillotte sealing the transaction by pouring a thimbleful of an uncertain drink for both the customer and himself, on the house. "Thus fortified," said Root, "we were ready for one other half-monthly rite, paying the rent, after which we could spend what remained of our $30 on riotous living."

Gillotte's was also a favorite site for holiday revelry. During one New Year's celebration Camille Haynes, an attractive blonde who at the time handled the *Tribune's* society news, brought a halt to festivities by tossing champagne in the face of William L. Shirer and stomping out after Shirer said something that angered her. Elliot Paul, offering his services as peacemaker, said he would bring Haynes back and Shirer could apologize. Neither Paul nor Haynes reappeared, though romance between them was sparked. Haynes eventually became one of Paul's many wives.

DEATH WATCH. "'Everybody Coming to Europe,' Says Nina W. Putnam" read a *Tribune* headline on May 14, 1929, with the story quoting the American writer, just returned to France after a trip home, on crowds jamming as never before the passport bureau in New York. The heady news would only survive the summer. After the Wall Street crash in October, *Tribune* staffers masked their apprehension about the future with an outburst of gallows humor. On a night with paychecks just out, a wild party ensued in the newsroom, with cheering over the doomsday reports on the wire and enthusiastic stories pounded out about American tourists finding themselves suddenly stranded and penniless in Paris. "As the evening wore on," reported Edmond Taylor, "the orgy grew more and more hysterical":

> Big firecrackers improvised from flashlight powder tightly
> rolled in copy paper and fused with an old shoe-string were
> set off under the copyreaders' chairs, or fired down a tube
> into the composing room. Several times some maniac set fire
> to the knee-high drift of old newspapers that littered the floor
> in places and a *bona fide* Götterdämmerung was narrowly
> missed. It was a good wake, if a little eerie.

That the orgy *was* a wake became clear with the steep slide into the depression. By the end of the year the *Paris Times* was a casualty while the *Tribune*, equally hit with declining circulation (according to Waverley Root, in 1930 the paper was claiming circulation of twenty thousand copies but actually printing eight thousand) and advertising revenue, staggered on. In January 1932 the paper insisted in an ad headlined "Steady Growth" in the Paris-American magazine *The Boulevardier* that "since 1929, the net sales of the European Edition of the Chicago Tribune have grown steadily. Even this year the

Tribune's circulation has increased and generally these haven't been boom days for Circulations." On July 4, 1933, in a page-one boxed note commemorating its founding sixteen years before, the paper claimed its circulation in the first half of the year had bettered the gains of 1932. Yet despite the sales and circulation bravado, in the spring of both 1932 and 1933 there were editorial pay cuts, and staffers who left the paper were not replaced. As early as the spring of 1932, Henry Miller noted in a letter home that "the *Tribune* is going out of business in a few months, so I am told"—a hardship from which he was free, since he had already lost his job.

Each day the *Tribune*'s front page still blazed with a banner headline no matter how trivial the accompanying story, and the paper carried the same eclectic mixture of American and foreign news. Regular columns continued to appear from Alex Small, Louis Atlas, and Hérol Egan; society was still chronicled by May Birkhead and horses ranked by the current Peter Pickem, James King; films were reviewed by Lee Dickson and fashions by Bettina Bedwell and Lisbeth De Morinni; and there were informed discussions of the arts by B. J. Kospoth and Irving Schwerké. But the paper's coverage of Left Bank cultural matters had fallen off; book reviews were now largely reduced to Waverley Root's "In the World of Books" section of the Monday paper; and, as of the summer of 1933, Wambly Bald's eagerly awaited "La Vie de Bohème" column was gone altogether.

With the Paris *Herald* equally weakened by the depression, it was obvious there was no longer room for two Paris-American newspapers. The *Tribune*'s business manager Jack Hummel several times approached Laurence Hills of the *Herald* about combining the two papers, and in 1932 Colonel McCormick told the *Herald*'s New York owners that without merger both papers would likely fold. Finally McCormick tried to buy the *Herald*, and when his offer was refused he reversed course and on October 26, 1934, sold the *Tribune* to the *Herald* for $50,000 and a provision that for nine months the surviving paper bear the titles of both papers.

The death watch for the *Tribune*'s final edition on November 30 nearly got out of hand when, as Ralph Jules Frantz reported, "younger, wilder members of the staff thought it would be fun to burn out the editorial room, and Waverley Root and I were kept busy putting out small fires which had been playfully set." Root recalled that during the last days, when staffers knew the paper was doomed, wastebasket fires were common, and on the last night "the ritual bonfire reached such proportions that it looked for a moment as though the whole building might be burned down."

TOO GOOD TO LAST. A boxed editorial statement at the head of page one, headlined "Hail and Farewell," blandly announced that with the issue the paper had reached its end. Just below, under the headline "'Tribune's Life of Service to Americans Ends Today" and an inside subhead reading "Amusing Period in History of U.S. Journalism Ended," ran Wilfred Barber's lengthy account of the paper's history. A warm tribute to the staff's skill and versatility came near the end:

> Toss them a French clipping on a murder, a little scrap of something new in Hitleria, a bit about French politics, politics anywhere, a few words about new developments of the new deal, toss them anything—they knew the background, they didn't have to pad (it's too easy) and a readable accurate story came out. French? There were as many accents as men in the office, but they knew how to twist a subjunctive into a reasonable animal or take an official's speech and make it, not a slice out of an encyclopedia, but an accurate piece of American.

The day before, in the first part of a two-part article, Alex Small had tried to strike a hopeful note amid the thick gloom with the thought that the local journalistic community of the interwar years might be recounted at some future time. The attention, he wrote, would only be just:

A separate chapter may some day be written about the
journalists who rode on the crest of that wave. Not only were
[they] the more modest laborers in the vineyard, who
contented themselves with thumping out copy for the . . .
small local products, but the more showy agglomeration of
special correspondents, special writers, feature writers,
traveling columnists, or whatever else a man might be on the
editorial side of a newspaper. For it was assumed in the
halcyon era that our people were hungry for copy about the
glamorous lands across the sea. In advertising jargon, it had
become "European-conscious." It was only just that the
journalists should have had their cut of fat and facility.

In the article's second part, under the heading "Americans Had Gay
Time, Eating Cake, Having It Too," Small linked the paper's fold-
ing to the end of an American era in Paris. The tide that began with
the "reverse migration" of World War I had now receded; left in
Paris were only "a few businessmen, a few incorrigible chasers of
the blue flower, a few opulent esthetes who can still afford to turn
old houses on the Ile Saint-Louis into annexes of the Cluny Mu-
seum. The rest have departed, as we are doing." The bonanza period when the Paris-American colony could support at least two
daily newspapers was simply over. "It was too good to last," Small
wrote at the finish, "and it is as well that it should be ended. A man
must live, fight and die with his own people."

In the final edition several other staff members signed off in
print. Carol Weld, under the headline "Girl Reporter Tells It All on
Last Day," recalled some of her colleagues' "conversational identi-
fications." Ralph Jules Frantz: "Did you get the story? Swell!" Louis
Atlas: "I'm fed up. Where you going to eat?" May Birkhead: "Be
that as it may . . ." B. J. Kospoth: "What's that? I've been at the Embassy all afternoon. But there's no story there." Edmond Taylor:
"Call me up if anything breaks." Wilfred Barber: "That was July 2,
1887 at 3:10 in the morning, and it was raining, because . . ." Robert

Sage: "There's not enough air in here, let's open a window." Alex Small: "My dear fellow! Didn't you know? Why of course. Louis XIV, when he built the palace at Versailles, said . . ." Robert L. Stern: "You can't write that! You gotta have a new lead." Mary Fentress: "American Hospital? Anybody dead?"

Four days earlier, Louis Atlas had used his final "Most Anything Can Happen" column to salute Sylvia Beach and her bookstore (". . . I decided to give her a boost while I still had a newspaper in which to do the boosting"), both fixtures of Paris-American life and both carrying on while the *Tribune* was not. For her part, May Birkhead carried on in the final issue with a densely detailed page-one story from London about the marriage in Westminster Abbey of the Duke of Kent and Princess Marina. A friend provided ringside seats just outside the Abbey entrance, allowing her triumphantly to see the procession "come and go, as it could have been seen nowhere else. Even those who had invitations to the ceremony inside the celebrated cathedral itself could not have had such a panoramic view of the spectacle."

VALEDICTION. In the wake of the death, staff members moved on. Carol Weld found a wire-service position with the Paris bureau of the Universal Service. Robert Sage, B. J. Kospoth, Robert Stern, and Louis Atlas went to the *Herald*. Wilfred Barber and Alex Small were promoted to the *Chicago Tribune's* foreign service. Ralph Jules Frantz was offered the position of assistant managing editor of the *Herald*, working under Eric Hawkins, but declined and left Paris for a job on the *Herald Tribune* in New York. Wambly Bald returned home as well, becoming editor of the "March of Events" section of the *New York American*. It was Hemingway, according to Bald, who provided his transit fare after a chance meeting outside the Luxembourg Gardens:

He fired questions at me. Where was everyone? The Dingo looked deserted. He had been back in Paris nearly a week and a lot of the old faces were gone. Where, back to the States? he wanted to know. I told him it looked that way, and rattled off names of those who had gone back. . . . How about me? Did I feel like going back? No, I told him, I still liked it here and always would. Then he threw me this thunderbolt out of the clear blue sky: "If you change your mind I'll pay your fare." He told me where he was staying. "Drop over tomorrow and I'll lend you the money."

Bald did drop over the following day and Hemingway "wrote out a sizable check, handed it to me, and a week later, after saying good-bye to my *Tribune* friends I was on the boat."

In his final "La Vie de Bohème" column on July 25, 1933, over a year before the *Tribune*'s death, Bald had, in effect, already said goodbye both to his newspaper friends and to the wondrous Paris days working for the paper had made possible. He was giving up the column (while, as he made clear, keeping his *Tribune* job) because, with Paris-Americans returning home in droves, Montparnasse now seemed like a worn handkerchief covering a corpse, and he was "tired of jiggling a corpse." Before his eyes, as he wrote his "vale-diction," was a "parade of silhouettes." As he would later do for Hemingway, Bald ticked off the names of some of them—and ended with a lone word that, in the disjointed yet at times oddly effective fashion of his column, provided a suitably melancholy epitaph for the *Tribune*'s end:

> What became of Flossie Martin, Harold Stearns, Homer
> Bevans, the Countess Eileen? What became of Samuel
> Putnam, who brought forth on this continent *The New*
> *Review*, conceived in liberty and dedicated to the proposition
> that almost anyone is literary. Where is Jolas now? Where is
> Link Gillespie, the unconquerable poet who fought so

valiantly that words might escape their spelling? Whither hath
fled flummery and mummery? Oh!

CHEAP AT THE PRICE. For Waverley Root, on the other hand, the end
was an opportunity. With the news of the *Tribune*'s sale he had immediately signed on with the Paris bureau of the United Press as an
overnight editor, and during the paper's final month, after finishing
his night's work, walked to the UP office in Rue des Italiens for a shift
ending at 8 a.m. At the same time he kept on as a correspondent for
Copenhagen's *Politiken* and as a contributor to *Newsweek*—all told
earning, by his calculation, $150 a week beyond his *Tribune* salary at
a time when one could get by in Paris on $25 a month. But the money
did nothing to dampen his angry reaction to the paper's death.

Root believed the *Tribune* in its latter days was gaining on the
Herald in circulation and quality, and consequently the death sentence was simply the result of "mismanagement in the business office while editorially [the paper] was still thriving." He set out his
view in a page-one editorial in a new weekly newspaper, the *Paris
Tribune*, mailed to former subscribers the day after the death of the
Chicago Tribune edition. The unassuming tabloid, conceived and put
together by Root and carrying features and columns by former staff
members together with some advertising from the old paper, was a
response to reader demand—or so Root claimed in his editorial. "A
flood of letters of protest" had poured into the paper with the news
of its demise:

> Perfect strangers all but wept on the shoulders of *Tribune*
> reporters whom they encountered at odd moments, chiefly in
> bars, whose lachrymose effect is well known. Critics and
> columnists had their private mail swelled by despairing
> appeals from previously unknown admirers who asked
> pathetically where now they might read their writings. They
> may read them here, in the *Paris Tribune*. . . .

The upstart newspaper was a valiant effort, and Root's editorial hyperbole had at least some basis in fact. A young woman in the Paris bureau of the United Press, Mary Knight, sent a subscription to the new paper together with a message that read in part: "Please accept my fifty francs, my hearty congratulations and my sincere admiration of your enthusiasm and spontaneity in kindling the fire of the new *Paris Tribune* on the bier of the *Chicago Tribune*, Paris Edition. . . . Your present initiative is the surest proof anyone could want that the Americans still in Paris are alive and kicking."

But without a news service or newsstand distribution Root's paper was fated to fail—and, after some two months and eight issues, did. Root claimed satisfaction in keeping the former paper's spirit alive, if only briefly—and in the fact that, in his sole venture as a publisher, he was only $100 out of pocket. "I thought," he concluded, "it was cheap at the price."

CHAPTER THREE

News in the Afternoon

We crossed the Boulevard Montparnasse
and sat down at a table. A boy came by
with the Paris Times, *and*
I bought one and opened it up.
—ERNEST HEMINGWAY,
The Sun Also Rises

AMERICAN BY VOCATION. The Americanization process under way at the Paris *Herald* in 1924 brought a prominent defection within the ranks. Absent for four years while serving in the French military in World War I, Gaston Archambault had returned to the paper to take up his position as managing editor, working now under Laurence Hills, the editor and general manager installed by Frank Munsey and retained by the Reid family. Short, wide, pipe-smoking, the British-educated Frenchman had a luxurious handlebar mustache and—as observed by Waverley Root—a sinister look caused by a permanently half-closed eyelid from losing sight in one eye during the war. He had been a key figure on the Bennett paper, reputed to know all the Commodore's supposed 483 taboos and a skilled deskman who could stretch skimpy cables into full, readable stories. He was also a loud and domineering personality with firm views about how the *Herald* should be run.

Once, making a rare visit to his Paris property, Munsey had asked Archambault about his nationality, the managing editor replying that he was "French by birth, English by education, American by vocation." Some thought his American side came wholly from regular reading of the *Saturday Evening Post*; in any case, it did not extend to embracing Hills's efforts to add more of his countrymen to the staff, switch to American rather than British spelling, and enliven the paper's stodgy makeup. As Whit Burnett and Martha Foley simply left it in their *American Mercury* article about the *Herald*, "there were differences" between Hills and the Frenchman. So when Archambault turned up a wealthy expatriate and collector of art, books, and rare stamps, Cortlandt F. Bishop of New York and Lenox, Massachusetts, who was willing to finance a new paper as a tax break, he walked away from the *Herald* to run his own shop his own way, taking Ralph Heinzen of the paper with him as business manager. In the summer of 1924 the *Paris Times* began publishing as an afternoon paper competing against the morning *Herald* and *Tribune*.

PARIS EVENING TELEGRAM. Just before, a paper bankrolled by Jefferson Davis Cohn had failed in the afternoon slot. The British-born exile whose godfather had been president of the Confederacy, Cohn, among other diversions, occupied himself with race horses. Said to have won his first race as an owner at age fourteen, in the French turf season of 1923 he led owners with thirty-two first-place finishes and over a million and a half francs in earnings. A magazine profile in the Paris-American magazine *The Boulevardier* in 1930 had it that Captain Cohn, as he was called, had taken control of the *Paris Evening Telegram* by appearing at the plant where its printer was refusing to print due to lack of payment, presenting a check for 100,000 francs, and asking, "Whom do I give that to?" Nobody seemed to know but, according to the article, the presses began rolling again. With flowing hair and typically puffing a cigar beneath a black top hat, the picturesque Cohn had recently invested

in a theater and a French sporting sheet as well as the newspaper—
enterprises, reported the magazine, that "left him with cheque stubs
and other sad memories."

Published seven days a week from offices at 123 Rue Montmartre,
the *Paris Evening Telegram*—the name, intentionally or not, echoing
that of the *Evening Telegram* begun in New York in 1867 by the father
of James Gordon Bennett—billed itself during a three-year run from
1921 to 1924 as the "Only Evening Paper on the Continent Printed
in English." A skimpy four-page, six-column publication, it carried
no bylines and attributed its main page-one news stories as coming
"From Our Own Correspondent by Wireless."

Standing-head columns of rewrite filled the inside pages: "People of Paris," "What To-Day's Papers Say," "London Gossip," "Paris
Gossip." Two columns treated local cultural matters: "Latin Quarter
Notes" and "Literary and Artistic Notes." Page four was given over
to sports, presumably one of the paper's major selling points as an afternoon paper. "A Day Ahead!" house ads repeatedly declared.
"American baseball reports 18 hours ahead of any other paper."

Matthew Josephson, who came to Paris in 1921 after Columbia
University and experience as a newspaper reporter in Newark, New
Jersey, caught on with the *Evening Telegram* after finding nothing
available on the other English-language papers. One of his main jobs
was translating racing results from the French press, another of the
Telegram's key ingredients. The paper itself struck him as a "poor
sheet" with a "small public," but it paid an "American salary," transforming his view of Paris from a "good place in which to starve" into
the "most miraculous city on earth."

The *Evening Telegram* seemingly had little impact on the Paris-
American colony beyond providing baseball and turf results. Even
mention of the paper's existence in historical accounts and memoirs
is limited to Josephson's brief notice and Al Laney's equally brief
comment in his book about the *Herald*—and to a single backhand remark: "It was he [Gaston Archambault] who persuaded Cortlandt
Bishop to become a newspaper publisher in spite of the recent failure

of the *Evening Telegram*, a venture in the afternoon field sponsored by Jefferson Davis Cohn, another American millionaire living in Paris." In contemporary publications references are similarly restricted to the profile, noted above, of Captain Cohn in *The Boulevardier*.

PASTEPOT AND SCISSORS. Gaston Archambault's negotiations with Cortlandt Bishop for a successor to the *Evening Telegram* were conducted in secret and caught Laurence Hills off guard. Thereafter he kept a close eye on the *Paris Times*, aware of Archambault's ability and troubled the *Herald* would be outmaneuvered on news stories. The concern was extreme—though *Time* magazine, in its 1939 article about the *Herald*, believed otherwise, singling out the *Times* as the paper's "most engaging competitor" in the late twenties. With only a tiny staff and meager resources, the paper was never a match for either the *Herald* or the *Tribune*.

Eric Hawkins, who had worked under Archambault on the *Herald* and followed him as managing editor, described the new rival as a paper whose "principal tools were imagination, a pastepot and scissors." Still, he believed Archambault managed to put out "a good, readable newspaper." Its staff, Hawkins added, "could do wonders with the barest one-line dispatches, filling them out with hundreds of words of detail that came to them from background files or, as sometimes happened, from their own prescience." Such insight now and then led to wondrous blunders. Hawkins recalled the time the paper built the bare cable information that Navy had defeated Army in their annual football game into a vivid half-column story ending with the Navy goat leading the victors in celebration. The following morning the *Herald* and the *Tribune* correctly reported that Army had won the game—leaving the *Times* to blame the cable company for the mistaken score while sidestepping the story's rich detail.

Waverley Root, an onlooker at the *Tribune*, thought the *Times*, unable to afford much of anything in cable and wire service and dependent on rewriting other papers, was forced to give stories more

depth or better packaging. This required able writers, and he credited Archambault with using his limited funds to hire them. The
Times paid better than the *Tribune*, or so Root was advised when
looking for a Paris job in 1927. "Go to the *Paris Herald* first," he was
told by Arno Dosch-Fleurot, then the local correspondent for the
New York World. "They pay best. If you don't make it there, try the
Paris Times. They're second best. If worse comes to worst, you can
always fall back on the *Chicago Tribune*. Bad pay, but some people
manage to live on it." Root took the advice and called on the *Times*
after no one was available at the *Herald* office. It was nearly press
time on the afternoon paper and no one was free to talk with him,
so he went over to the *Tribune*—and signed on with the poorest
paying and most interesting of the Paris-American papers.

With French papers, rewrite implied an ability to handle the
language—a basic Archambault requisite for new hires. A deskman
recently let go by the *Tribune* was immediately fired at the *Times* for
translating "petit-fils" as "little son" rather than "grandson." Another necessity was knowing how to spell, with the editor's standard
test a single word: accommodate. For women, the bar was higher:
Archambault would allow only one at a time on his staff.

Once hired, most staffers found the editor a difficult taskmaster.
Hawkins thought he adopted the manner of an English schoolmas-
ter and treated his staff as pupils—or, the metaphor shifted, he was
a military leader ordering subordinates: "The trouble was that his
love of authority transformed him into something of a top sergeant,
and the orders he shouted often sounded more appropriate to the
drill ground. He was fond of displaying knowledge and erudition,
with which he was amply equipped." Offending writers were summoned before the editor's desk and lectured about their deficiencies
sentence by sentence.

OUR PROGRAMME. The seven-column, usually eight-page *Paris
Times* began publishing on June 5, 1924, the masthead announcing it
would appear every afternoon and Sunday morning from the Euro-

pean Publishing Company at Right Bank offices near the *Herald* at 33 Rue Jean-Jacques-Rousseau. Later, Cortlandt Bishop was listed as the company's president. Despite four degrees from Columbia University, including a law degree and a doctorate, the proprietor's interests were outside the academy, with newspaper ownership—the *Times* was his sole venture—only a fleeting one. Among the several others were automobiles, and he was said to average 25,000 to 30,000 miles a year driving about in Europe and elsewhere. Not surprisingly, for some years he was the European representative of the American Automobile Association.

An editorial in the paper's first issue, "Our Programme," took up three questions: "Why another newspaper? Why in Paris? Why the Paris *Times*?" The answers were that an afternoon paper was needed; Paris was the key location in Europe; and "the outlook of The Paris *Times* will be that of the man of the world; its attitude will be based on reason born of reflection, on sympathy tempered by judgment, on common sense developed by experience, and, above all things, on independence fortified by honesty of purpose and the desire to serve." The inflated statement about the paper's outlook would appear in an editorial page box in all future editions.

The first issue established a format that was only marginally changed over the next five years. Major stories on page one were attributed to the "Paris *Times* Cable"—replaced in later issues by a radio source, the "Paris *Times* Radio"—or vaguely announced as a "Paris *Times* Special." Like the *Evening Telegram*, inside pages carried a collage of standing-head columns: "Boulevard Gossip," "Gossip from Washington," "Mainly About People," "In Little Old New York," "The Talk of London." In the manner of Bennett's *Herald*, page six appeared entirely in French and included a separate editorial, though within a year the French page would shrink to three columns.

OVER THE RIVER. The lone signed column in the initial issue was Arthur Moss's "Over the River," a collection of Left Bank and beyond observations that developed into a daily feature of the paper. A caricature or photograph usually accompanied the column—with one especially effective photo catching a dapper looking Sinclair Lewis buying the *Paris Times* at a kiosk and the caption reading, "Without it he can't enjoy his apéritif." Moss's manner was generally light and chatty, as in a typical item from an early column:

> If you think the Left Bank is the home of only pallid
> aesthetes, take a trip over to the tennis courts near the Porte
> de Versailles. You'll see a number of Quarterites slamming
> 'em but on the coldest days. Or watch them playing basketball
> in Gaston Francois' gym.

Morrill Cody thought Moss's work rivaled Wambly Bald's "La Vie de Bohème" column in the *Tribune*, but while "Over the River" was a bright spot in the *Times* it exhibited nothing of Bald's verve, style, and flashes of insight. Moss's cultural interest was ordinarily limited to news notes about recent issues of such journals as the *Double Dealer* in New Orleans or the *Criterion* in London. In Parisian literary matters he reached for little more analysis than placing Robert McAlmon in the front rank of young American writers following publication of his book *Village* and finding Lewis Galantière instructive on the biographers of Arthur Rimbaud in an issue of the *Dial*. With the appearance of Ezra Pound's *Sixteen Cantos* from Bill Bird's Three Mountains Press, Moss congratulated Bird on his typography but shied away from a critical view of the poetry: "As to the verse; well, who doesn't know the erudite Ezra?" The book was expensive, however, and "there's a rub":

> Well, for people who like Ezra's poetry that well, that sort of
> tariff is all right. A good bargain for millionaire lumbermen or
> wealthy journalists like Ernest Hemingway, whose name, by
> the way, is printed as the owner of No. 10 [of the limited
> edition of the book]. Does anyone know what income tax
> Hemmy paid.

Harold Stearns's rumored exposé of expatriate life came in for attention, with Moss reporting that Stearns had recently traveled to Havana and possibly was "working on the fifth chapter of that great book he's been telling me about for so many years." In a column a month later, Stearns now back in Paris, Moss had it that "Harold's new book, which he has talked about for a long time, is at last really on the way. It is a collection of psychological studies based on expatriate American types, and it will be published early in the autumn." The book failed to appear in that season or any other.

In time, other signed columns appeared in the *Times'* pages, with "Sportorial" developing into another daily feature, though one left unsigned until Sam Spivvis (or, now and then, Sam Spivis) was listed as the writer. Over the years a long line of others would turn out the column: Spencer Jones, Sedley Peck, Ray McCarthy, George Chadwick, Galen Bogue, Dick Hyland, and Sparrow McGann. Wisely, McGann avoided Sparrow Robertson's zany manner but, like Sparrow, wrote often about boxing.

The first Sunday issue of the *Times* on June 8, 1924, initiated a four-page photo supplement—with one photo of Robert McAlmon, William Carlos Williams, and Lawrence Vail billed as "An American Literary Trio in Paris." A sporting column, "Through the Sportoscope," became a Sunday staple under the names of George Rehm, who had come over from the sports desk of the *Herald*, Sedley Peck, and James G. Conner. Conner would become nearly as visible to *Times* readers as Arthur Moss through another column, his daily "In the Margin" that both bore his signature and frequently printed his disparate musings ("'Women Talk on the South Seas,' says a newspaper headline. Why not, we should like to know. They talk in every other place") and homespun verse. As a hodgepodge of brief bits of prose and poetry and reader contributions, the column seemed modeled on the *Chicago Tribune's* familiar editorial page feature "A Line O' Type or Two."

Columns also eventually appeared about the arts—all mostly gatherings of news notes, unsigned and impersonal: "Cinematters,"

"Art and Artists," "Matters Musical." A column devoted to students in the city, "With the Students," was largely handout material ("The alumnae of Chicago University will have a tea on Thursday afternoon at 4:30 o'clock at the American Women's Club of Paris"). A modest exception to the flat information quality of most columns was "The Gourmet," a critical dining column signed with the initials "C. W.," the initials that also appeared beneath a people column called "Parisian Silhouettes."

More substantial were "The Man of the Day" and "The Woman of the Day" columns, both typically given over to such distant figures, with photographs, as Thomas Hardy and George Bernard Shaw. "The Topic of the Day" column provided a solemn essay set two columns wide and treating such weighty matters as "How the Kellogg Pact Developed," "English Terms for Debt Settlement," and "Florida's War on an Insect Enemy." Only rarely did a Paris event become the subject, as it did in a column reviewing in straightforward fashion the first issue of Edward Titus's literary journal *This Quarter*.

PLANTING GENIUSES. Keeping a competent staff together was a perennial problem on Paris-American papers, with newsmen jumping from paper to paper or vanishing altogether. On the *Paris Times*, with the smallest staff and tightest budget, the problem was compounded by having Gaston Archambault as editor. For Bravig Imbs, who came to the paper from the *Tribune*, working under Archambault—who he characterized as a "crusty, stubby, obese French Jew, who was irascible but fundamentally kind"—went along smoothly enough until, as Imbs recounted it, his "nonchalance got on the nerves of the editor and I became his pet bête noire." His daily job was to produce the columns on the man and woman of the day, and he quickly got the hang of conducting rapid interviews and putting down his impressions if the figures were local, ransacking other papers and publications if not. His only problem was that "once I had the formula, the job became a great bore, and it was impossible for me to take it seriously."

"Why the good Lord always plants geniuses on me, I don't know," Archambault lamented to Imbs one day. "Good God, give me some garden variety of newspaperman; I know they don't exist in Paris, but couldn't you find one for me, just the same?" Imbs was hardly a garden-variety newsman, either. When he came up with an effective interview of a French entertainer, the editor was pleased enough to name him the paper's music critic, yet after a few weeks of contentment the new work revealed to Imbs its "ghastly side": "Music which had been my greatest joy became an arduous task; it was most unpleasant to go to a concert one had no desire to hear, or to wrench away from one that was a pleasure. The strain, too, of going out night after night and working all day long began to tell, and struggle as I would I kept coming to the office later each day." Before long Imbs was sacked.

One of the prime geniuses Archambault felt himself burdened with was Vincent Sheean. After the former Paris *Tribune* staff member and *Chicago Tribune* foreign correspondent had lost his job with the latter and was making his way as a freelance correspondent, he frequently returned to Paris between assignments for bill-paying work with the *Times*. "There existed in Paris in those years," as he described the work, "a refuge to which I could always repair in difficulty—the Paris *Times*":

> It was an evening newspaper in English, created by the whim
> of a millionaire, and edited by a small staff made up of old
> friends from my earliest days in Paris. The whimsical
> millionaire did not allow his generosity to run away with him,
> and there was little money to run the paper with;
> consequently salaries were tiny, and essential expenses (such as
> telegraphic service) cut to a minimum. But however small and
> poverty-stricken, it was a friendly world in which I could
> always find a place.

Sheean's friends on the paper were an able group who later made names for themselves as accomplished journalists and writers: Martin Sommers, Hillel Bernstein, Lawrence Blochman, H. E. Monahan, Allen Raymond. The paper itself, with almost nothing to go on beyond the skills of its staff, struck him as a "superior conjuring trick." As with the *Herald* and the *Tribune*, cables had to be worked into full stories, and when the cable service was shut down completely nearly the whole paper was rewrite from other papers. "How that newspaper was daily invented and spread in print upon paper," Sheean marveled, "was daily issued forth to its minute circle of readers, was daily condemned to death and still kept going, was a journalistic phenomenon that amused us all when we thought of it."

Perhaps because the staff was tiny and overburdened, it spawned what seemed to Sheean a self-enclosed, communal style of Paris life, with everyone housed in hotels near the office and associating almost exclusively with one another. When someone overslept, an office boy roused him from bed and led the way to the office for a workday that ran from eight in the morning to four in the afternoon. After the paper went to press the staff gathered in a downstairs café for beer and talk. "The conversation (like the life) was as aimless as a goat track," said Sheean. "We talked about everything and nothing, but it seemed to take up the whole time left over from work." On Saturdays there was double duty, the staff returning to the office after dinner to put together the Sunday edition. The favored Saturday evening eating place was the Petite Escargot in Les Halles, where food was good and service slow, with the result that on-time office returns were uncommon.

Another of Archambault's staff burdens, though only briefly, was Alvah Bessie. An aspiring writer who had attended Columbia University, he had come to Paris in 1927 and was hired by the *Times* after dropping Vincent Sheean's name and inventing a wealth of experience on papers such as the *Boston Globe* and *Baltimore Sun*. Archambault instructed him that he wanted "good stories, no matter how you tell them," but when Bessie complained about editing performed on his work, Archambault shouted at him, "Are you telling me how to run my paper! Go to the caisse and get your pay." Whit Burnett, at the time working on the *Herald* and frequenting the same cafés as Bessie, thought the firing came about when Bessie, in the dateline of a dispatch, located Annam in China, a blunder Archambault was unwilling to overlook.

Bessie returned to America in 1929, the same year his short story "Redbird," written aboard the ship that had brought him to France, appeared in *transition*. Later he joined the International Brigade during the Spanish Civil War and gave an account of the experience in *Men in Battle*. He recalled leaving Spain for France in a sealed train of war veterans, and in Le Havre finding Vincent Sheean passing out whiskey, cigarettes, chocolate, and sandwiches at the station. Later still, working in Hollywood as a screenwriter, Bessie was one of the Hollywood Ten who served prison terms and were blacklisted for refusing to answer questions about Communist affiliation before the House Committee on Un-American Activities. His bitter memoir of the experience, *Inquisition in Eden*, appeared in 1965.

HONEST-TO-GOODNESS NEWSPAPER. An editorial on the *Paris Times*' first anniversary in June 1925 declared the paper was succeeding because "readers have realized The Paris *Times* is an honest-to-goodness newspaper and nothing else." Presumably Archambault favored a strict just-the-news policy to distinguish his paper from the personal flair in columns, reviews, and reporting that marked the *Tribune* and now and then enlivened the *Herald*, and in fact the *Times* was a reasonably competent example of largely copy-desk, rewrite-and-expand journalism.

What the paper markedly lacked was its own local reporting, let alone local commentary. Seldom was the paper's local news more than a passing notice in Arthur Moss's "Over the River" ("Last evening a group of journalist Left Bankers staged a *gourmet* session at Mme. Grimm's 'Cabaret Furet,' one of the oldest restaurants in the Latin Quarter")—or, at its most expansive, an account on July 10, 1929, of the poet Hart Crane's release after several days in La Santé Prison following a wild altercation with police at the Café Sélect. Crane's release came about, so the newspaper reported, after the poet's attorney produced letters from his publishers saying he was a "diligent worker." Crane himself, asked by the presiding judge what he had done to provoke the policemen, said he was unable to remember.

Café rows were nothing new for the poet. Janet Flanner remembered a drunken Crane making such an uproar in one over a mislaid overcoat that she hoped never to see him again—and added that, to her lasting regret, she never did. But what had taken place in the Sélect was far more violent than the *Times*' story revealed. According to a Crane biographer, police were called to the café when the poet found himself unable to pay his bar bill, with a brawl following that ended only when Crane was "clubbed insensible" and "police reinforcements were able to drag him away by his feet to the waiting vehicle." At the prison he was "thrashed with a rubber hose, thrown into a cell and held incommunicado." When it became known that Crane was under arrest, admirers put together a defense fund, hired a lawyer, and a delegation headed by e.e. cummings called on the police but learned the poet could not be set free without a trial.

A firsthand account of Crane's eventual release would appear in the published Paris diaries of Harry Crosby, the eccentric expatriate writer and proprietor of the Black Sun Press. In a July 10, 1929, entry, Crosby—who at the time was preparing to issue Crane's long poem *The Bridge* from his press—recorded that at his trial the poet was "magnificent. When the Judge announced that it had taken ten gendarmes to hold him (the dirty bastards, they dragged him three blocks by the feet) all the court burst into laughter. After ten minutes of questioning he was fined 800 francs and 8 days in prison should he ever be arrested again."

Crane was returned to the prison before he was released, and so Crosby, in the company of Whit Burnett of the Paris *Herald*, drove there to "wait and to wait from six until long after eight (we spent the time drinking beer and playing checkers and talking to the gendarmes)":

> At last the prisoners began to come out, Hart the last one, unshaved hungry wild. So we stood and drank in the Bar de la Bonne Santé right opposite the prison gate and then drove to the *Herald* office where Burnett got out to write up the story for the newspaper, Hart and I going on to the Chicago Inn for cornbread and poached eggs on toast . . . and Hart said that the dirty skunks in the Santé wouldn't give him any paper to write poems on. The bastards.

FINALE. In 1929 the *Paris Times* was still putting out an eight-page paper, with page-one news now attributed as a "Paris Times Special" or coming via "Paris Times Special Cable." James G. Conner's "In the Margin" column was reduced in length but a continuing daily feature, as was "Looking Through the Sportoscope," written now by Sam Spivvas. But Arthur Moss's long-running "Over the River" column was gone, replaced by "On the Left Bank" by "Montparno." On October 30 a page-one headline ominously announced that "Wall Street Slump Nearing Panic Stage." When the slump became collapse and the panic arrived with full force, Cortlandt Bishop presumably realized a tax break was no longer a pressing need, and before the year was out he shut down the paper.

In a *New York Times* report about the closing, Bishop was said to have confided to a friend two years earlier that he was losing $50,000 a year on the paper yet had hopes of breaking even within another year or so. The *Paris Times* staff, the news story added, was expected to be absorbed by the remaining English-language papers operating in Paris. No mention was made of the fate of Gaston Archambault. The *Herald* was unlikely to welcome the editor back, and there is no indication he tried for a position with the *Tribune* or the *Daily Mail*. During World War II, however, he would have prominent journalistic stature as a European correspondent of the *New York Times*. As for the publisher, his name surfaced in the Paris-American papers in 1931 when he was reported gravely ill in a noted French surgeon's private clinic in Paris—and again in 1935 with his death at age sixty-four just after returning to America.

CHAPTER FOUR

Short Cut to Paradise

*The dream of becoming a "writer" had
helped lure me to Paris. The hope
of becoming a foreign correspondent
held me there.*
—EDMOND TAYLOR,
Awakening from History

JAKE'S ORIGINAL. Jake Barnes's newspaper work in *The Sun Also Rises* is not drawn from Hemingway's own Paris journalism so much as his friendship with Bill Bird, a Paris-American who after finishing Trinity College in Connecticut had co-founded with David Lawrence the Consolidated Press Association. When the *New York Evening Post* dropped syndication of Lawrence's Washington political column in 1919, the wire service was formed to transmit the column to subscribing newspapers around the country. Soon the service added news, features, and market quotations, operating from Washington and a Paris office at 19 Rue d'Antim where Bird, Lawrence's longtime friend, was the European director. In material about Jake's journalistic background that Hemingway cut from galleys of *The Sun Also Rises*, the Consolidated Press Association is the

Continental Press Association, David Lawrence is Robert Graham, and Bill Bird is essentially Jake Barnes:

> In 1916 I was invalided home from a British hospital and got a job on *The Mail* in New York. I quit to start the Continental Press Association with Robert Graham, who was then just getting his reputation as a Washington correspondent. We started in one room on the basis of syndicating Bob Graham's Washington dispatches. I ran the business end and the first year wrote a special war-expert service. By 1920 the Continental was the third largest feature service in the States. I told Bob Graham that rather than stay and get rich with him the Continental could give me a job in Paris. So I made the job, and I have some stock, but not as much as I ought to have, and I do not try to run the salary up too high because if it ever got up past a certain amount there would be too many people shooting at my job as European Director of the Continental Press Association.

Hemingway and Bird first met in April 1922 when Hemingway joined a group of experienced correspondents covering a postwar economic conference in Genoa. In the summer of 1923 Bird, Hemingway, and Robert McAlmon followed the bullfights in Spain. Shortly thereafter Bird and his wife appeared in two *Toronto Star* stories Hemingway wrote about trout fishing in the Black Forest of Germany. In the summer of 1924 Bird and Hemingway were again in Spain, their wives with them, for the San Fermin festival in Pamplona. "Since seeing his first bull-fight," Hemingway reported in the *transatlantic review*, "Mr. William Bird . . . no longer finds it necessary to read the cabled base-ball reports from New York."

Other Paris-based correspondents were also part of Hemingway's circle of friends. Frank Mason, the Paris chief of Hearst's International News Service, had hired him in the fall of 1922 to send cable news from Constantinople on war between Greece and Turkey. At the same time Hemingway wrote about the conflict for the *Toronto Star*, the double duty an ethical issue, though one that failed to prevent him from providing the Hearst organization with more wire coverage from Greco-Turkish peace talks in Lausanne (the work prompting a letter from Hemingway to his wife bemoaning the effort required: "Evrybody else has two men or an assistant, and they expect me to cover everything by myself. . . . It's almost impossible cause they happen at the same time and far apart and evrything"). Mason, who frequently lunched with Hemingway in Paris and talked writing, believed himself the original of Krum, one of the two correspondents in *The Sun Also Rises* who share a taxi with Jake after a press briefing at the Quai d'Orsay. In the scene, Krum, saddled with wife and children, asks Jake about nightlife in the Latin Quarter and longingly anticipates a future when he is free of working for a news agency.

At the Genoa conference where he met Bird, Hemingway spent considerable time with Guy Hickok, the European correspondent for the *Brooklyn Daily Eagle* who worked from a Paris office at 53 Rue Cambon, bore a luxurious black mustache, and matched Hemingway's enthusiasm for boxing and horse racing. (An article of Hickok's, "Herriot in the States," appeared in a 1924 issue of *transatlantic review*, the journal that in the same year carried some of Hemingway's earliest stories.) At Lausanne Hemingway again kept company with Hickok and with Hank Wales, the tough-talking former New York police reporter who had been an International News Service correspondent during World War I and was now Floyd Gibbons's assistant in the *Chicago Tribune*'s Paris bureau. In a letter in 1925, Hemingway informed Scott Fitzgerald that Wales had come to France in 1918, "taught himself to read, write and speak French and is a hell of a good newspaper man. I used to hate him when I first knew him and now I am fonder of him than any other newspaper man except Bill Bird and Guy Hickock." (Hemingway's fondness for Hickok was shared by Henry Miller, who knew him in Paris in the early thirties. In a letter Miller noted that Hickok told him nobody deserved to have such a good time in the city as Miller was having. He added that "Hickok is a great guy—knows everybody.")

Wales had figured in a much ballyhooed *Chicago Tribune* news scoop of 1919. Negotiations in Paris for the Treaty of Versailles, conducted in deep secrecy, raised concern in the United States Senate and elsewhere about possible hidden provisions that might entangle the country in a future war. Wales's coverage of the peace conference carried in the Chicago and Paris papers had persuaded unhappy delegations that the papers shared their dissatisfaction, with the result that one day a Chinese delegate carried an official copy of the unsigned treaty to the *Tribune*'s newsroom and left it with Spearman Lewis, the man in charge in Gibbons's absence. A *Chicago Tribune* correspondent just back from reporting on revolution in Russia, Frazier Hunt, was entrusted by Lewis with carrying the treaty to Chicago. With the treaty wrapped in an old dressing gown and hidden in his luggage, Hunt paused for a farewell drink with colleagues at Harry's New York Bar before heading off. From Chicago he took the treaty to Washington for presentation to the Senate.

TRIBUNE HAS TREATY screamed a banner headline in the paper the following morning over an edited version with Hunt's byline. (In a scoop of its own, the *New York Times* subsequently printed the entire treaty, taking up nearly eight pages of the paper.) Spearman Lewis got a $1,000 bonus for his role in the feat; Frazier Hunt's reward was merely public notice. Hank Wales, kept in the dark about how the *Tribune* had come by the treaty, could plausibly deny any knowledge when called before conference officials investigating the leaked document.

A NICE JOB. In Genoa, Constantinople, Lausanne, and from the German Ruhr where he did extensive reporting for the *Star* in 1923, Hemingway worked as a foreign correspondent, drawing wages and expenses. His per-piece work for the paper was of a different order—not factual reporting but feature stories written in a freewheeling personal style. For its regular foreign news coverage the *Star*, as most Canadian and American papers of the time, depended on wire services of the sort conducted from Paris by Frank Mason. From Hemingway, the *Star*—as concluded by another reporter later sent abroad for the Toronto paper—"only wanted froth," and froth Hemingway gave them.

A different sort of journalistic job was needed for Jake Barnes—work setting him decidedly apart, as part-time feature writing might not, from the occasional workers in Montparnasse. Jake could not, however, be a journalist tied to the ordinary workaday routine of a Paris-American newspaper office, unable to easily cut free for adventures in Spain. An experienced and independent Paris-based foreign correspondent was the better choice, all the more so since correspondents had an air about them of worldly knowingness, a style emulated by Hemingway and manifest by Jake.

Tall, scholarly-looking, reserved, Bill Bird fit the bill as Jake's original better than any of Hemingway's correspondent friends. He was also that uncommon thing, a Paris journalist without ambition as a poet or fiction writer—a lack not shared by Jake but one Hemingway, edgy with competitors, may have found agreeable. Writers of all sorts, including volatile Ezra Pound, thought Bird an attractive figure. Martha Foley, hired by Bird with her husband Whit Burnett to work in Vienna for the Consolidated Press as Central European correspondents, warmly praised him for shielding them from main-office reservations about the literary work they did at the same time as founders and editors of *STORY* magazine. John Dos Passos gave the Birds, husband and wife, at least a passing grade: "The Birds were all right even if they were expatriates."

Two serious avocations bolstered Bird's appeal: French wines and fine printing on an aged press in his own cramped shop on Quai d'Anjou. He printed in 1922 his *A Practical Guide to French Wines*, and when Hemingway brought him together with Ezra Pound he began publishing, under the imprint of his self-financed Three

Mountains Press, a series of six short books led off by Pound, Ford
Madox Ford, and William Carlos Williams and concluded in March
1924 with Hemingway's book of prose miniatures, *in our time*. Bird
also found space in his shop for Ford to edit *transatlantic review*, a
gracious gesture from a man Ford considered "everybody's uncle":
"He was what the *Assistance Publique* would be if it were worthy of
its name. In public he was a stern and incorruptible head of a news
agency. . . . In private he had a passion for a hand printing press that
he owned and his hands and even his hair would be decorated with
printer's ink."

Bird's overriding attraction as Jake's original may simply have
been his special situation as a journalist. As European director of a
news service he helped found, he had a degree of independence unusual even for a foreign correspondent, able to set his work hours
and subjects he wrote about while drawing a comfortable salary that
permitted pursuit of his twin avocations and travels with Hemingway. As Jake would remark of his own work in the discarded draft
of the novel, Bird had "a nice job":

> When you have a title like that [European Director of the
> Continental Press Association], translated into French on the
> letter-heads, and only have to work about four or five hours a
> day and all the salary you want you are pretty well fixed. I
> write political dispatches under my own name, and feature
> stuff under a couple of different names, and all that trained-
> seal stuff is filed through our Office. It is a nice job. I want to
> hang on to it.

LONDON TO PARIS. Bill Bird gave up book publishing in 1928—the
year he served in Paris as president of the Anglo-American Press
Association—when he sold his printing operation to the British
aristocrat and poet Nancy Cunard, who gave it continued life as the
Hours Press. He clung to his job with the Consolidated Press until

the service closed down in 1933, then stayed on in Paris as chief foreign correspondent of the *New York Sun*, a position held through the rest of the interwar years. (After several years in Tunisia after the war, he returned to France and died in Paris in 1963.) In its duration, Bird's Paris period was unusual for expatriate American journalists, and especially so for correspondents typically shifted about in foreign postings. It was not unusual, however, that, at the start of his career abroad in 1920, Bird chose to post himself to Paris.

Before the war, London had been the center of American journalism in Europe, with Paris nonetheless having a sufficient number of American correspondents in 1907—nine together with sixteen British correspondents—to form the Anglo-American Press Association, the presidency alternating yearly between newsmen of the two countries. Yet, save for the wire services and a few leading newspapers and magazines, foreign bureaus in London or elsewhere were considered luxuries for American news organizations—and for journalists little more than sideways moves in their careers. A reporter-adventurer like Richard Harding Davis might find fame and fortune overseas, but for most journalists the action was at home. A foreign assignment meant largely routine work in outposts of limited news value. Raymond Gram Swing remembered the prewar European bureaus of the *Chicago Daily News* as mostly meant to advertise the paper and provide reading rooms and toilets for visiting Chicagoans, with his main duty cabling back each day a list of visitors who had registered their names. When he undertook an ambitious series of articles about the likelihood of war in Europe, the home office edited them down to tame travel pieces.

With the war came dramatic change. Widespread interest in foreign news brought the rushed creation of overseas bureaus and elevated the correspondents manning them to new stature. Now they were members of an exclusive club, the most envied of American newspapermen while remaining—as one of their favored number, George Seldes, observed—the freest figures in any news organization, distant from home offices and insulated by their insider knowledge from meddling editors and publishers with limited awareness of world events. At the same time the expansion of foreign news stimulated by the war and its long diplomatic aftermath decisively shifted the center of American journalism in Europe to Paris. For Webb Miller of the United Press, in charge of the wire service's London bureau in the period immediately after that war, that city was only a "peaceful backwater eddy of the news." When he learned he would be moved to Paris, he happily began taking night-school classes to learn French. George Slocumbe, in the twenties the *London Daily Herald*'s man in Paris, marveled both at the number of incoming American correspondents and the overflowing journalistic vigor they brought with them:

> The American newspaper men swarmed all over the still-ravaged territories of the European belligerents. They came hungry for adventure, for news, for experience, for sensation, for novelty, for sex. They came with their bright and cynical eyes, their calm, unworried faces, their tireless industry, their cool courage, their infinite capacity for drinks, jesting, poker, and work, their insatiable curiosity, their generosity to a comrade, American or European, their professional pride, their calm assumption of equality with any king, president, statesman or newspaper reporter under the sun.

"Every man of them," added Slocombe, ". . . saw the world as high adventure, journalism as an Open Sesame, and Paris . . . as a newspaperman's short cut to Paradise."

DESK WORK. Although the popular conception was exactly otherwise, George Seldes estimated that 90 percent of a foreign correspondent's time was spent tied to his office desk rather than out and about having high adventures. There he scanned newspapers and handouts, watched reports coming in from wire services, worked the telephone, edited and rewrote the stories of assistants and stringers, did his own writing. Ninety percent of a correspondent's time, in other words, was spent in routine work, "leaving only ten percent for war, revolution, *coup d'etat*, violence, and romantic adventure which occupy ninety percent of the volumes of personal history, memoirs, and autobiography which in the course of time make their best-seller appearances."

Paul Scott Mowrer's long career as a Paris-based correspondent matched Seldes's description in that it was heavily weighted on the side of commonplace deskwork. He had, nonetheless, real adventures during World War I and later, yet when he came to record his memoirs he wrote in an unobtrusive journalistic manner and called only minimal attention to his romantic exploits. Published in 1945 with the uninspired title *The House of Europe*, the work drew critical praise but failed to become one of Seldes's "best-seller appearances." Such, as Mowrer ruefully noted in its pages, was the usual fate of his books.

"I don't think they'll give me the job," Mowrer had cautioned his wife in 1910, "but if they should, we might try it a year." He was just twenty-two but already a veteran newspaperman who had been editor of the student paper at the University of Michigan and was now a city reporter on the *Chicago Daily News*. A colleague told him the paper's Paris correspondent, Lamar Middleton (one of the founding members of the Anglo-American Press Association), had died, and suggested Mowrer, who spoke French, apply for the job. He did and was promptly accepted with a comfortable salary of $50 a week.

A fellow newsman put a damper on Mowrer's Paris-bound celebration by insisting a foreign posting was a major career mistake. He had, said the newsman, seen this happen before:

A fellow goes to Europe to stay a few months, and he stays years. He may be a pretty fair newspaperman when he leaves. He comes back at last, wearing spats and carrying a cane, too good for reporting, no good as an executive, no place for him

anywhere, his career wrecked. What do you want to go to
Europe for? What do we care about Europe? What's the
matter with Chicago?

Daily News staff members took the matter further, forwarding a petition to the publisher urging him to keep the young reporter in
Chicago. Victor F. Lawson, a farsighted press chief with a rare interest in overseas news, ignored it and Mowrer set off for France.
Before he worked again in the home office, his planned year abroad
would mushroom into nearly a quarter-century.

Mowrer joined a well-regarded foreign service that Lawson had
organized at the turn of the century when he installed Edward Bell
in London as a resident correspondent and director of the paper's
European operations. Headed by Lamar Middleton since 1901, the
Paris office, with a prominent Right Bank location at 10 Boulevard
Des Capuchines, included a clublike area of potted palms, Oriental
rugs, and leather armchairs where visiting Chicagoans signed a register and had their names cabled back for home printing. As the new
man in charge, Mowrer struck Middleton's widow as unusually
young when she turned over the office to him—a view he did not
share—yet, to at least look the correspondent's part, he bought a
pair of spats and a cane and began a mustache.

As the office manager, Mowrer's duties included ushering visiting firemen about town and dealing with supplicants wanting jobs
or aid with business schemes. As a correspondent, his instructions—
the orders coming from Chicago and Edward Bell in London—
were to downplay politics and supply the paper with entertaining
features. At the same moment that war broke out in North Africa,
the home office asked him to forward good jokes from the comic
sections of the French papers, a request he dutifully fulfilled even
though the best ones were too racy for a family publication.

The undemanding office routine left abundant time for travel
about Europe and getting on with Mowrer's ultimate plan of becoming an author. He read widely in French and German literature

and submitted fiction and poetry to magazines. But when his poorest work was accepted and best rejected, he found himself disillusioned. Newspaper writing for a good paper—as he thought of it, the setting down in plain language and good order what he saw and heard—offered more gratification. He would nonetheless keep on with literary work, with poetry his main interest.

His first action as a war correspondent—Mowrer properly outfitted with gold in a money belt and a Colt .38 in a holster—came when he convinced Chicago to send him to the Balkans to report the fighting with Turkey. Back in Paris, he found his dispatches, prominently played in the *Daily News*, had carried bylines, his first in the paper. With the outbreak of World War I, frenzied tourists besieged the Paris office demanding help with cashing checks, booking passage back home, even glimpsing the war. Eager himself to reach the war zone, Mowrer pressed into service his younger brother, Edgar Ansel Mowrer, a University of Michigan graduate who was studying literature in Paris and was fluent in French. With Edgar running the office and rapidly schooled in the work of a correspondent (all he knew before, recalled his wife, was the principle editors impressed on new correspondents: "When there is no news don't cable it very fully"), Paul—without press credentials as a journalist of a neutral nation—made a dangerous undercover journey to the western front. He gathered firsthand material but, unable to wire his reports, caught a ship to Britain and wrote them in the paper's London office.

Back in Paris, Mowrer put together a network of correspondents working in the war zone, adding to the edge the *Daily News* had over competitors by already having a foreign service in place. Among the new men was Edgar. Paul had read the carbons of dispatches his brother had sent from Paris, judged them acceptable, and sent him off on a bicycle to visit recent battlefields. Edgar's subsequent war reporting from Flanders brought the offer in 1915 of a permanent position with the *Daily News* in either the Rome or Vienna bureau. Edgar took Rome.

WAR AND POETRY. When America joined the war Paul Mowrer was one of four American correspondents chosen for an Anglo-American Press Mission attached to the French military, and for the rest of the war he lived and worked in the military zone. While disappointed he was not assigned to American forces, his war reporting drew praise even from a rival Chicago paper, the *Evening Post*, where his dispatches were determined equal to the war dispatches of Rudyard Kipling and Richard Harding Davis. From the French came, in 1918, the Legion of Honor. Throughout the war Mowrer also kept on with his poetry. A collection of fifty lyrics written since his arrival in France, with some drawn from battlefield experience, were sent off in 1918 to E. P. Dutton in New York. Quickly accepted, they were published as *Hours of France in Peace and War*, his first book.

After the war, back in charge of the Paris office, a member of President Wilson's entourage passed Mowrer a printed, unbound copy of the secret peace treaty. He cabled Chicago with an account of its main parts and returned the copy. To his surprise, three weeks later the *Chicago Tribune*'s Frazier Hunt was credited with a major scoop by smuggling a copy to the waiting U.S. Senate. Mowrer scoffed at what he considered a cheap stunt:

> As there was nothing of importance in it that I had not
> already sent, and as by this time almost anyone who wanted
> to, by deceiving a friend and betraying a confidence, could
> have done likewise, I was not impressed. Yet in America, the
> stunt had created a sensation. I didn't blame the reporter. He
> was a decent fellow, personally, and I liked him. But what a
> degradation of our profession—playing cheap politics, to no
> constructive purpose!

On a six-month leave with pay in America—replaced in the Paris office, to Mowrer's ironic satisfaction, by the *Daily News* colleague who had warned against a correspondent's job—Chicago seemed scattered and squalid, the *Daily News* plant unappealing compared to the paper's quarters abroad, the food poor. All the same, he was wined and dined by important figures, sought after as a speaker, admired by newspaper colleagues—and, from his publisher, came a salary increase and a $5,000 bonus.

FIELD COMMANDER. In 1921 Mowrer produced a study of postwar European politics, *Balkanized Europe*, with a steady regimen of working three hours each morning before heading to the office. It was also a time of travel to the parade of international conferences in the aftermath of postwar diplomatic failures—all based, as a doubtful Mowrer saw it, on mystical faith in men around a conference table bridging the chasm of interest and emotion that divided nations. At one of them, in Genoa, he met for the first time Hemingway of the *Toronto Star*.

Shortly thereafter, Edward Bell left his London post and Mowrer in Paris was named European head of the *Daily News* foreign service. He now felt like a military field commander, directing his troops to action around the continent. One major move was to switch his brother from Rome to Berlin. Edgar Mowrer would remain in that increasingly important post for ten years, and in his dispatches and the book *Germany Puts the Clock Back* send out early alarms about Hitler.

When an auditor in Chicago questioned his expense accounts and those of his correspondents, Paul Mowrer angrily cabled his resignation from the *Daily News*. To persuade him to stay on, Victor Lawson raised his salary to $12,000, agreed to Mowrer's wish to shed his duties as head of the foreign service, and asked what he would rather do. "Oh, big assignments, I guess," replied Mowrer. "Travel. Go where interesting things are happening, and write about them." Subsequently named a roving correspondent and able to choose his own assignments, Mowrer was openly delighted: "No more office cares! No more fussing with other people's copy and cable quotas and accounts! I was fit, I was free. The world . . . was mine to write of, move in, as I pleased. What more could a newspaperman desire?"

One other desire was to write more books. In 1923 Dutton agreed to publish a second collection of poems, *The Good Comrade and Fairies*, if Mowrer would produce another political work, which he promptly did the following year with *Our Foreign Affairs*. As for his reporting, he decided he had written enough postwar stories on reparations, war debts, currency stabilization, and the like. He wanted action and adventure.

He found it in Morocco where the Riffs were engaged in a two-front conflict with Spain and France. In Arab dress and traveling by camel, he made a hazardous journey through battle zones, gathering material and finally interviewing the rebel leader Abd-el-Krim. His reports in the *Daily News*, richly promoted by the paper, caused a considerable stir that left Mowrer hungry for more of the same. But subjects befitting what the French called *grands réportages* were not easily come by. He rejected interviews with great men and instead traveled and reported on conditions in Europe in the wake of the Russian Revolution and the rising tide of fascism. His reporting on German reparations would gain him, in 1929, the first Pulitzer Prize given for foreign correspondence. The same award, four years later, went to Edgar Mowrer.

Weary of travel, Paul Mowrer had now returned to heading the *Daily News'* European foreign service in Paris. In the paper's Chicago office reporters were clamoring for overseas assignments, with Paris always the most desirable posting—as it continued to be for Mowrer. "We newspapermen," he remarked with characteristic understatement, "with our fringe of diplomats, artists, writers, politicians, economists, dancers, army officers, and visitors from abroad, had jolly times." He was a regular at Anglo-American Press Association luncheons and dinners and a member of the Trough, later grandly renamed the Royal Gastronomical Society, a group of twenty organized by Bill Bird that entertained itself monthly in Paris restaurants. The eating excursions were balanced with tennis on courts in the Boulevard Arago. Here the newly divorced Hadley Hemingway would catch Mowrer's eye and in 1933 become his second wife.

With the stock market collapse, Mowrer found his dream of giving up journalism to write poetry full time put on lengthy hold. He kept his Paris position through 1933 when he was brought back to Chicago as associate editor and then editor in chief of the *Daily News*. The Paris office remained in the family with Edgar—recently removed from Berlin under Nazi pressure—in charge and Paul's son Richard, bent on becoming a correspondent, now on his staff. (After retiring from the *Daily News* in 1944, Paul Mowrer returned to Paris in 1945 as editor of a new European edition of the *New York Post*, an afternoon tabloid that folded within six months.)

HEROIC PORTRAITS. A not inconsequential side benefit of the new prominence of correspondents, as George Seldes pointed out, was the possibility their work could be recounted in popular books for homebound readers hungry for tales of foreign lands. Many of the "noblesse of the reportorial profession" who had produced such books, Seldes added with thick irony, had been his colleagues:

> For fifteen years I worked with them in Europe, and now as I
> read their best selling books I too am carried away by the
> excitement, physical or mental, the spirit of adventure, the
> thrill of history in the making, and at times the tropical
> romantic pages which have brought such unprecedented
> popularity to the noblesse of the reportorial profession, the
> foreign correspondents. If these books affect me in this way,
> how much more fascinating must they appear to the lay
> reader? And what a heroic portrait they must give of the
> authors!

One of those colleagues, Vincent Sheean, was the first of the Paris-based correspondents to capitalize on the market opportunity with a spirited work that cast himself squarely at the heroic center. Aptly if simply titled, his 1935 book *Personal History* was a tale of journalistic pursuits through the twenties that propelled Sheean from ordinary newspaper chores to passionate and personal report-ing on the world stage. Hugely popular, the work also drew wide critical approval. Malcolm Cowley in the *New Republic* was typical in calling attention to Sheean's concentration on his own intellec-tual and emotional journey as a correspondent rather than a de-tached recording of places seen and events covered. "It is this drama," said Cowley, "that makes the book vastly more appealing than the usual war correspondent's memoirs of things romantically seen and dangers escaped by the breath of a keen Damascus blade."

Among fellow journalists Sheean's emphasis on the self brought mixed comment. Kenneth Stewart, in Paris during the same period of the twenties when Sheean was in and out of the city, recalled a newspaper executive complaining, "Who gives a damn about Sheean! . . . His job is to tell what he sees, not what he feels." Stew-art himself leaned the other way, as did many younger journalists, holding that Sheean's book freed them from narrow, stenographic conceptions of their role. "Sheean established as nobody before him," wrote Stewart, "that what counts is what a reporter thinks. I should guess that no book published in our time had a greater di-rect response from the working press itself or gave the public bet-ter insight into a newspaperman's mind."

After education and student journalism at the University of Chicago, the red-haired Sheean—Jimmy Sheean to friends—drifted off to New York and a reporter's job on the *Daily News*. In the hot-house atmosphere of Greenwich Village, hearing political talk of radical figures who had experienced the war and seen firsthand the Russian Revolution and the making of the Treaty of Versailles, his world was enlarged. Irresistibly attracted to Europe and great events, he was off to Paris in the spring of 1922.

The city seemed to him instantly familiar, "a *patrie* of the imag-ination," and after three months of seclusion in the north of France writing, by his own estimate, a bad first novel and then travels in Italy, he returned to it as a job seeker. He needed money but equally something to do, especially "something definite—tasks with a beginning and an end—to fill the hours," and newspapering was the only work he knew. When he applied at the Paris *Tribune*, drawn there by his time in Chicago, he was taken on as a handyman on the local newspaper and office assistant to Hank Wales, who had followed Floyd Gibbons as the *Chicago Tribune*'s chief foreign correspondent in Paris.

For a time Sheean worked with the split duties, his days running from noon until two or three o'clock the next morning, then moved full time to the Chicago paper's foreign service, based with Wales in Paris and covering political news throughout Europe. It was a choice assignment, one that would become all the more so as the foreign service gained in prestige. Few were named to the select group—and once in, few left voluntarily.

LIFE WITH THE COLONEL. Colonel Robert R. McCormick had organized the foreign news service shortly after the end of World War I, with swashbuckling, eye-patched Floyd Gibbons running operations from a hub in Paris and bureaus in London, Rome, Madrid, Berlin, and other major European cities. Soon McCormick had at his command a skilled and youthful group of men (and, in Sigrid Schultz in Berlin, a talented woman), able to boast that of all foreign dispatches cited in the European press, 70 percent were from *Chicago Tribune* correspondents. In turn, he paid his troops well—promotion from the Paris *Tribune* to the foreign service meant at least a doubling of salary—and they traveled first class and stayed in top hotels, McCormick reasoning that anything less would cause Chicago to be frowned upon about the world.

The job's downside was that McCormick ran the foreign service with little consultation with *Chicago Tribune* subeditors, the correspondents directly under his unpredictable thumb. In his baronial Chicago office a world map with colored pins tracked his overseas network, the pins frequently restuck as he shifted men about. Each was expected to send McCormick a weekly letter about his work and attend biannual conferences in Paris, gatherings dreaded by the correspondents but ordinarily held in the plush setting of the Hôtel Ritz. Every few years correspondents were expected to return to Chicago for "re-americanization"—a period of routine work as ordinary reporters meant to peel away the taint of European corruption and refashion them as genuine Americans.

In the field, correspondents were subject to sudden commands from Chicago to drop whatever they were working on and dig up evidence to support McCormick's belief of the moment. When George Seldes, the *Chicago Tribune*'s bureau chief in Berlin, was told to cable information on the failure of government ownership of railroads in Germany, he responded with a three-hundred-word report saying the German system worked well. McCormick cabled back that he wanted a different story, one pointing out that German railroads were bankrupt, inefficient, and dangerous—a story to strengthen his opposition to government operation of American railroads. Seldes cabled a long report even more supportive of government ownership and, to his surprise, heard no more from his boss.

One of McCormick's enduring beliefs was that he could sense where a story would break and so place a correspondent on the spot in advance. If he sensed wrong, a correspondent got what amounted to a lengthy vacation, as David Darrah did when in 1929 he was dispatched from the Rome bureau to Madrid to report on the coming Spanish Civil War. The war came, but seven years later. When Wilfred Barber, then based in London, was told to head to Ethiopia to cover a coming invasion by Mussolini's Italy, he sensibly asked to delay departure for two weeks for inoculations against tropical diseases. ARE YOU A HISTORIAN OR A NEWSPAPERMAN? McCormick wired back. The next day Barber left for Addis Ababa, where he waited for six months for the invasion. On the day it came he died of malaria in a Seventh Day Adventist hospital. In 1936 Barber was posthumously awarded the Pulitzer Prize for Correspondence.

McCormick's ultimate hold on his correspondents, sudden dismissal, could come for whimsical reasons, as could sudden elevation. After Floyd Gibbons, at the time the *Chicago Tribune*'s chief roaming correspondent, was not unreasonably fired for running up $20,000 in expenses during a Timbuktu safari (he had told his mother, Gibbons jauntily explained, that he had long wished to send her a postcard from Timbuktu), McCormick gathered his troops at the Ritz in Paris to pick a replacement. The job—in George Seldes's view, possibly the best newspaper job in the world at the time—came with Gibbons's former freedom to go anywhere in the world after breaking news, expenses paid and with a salary that topped that of bureau chiefs. McCormick began the session by asking how many of the correspondents spoke French, then in turn German and Italian. After brief hesitation he announced, "I think I will appoint Larry Rue chief roaming correspondent of the *Tribune*." Silence was deafening until someone pointed out that Rue spoke no foreign language. "That," said McCormick, "is exactly what I want. I don't want my fine young American boys ruined by these damned foreigners."

A military flyer in World War I, Rue would do his roaming as the pilot of a *Tribune* plane, the first European correspondent to fly to the news. Two years into his prominent new position, however, he was fired. The explanation seemed to be that McCormick was disappointed over Rue's failure to fully utilize the plane's newsgathering potential.

TO THE RIFF. As one of the Colonel's fine boys with the foreign service, Vincent Sheean's first assignment was to Lausanne. For two months he covered the latter part of the peace conference of 1924, happily finding the work required no writing but only phoning information to Paris each evening. Subsequent assignments took him to the Rhineland, Geneva, Rome, and Madrid with returns to Paris where, in Hank Wales's absence, he covered routine press briefings at the Quai d'Orsay. Late in 1924 he went to Tangier to cover fighting between Spain and Riffian tribesmen under Abd-el-Krim, a long and perilous adventure that would make his name as a correspondent.

Since Paul Mowrer had traveled through Spanish territory to interview the rebel chief, Sheean in Tom-Sawyerish fashion picked a more difficult route from the French zone of the country. At first the *Tribune*'s Paris bureau refused authorization, then told him to use his own discretion; with that Sheean disappeared on a journey that took him across the Riffian mountains to the coastal village that was Abd-el-Krim's stronghold. Two months later, back in Tangier, he cabled Paris that he had a good story and began firing off dispatches. When he eventually reached Paris he found his work held in such high regard that one evening McCormick wined and dined him at the Ritz.

A few weeks later he was fired. The reason—in the brief, and obscure, explanation Sheean would give in *Personal History*—was "a disagreement between my immediate superior [presumably Hank Wales] and myself over the length of time I had stayed out to dinner." Asked to write and sign a letter requesting a leave of absence "in order to make everything look smooth and amicable to the home office of the paper," he oddly enough complied and produced the letter ("what were a few words more or less?"), thereby ending his days with the foreign service.

After writing a book on his Riffian adventure, Sheean resumed his career as a correspondent, reporting now largely on a freelance basis for magazines and news syndicates while returning to Paris for brief spells of newspaper work on the *Paris Times*. This would be the pattern of his life through the rest of the twenties—routine newspaper tasks, and reconnection with the agreeable life of the Paris-American journalistic community, between far-flung assignments as a correspondent. His hopes to become a fiction writer had faded but were not forgotten. A chance meeting with Hemingway in a Berlin railway station while Sheean was on assignment to Russia brought them vividly back to mind—and with a sense of an un-bridgeable chasm between a fiction writer's preoccupation with a private world and a journalist's with the public stage:

> Why couldn't I (allowing for the general inferiority of my
> equipment as a writer) do what he did—shut out the whole
> world and live, both as a writer and as a human being, in the
> restricted company of my own kind? . . . He wrote prose with
> the precision and power of poetry, upon subjects of the
> narrowest individual significance. . . . He was, of all the
> writers or artists of his approximate age, the one who had
> most amply developed and exactly applied the gifts he
> possessed. . . . The question arose, then: wasn't his way the
> best way, perhaps the only way, for an American bourgeois
> writer in the first half of the twentieth century to find his
> certainties and act upon them? What did he care about
> Chinese coolies? He had written *My Old Man*.

THE INSIDER. John Gunther shared Vincent Sheean's literary ambition and University of Chicago education, and like Sheean his breakthrough book was not a novel—though he had published novels before it appeared—but a foreign correspondent's work of personal reporting. Published the year after Sheean's book, *Inside Europe* was an immense success, leading to a string of "Inside" books that propelled Gunther, as *Personal History* did Sheean, from newspaper work to the new career niche of book journalist.

Gunther would credit Sheean and such fellow correspondents as Walter Duranty and George Slocombe with paving the way for a style of work in which the correspondent switched from news gatherer to reflective self, allowing himself the luxury of going beyond time-bound copy and the pursuit of scoops to write with more depth and individuality. "Rationally considered," he maintained, "it is utterly preposterous to ask a man to write and cable a fair and accurate interpretation of a great event a few minutes or seconds after it has happened—or a few minutes or seconds before." Book writing permitted correspondents to "go back, to write in more detail of the things they have seen, to express themselves on what is after all the most important thing, their own relation to the events they participate in."

Gunther was the *Chicago Daily News* correspondent in Vienna and London when *Inside Europe* was conceived and written, working under the paper's European director in Paris, Paul Mowrer. Eager for assignment as a correspondent, he had left the Chicago home office in 1928 and was taken on in London by the United Press before rejoining the *Daily News* as a junior member of its London bureau. When bureau chiefs around Europe went on home leave, Gunther filled in, and as a roving correspondent he covered breaking news throughout the continent. Mowrer, who considered him better at features than spot reporting, also gave him lengthy assignments to write impressionistic stories that could be dispatched by mail.

By 1930, now with a bureau of his own in Vienna, the large, fair-haired, outgoing Gunther considered himself a well-traveled correspondent who had "picked up dust from almost every European country." His new coverage territory was vast, Central Europe and the Balkans, and he depended on rival newsmen for tips and information. Other correspondents did as well, but Gunther's need was more acute since, in the five years he would spend in a German-speaking country, he failed to pick up the language. Travel was constant yet he found time to send off articles to a variety of American magazines and continue with fiction. Martha Foley, who with Whit Burnett was now running the Vienna bureau of the Consolidated Press, found Gunther working on a novel when she phoned to see if he had his radio on to news of the Nazi takeover of the German Reichstag. "No, I don't!" he moaned. "I'm trying to finish a chapter! Now this crap! Why did you have to tell me?"

The unexpected success in 1931 of *Washington Merry-Go-Round* by Drew Pearson and Robert Allen caused a stir among publishers.

When Harper & Brothers approached Gunther with a proposal for a similar broad-scope survey directed to Europe, he begged off on grounds of not knowing enough for the job and recommended a fellow correspondent in Berlin, H. R. Knickerbocker. The publishing house returned to Gunther when Knickerbocker declined, but he continued to hold off. Besides limited European experience, he saw his future in fiction rather than fact writing.

In America on leave in 1934, Gunther was asked to name a publisher's advance that would bring about a change of mind. He picked what he thought was the outrageous figure of $5,000. When Harper agreed to $3,000, with the rest made up by the British publisher Hamish Hamilton and *Harper's Magazine*, which would draw three articles from the book, Gunther still resisted. Finally, just as he was about to return to Vienna, Cass Canfield of the publishing firm arrived at Gunther's New York hotel room and refused to leave until he agreed to the book.

Back in Vienna, Gunther began work while holding down his position with the *Daily News*, one that turned more demanding when in 1935 the paper abruptly transferred him to London as bureau chief. Gunther used vacation time for research travel and gathered material from correspondents in other European capitals. At night and on Sundays he did his writing, and within seven months he had a manuscript to send to Harper in New York and Hamish Hamilton in London. Meant to be timely, the book required revisions up to the last moment, including settling on *Inside Europe* as the title. Finally the proofs were closed just before Christmas 1935, with the book appearing early in the new year to immediate success in America and Britain. In various editions it would sell over a million copies.

Even before the book's appearance Gunther had suggested to Harper that its pattern might be applied to other continents. To find out, he resigned from the *Daily News* and returned to America in 1936. Financed by publisher advances, lecture tours, and magazine articles, he began the travel and reporting that would go into

Inside Asia. Three years later, the book published and *Inside Latin America* just ahead, he returned to Europe with assignments from the North American Newspaper Alliance, *Reader's Digest*, and the National Broadcasting Company to gather impressions of the continent on the brink of war. In Paris, where he was a featured speaker on the Sino-Japanese conflict at a weekly luncheon of the American Club, the *Herald* reported that Gunther was a "widely-known newspaper correspondent and author" whose *Inside Europe* was still a "widely-selling book in the United States."

CONTEMPORARY HISTORY. William L. Shirer shared with John Gunther a Vienna posting as a correspondent, and with Gunther and Vincent Sheean dreams of writing fiction. Yet early on, after a year of producing short stories and some poetry while working on the Paris *Tribune*, he concluded he was unlikely to become another Hemingway or Fitzgerald; his natural bent was to turn outward to contemporary events, not inward to a private vision. Eventually he thought he might recreate the public world in fiction, but for the time being he lowered his sights to newspaper writing about Europe for an audience back home. This meant, he realized, he needed to "graduate from the somewhat frivolous Paris *Tribune* and become a foreign correspondent."

Promotion to the *Chicago Tribune*'s foreign staff—only a walk to an office down the hall from the *Tribune* newsroom yet a rise to lofty status and pay in dollars instead of francs—was no easy matter since the bureau chief, Hank Wales, chose an assistant from the daily paper only every couple of years. To catch his eye Shirer worked at improving his local reporting, wrote articles for the paper's Sunday literary page, and tried to master the toll-saving narrative style of cables. Each day he examined the file of cables Wales had sent to Chicago, deciphering such cryptic mysteries as an interview with the French president, Raymond Poincaré, about war debts:

EXCLUSIVE POINCARE CHICATRIBWARD UNTRUTH UNPAY
WARDEBTS AMERICAWARD STOP FRANCE UNINTENDS
UPGIVE REPARATIONS DUE EXTREATIES STOP TWO
LINKED QUOTE UNREPARATIONS UNWARDEBTS PAYABLE
UNQUOTE UNBELIEVES GERMANS UNFUNDS PAY FULLEST
STOP UNBEFORE POINCARE ADAMANTEST REGERMANS
DELIBERATE STALLING STOP BRISTLING CHICATRIBWARD
UNEXCUSES EXGERMANS. . . .

As it happened, it was not cabalese that brought about Shirer's elevation in the summer of 1927 but special reporting for the daily paper on the French tennis championships—with his bylined story of Bill Tilden's loss in the singles final making page one—and, that same year, Lindbergh's Paris landing. For the latter Shirer prepared himself by working up background material in the company of Wales and Jay Allen, the bureau assistant who had followed Vincent Sheean. The two correspondents had settled on a reporting strategy in which they would cable dispatches to Chicago in short takes rather than first writing full stories, and they would avoid the usual cable services, certain to be overrun with demand, in favor of the seldom-used Commercial Cable. It proved a wise scheme and gave Shirer a key lesson as a correspondent: getting a story was one thing, getting it through, preferably ahead of the competition, was another.

"And when you're through with your story for the lousy Paris edition," Wales ordered Shirer as they ended a planning meeting, "get the hell over to Commercial Cable and give me a hand." Wales's side-of-the-mouth growl was music to Shirer's ears. In the frenzy that followed Lindbergh's landing, Shirer both wrote his report for the Paris *Tribune* and teamed with Wales and Allen. The three ended up in an all-night café, and over coffee and croissants Wales read Shirer's page-one account. "Not bad," he allowed. "In fact, damn good." Then he added: "Willy, I think maybe you got what it takes. The secret of this business is to turn it out fast under pressure.

Maybe—maybe I can find room for you." The next day, age twenty-three, Shirer became a *Chicago Tribune* foreign correspondent with a salary boost from $15 in francs a week to $50 in dollars.

ISADORA. Hank Wales grasped the news value in Lindbergh's landing but missed it entirely in Isadora Duncan's Paris funeral a short while later. After the famed American dancer's bizarre death by strangulation on the Riviera when her dangling scarf was caught in the wheels of a car, Shirer, who had come to know and admire her, pleaded in vain with both Wales and the Paris *Tribune* to cover the burial service in Père Lachaise Cemetery. "What the hell," snapped Wales, "she was only a dancer."

At the time of the death the Paris papers and new bureaus were occupied covering the tenth-anniversary American Legion convention in Paris, a boozy, boisterous gathering of twenty thousand that culminated on September 19 in a parade down the Champs-Elysées. That same day Duncan's funeral procession of a few hundred, rerouted around the parade, made a long walk in a drizzle to the cemetery where a great mass of her fans had gathered. None of the American papers could spare a reporter for the procession, and the *Herald* buried a story on an inside page under a misleading headline: "Few Attend Isadora Duncan's Rites as Compatriots Parade." Later, in her Paris letter in *The New Yorker*, Janet Flanner clarified what had taken place:

> Since Isadora was an American, it was regrettable that both the [morning] Paris American newspapers . . . busy doubtless with the gayer Legion matters, did not send reporters to follow her funeral cortege to its destination. Thus Americans next morning read that Isadora was followed to her grave by a pitiful handful. Only five carriages made up the official procession; but four thousand people—men, women, old, young, and of all nationalities—waited in the rain for the arrival of her body at Père-Lachaise.

APPRENTICE DAYS. For Shirer, becoming a foreign correspondent promised travel, adventure, glamour, but at first it meant only fitting into the repetitive routine of the *Chicago Tribune*'s Paris bureau. As head man, Hank Wales's workday began late and ended early. About six o'clock each evening, after writing a piece drawn from the afternoon papers or some political event, he repaired to Harry's New York Bar in the company of such fellow bureau chiefs as the dapper boulevardier Edwin L. James of the *New York Times*, soon to become the paper's managing editor, and former war correspondents like Floyd Gibbons, now a magazine freelancer.

As Wales left the office Shirer, who started work at 3 p.m., returned from checking in with the American embassy, the French Foreign Office, and other news sources. He would phone Wales at Harry's, discuss what and how much to file, and after an evening meal read the French morning papers and Havas wire reports. Final editions of the French papers came in at 2:30 a.m. and had to be rapidly scanned before deadline. If an important story surfaced, Shirer informed Wales, locating him in whatever bar he now inhabited. Shirer could handle the story himself, was Wales's usual response, yet when Shirer did, the printed dispatch in the Chicago always carried the bureau chief's byline.

With apprentice days behind him, Shirer became a roving correspondent, working out of Paris with assignments that took him about Europe. After covering the Winter Olympics in St. Moritz he moved on to Geneva for a session of the League of Nations. He was now, for good reason, feeling his journalistic oats: "At twenty-four . . . I had reached the big time in journalism, hobnobbing with veteran and renowned correspondents and statesmen twice my age or more, and daily recording history for the 'World's Greatest Newspaper.' For an American youngster less than three years out of a prairie college, I was not, I thought, doing badly."

In Chicago, McCormick believed otherwise and fired off a cable to Wales in Paris: WALES. SHIRER'S STORIES FROM GENEVA HEAVY AS A BRIDE'S CAKE. PROCEED THERE IMMEDIATELY AND

TAKE OVER. Shirer slunk back to Paris, expecting to be fired. He would be, but not for years; for the present he stayed on as Wales's roaming correspondent, assigned to the French Riviera to cover a funeral and then staying on to report on the rich and famous. Wales considered the latter task a paid vacation, but Shirer was only bored. His reprieve came one day with a telephone call from Wales: "Willy, I've got good news for you, since you claimed to be so miserable down there. Get up to Vienna as fast as you can and take over the bureau there for a while."

VIENNA DAYS. The postwar city was battered and impoverished but appealed to Shirer nearly as much as Paris. His work was demanding, with a coverage area that included countries to the east along the Danube River as well as Austria, but he had the aid of an assistant for office work and translating. Vienna itself offered abundant feature material to mail off to Chicago about temperamental opera stars, playboy aristocrats, and ongoing feuds among Freud's disciples. It provided as well a community of fellow correspondents who regularly gathered at a permanently reserved table in the Café Louvre close by the stock exchange and the cable office.

The group clung to one another for ideas, information, the logistics of daily life in a foreign country, and—far from least in the importance they attached to it—moral support in their long-term plans to switch from reporting to fiction and poetry. Along with Shirer and John Gunther, the Vienna literary circle included Whit Burnett, Martha Foley, and Dorothy Thompson, over frequently from her Berlin posting as a correspondent and now the wife of Sinclair Lewis. (The heights and depths of the marriage would be chronicled years later by Vincent Sheean in *Dorothy and Red*.)

Bill Bird had noticed and liked Whit Burnett's short stories in *transition* and his feature writing for the Paris *Herald*, and late in 1929 offered him a job in the Consolidated Press Association's Vienna bureau at double his newspaper pay. When Martha Foley caught on with another wire service in Vienna, the pair left Paris together. Later, Foley joined Burnett with the Consolidated Press, and while working together as Vienna correspondents they produced their warts-and-all magazine portrait of the *Herald* and began their long venture as founders and editors of *STORY*, the magazine of short fiction that over the years published a glittering list of writers.

The tight-knit group of Vienna correspondents were all young, Martha Foley pointed out, because the city "did not rank in importance with London, Berlin, or Paris, where news bureaus were headed by older, more established journalists. But we didn't care. We looked beyond newspaper work to more important writing. . . . We wanted to produce literature." Whit Burnett would repeat with approval John Gunther's remark that nowhere were journalists more engaged in literature than in Vienna—and add himself the qualification that what consumed their time "was not all literature, but it was not, as in Paris, all drink and talk, either."

A LITTLE YOUNG. During a month's home leave late in 1929, his first return to America after four years in Europe, Shirer was summoned to a meeting with Colonel McCormick in Chicago. In his lofty perch in the *Tribune* Tower, McCormick moved to his wall map, directed a finger to Europe, and announced, "I want you to go there. I want you to take over the bureau." When the tall, bulky editor-publisher theatrically stepped aside, Shirer could see that "there" was Vienna. Elated at returning to the city, now with command of the bureau, he could only stammer, "I think there will be a lot of news there." "That's why I'm sending you," replied McCormick.

Before Shirer could escape the office McCormick asked him his age. Shirer told the truth. "A little young," McCormick mused. "But give it a try. On the *Tribune*, Shirer, it doesn't make much difference. If you're good enough to make the paper, however young, you're good enough to take on any assignment." Shirer thought so too, and though the Colonel had struck him as odd he left the office in a pleasurable daze. "But he gave me Vienna!" he kept saying to himself. "Not bad for twenty-five."

In August 1930 a two-word cable arrived from McCormick: FLY INDIA. Jay Allen had fallen ill and Shirer had been plucked from Vienna as his replacement. He would do impressive reporting on Gandhi's resistance movement and on Afghanistan, where he gained rare access to the country and wrote exclusive dispatches the *Chicago Tribune* vigorously promoted and the Paris *Tribune* played on page one. When he developed health problems of his own, he proposed to McCormick a return to Vienna on an overland route through the Middle East, writing colorful stories along the way. The message this time from Chicago was slightly longer: SHIRER COME BACK VIA BABYLON. MCCORMICK.

In Vienna, Shirer married—his wife, a young Austrian journalist, had been an assistant to the Vienna correspondent of the *London Daily Telegraph*—and got the bureau up and running again. Another cable—SHIRER. RETURN INDIA—sent him packing for a second Asian interlude, now reporting on the aftermath of Gandhi's release from prison, before he settled again into his work in Vienna. Ominous political developments under way across the border in Germany and elsewhere along the Danube provided plentiful material, his somber reports balanced by a relaxing period of writing entertainment articles from the Mozart festival in Salzburg.

Now and then a specific assignment came from McCormick. One took the form of a challenge—a picture from a French weekly of a fallen bridge over a small stream, the text cut out, and a scrawled message: *Shirer—go there*. Luckily, Shirer remembered a picture of a similar bridge in Russia, and there had been recent reports of Moldavian peasants fleeing forced collectives. Together with a Russian-speaking friend he went to the Ukraine, located the bridge, and spent a week recording the woes of refugees from the Soviet paradise.

Shortly thereafter the bottom dropped out of his life. A serious skiing accident in the Alps left him with permanent loss of vision in one eye and for a time threatened both. Then in October 1932 came a cable from the *Chicago Tribune*'s managing editor informing him he was fired, effective at once. Stunned, Shirer wrote back asking why; the managing editor took five weeks to reply, and then in generic fashion: "The reason you were dropped from the staff was that your recent dispatches and mail articles had not been satisfactory to the management." There was also a particular reason: a dispatch about a traffic accident had misidentified the American film star Anna May Wong, caused her to sue, and forced the newspaper to pay out $1,000 and print a retraction.

Shirer thought the mistake trivial—other American papers had carried the same story—especially when balanced against McCormick's praise for his recent work and the fact the *Chicago Tribune*, on the day he was fired, was preparing a full-page house ad acclaiming one of his stories. In the final analysis it was the depression that had done him in, Shirer concluded, the paper cutting back on foreign news and overseas staff. Hank Wales had been fired, as had Shirer's successor in India, and Jay Allen was soon to go. Other American papers were retrenching as well, as were the wire services—reductions Shirer learned to his dismay when he began hunting for a new job.

With no immediate prospects, he and his wife decided to use their savings for a year in Spain, living cheaply while Shirer wrote a novel, seeing if he could make his future way as a fiction writer. They had booked passage to Barcelona when a chatty letter arrived from McCormick implying the firing was a mistake or had been forgotten and Shirer still had his job. McCormick noted that after "some excellent work in India . . . you have almost vanished from the picture as a European correspondent," and wondered if a transfer to a new post was in order. Elated, Shirer responded that he believed Vienna could still produce good material. A cable immediately came from

Chicago: SHIRER DISREGARD LETTER THIRTIETH. MCCORMICK. A letter followed from McCormick's secretary explaining that when the letter of the 30th was written the Colonel had not realized Shirer was off the payroll—clearly a fabrication, in Shirer's outraged view ("What a contemptible son-of-a-bitch!"), since McCormick alone decided who was on or off the foreign service.

SHORTER ENGLISH SENTENCES. As Hank Wales's successor as head of the *Chicago Tribune*'s Paris bureau, Edmond Taylor was Shirer's superior, and McCormick maintained to him that he had gone the last mile in trying to give the Vienna correspondent a "square deal." Taylor himself seems to have sidestepped any involvement in Shirer's sacking, perhaps alert to the likelihood his own relationship with McCormick would eventually sour. At age nineteen he had left a good $35-a-week job as a deskman and feature writer on the *St. Louis Times* when, as he put it, "my imagination was beginning to feel confined. The traditional remedy for this state was Paris. In the summer of 1928 I decided to try it." Hired by the Paris *Tribune*, his ambition soon switched from local reporting to becoming a foreign correspondent—and he realized the Paris paper could be a stepping-stone since Sheean, Shirer, and Jay Allen, with scarcely more journalistic background than he possessed, had managed the transition.

On the *Tribune* Taylor rose to the news editor position and started work on a sorely needed style book regularizing the paper's spelling and usage. When Hank Wales took him on as an assistant in 1930, Waverley Root—just back with the *Tribune* after giving up his correspondent's position in London—moved into Taylor's position and completed the style book while Taylor began spending long, routine nights in the bureau office scanning early editions of the French papers that had been rushed from the presses by a cycling messenger. If anything of importance turned up, he followed Shirer's procedure of calling Wales in one of his favored nightspots (the "oddly straitlaced" bureau chief, he soon realized, was a "pillar of the Presbyterian Church—as well as of several Montmartre nightclubs") and occasionally filing human interest dispatches under Wales's name.

When Wales fell out of favor with McCormick, Taylor replaced him in the Paris bureau, and the level of his work sharply increased. He covered sessions of the League of Nations in Geneva and traveled throughout Central Europe on assignments. In Vienna he joined nightly with John Gunther and other correspondents in the Café Louvre, gathering background information on what seemed the "depression-pauperism" of the stricken city and on contemporary European politics in general. In October 1931, in Berlin backing up the *Chicago Tribune*'s correspondent Sigrid Schulz, he got his first look at Hitler, who struck him while reading a speech as a comic "Chaplinesque figure" with "jerky, robot gestures." Nonetheless, when he returned to Paris he brought with him deep forebodings about the future of Germany.

Just before, in the summer of 1931, Taylor had his first encounter with McCormick during one of his leader's European swings. "Taylor, do you get sick when you fly?" said a voice on the phone in the Paris bureau. Taylor, who had never before heard McCormick speak but recognized him instantly, said he did not. "Meet me at the Ritz at eleven o'clock then. I want you to fly to London with me." They made the flight in a private plane and were met by John Steele, the *Chicago Tribune*'s London correspondent. At a late lunch in the London Ritz, McCormick mused on the Roman period in Britain, and it was decided to inspect the ancient ruins at St. Albans before heading to the paper's London office. A side trip followed to Ludgrove, McCormick's old school, and then there was a stop at a cricket match in progress on the way back to London. "I know you two boys will want to get out on the town tonight," McCormick informed the weary correspondents when the three at last arrived at the Ritz, "so I'll let you off now."

The following morning there was a demonstration of a British color camera McCormick thought might prove useful for the

Chicago Tribune's Sunday paper, then another lunch and a return to the airport. On the way Steele managed to get in a few questions about office matters, one of which involved what McCormick planned to do about the Vienna bureau while William L. Shirer was in India on assignment. McCormick cocked his head toward Taylor and replied, "I think I'll send this fellow." Taylor was pleased with the assignment but still in the dark about why McCormick had brought him along on the trip. The answer came while rain pounded the plane over the English Channel. "I've noticed that when you translate from the French you sometimes follow the original sentence structure too closely," said McCormick. "You should break it up into shorter English sentences."

SUGGEST YOU JOIN. . . . As the *Chicago Tribune*'s Paris bureau chief through most of the thirties, Taylor learned, as had others before him, that he was a soldier in McCormick's private army and subject to frequent letters or cables from the commander. Some were merely trivial or possessed what Taylor shrugged off as having a "cosmic irrelevance that suggested the indecipherable cliff-writings of some vanished civilization"; others were unambiguous reminders that his dispatches were not to stray from McCormick's isolationist vision and his newspaper's editorial policies. With the crumbling political situation in Europe, and the Spanish Civil War in particular, Taylor found himself increasingly at odds with McCormick in both areas.

A passionate anti-Franco speech that Taylor delivered to an audience heavily made up of businessmen at the American Club of Paris in 1936 ("The spirit of Franco's army is the spirit of a mob of lynchers in our own South hunting for a Negro murderer") brought a terse cable from McCormick: TAYLOR WHAT'S THIS ABOUT YOU MAKING SPEECH AT AMERICAN CLUB PARIS QUERY. When Taylor forwarded a copy of the speech, McCormick pointed out in a lengthy letter that grim and irrational acts were carried out on both sides of the conflict, a truth Taylor did not dispute. (When Taylor subsequently asked to be relieved of his assignment of reporting the war from the Nationalist side, McCormick replaced him with Alex Small, now with the *Chicago Tribune*'s foreign service, who soon thereafter found himself officially banished from Nationalist-controlled areas of Spain.)

With Hitler's annexation of Austria in 1938 and other cross-border interventions, Taylor in Paris was on the receiving end of letters and cables from Chicago maintaining that, while the paper still printed most of his dispatches, he was losing objectivity and falling prey to European war fears. A total break came with Germany's Moscow Pact with Stalin and the invasion of Poland. When a think piece he cabled to Chicago—one admittedly short on critical analysis and long on editorializing—was rejected as a "bedtime story," Taylor replied with a cable both defending the piece and unwisely suggesting its publication would advance the political knowledge of the paper's editors. McCormick's swift response was that Taylor was a victim of hysterical European propaganda designed to drag America into war—and added an unmistakable recommendation: SUGGEST YOU JOIN FOREIGN LEGION OR TAKE REST CURE IN NEUTRAL SANITARIUM. Taylor understood the message and resigned. He was without immediate job prospects but, as he wrote, relieved

> to be freed from the nightly gymnastic of searching for some
> perspective on the day's events that would be compatible
> enough with Col. McCormick's to run the gauntlet of the
> *Tribune*'s copy editors, and at the same time valid in terms of
> my own professional or political conscience. Moreover . . . in
> abandoning the hopeless struggle to open the Colonel's mind
> to the truth as I saw it, I eliminated a factor of excess and
> distortion in my own.

Larry Rue, back in McCormick's good graces, took over the Paris bureau. Taylor remained in the city and, with his Swiss-born wife holding a job to pay the bills, produced a book of political reporting that was published in 1940 as *The Strategy of Terror*. In the summer of the year, German troops advancing on Paris, he was briefly back in a correspondent's role as a colleague of Eric Sevareid with CBS radio. Another dramatic swing in Taylor's career took place the following year when, now in America with his wife, he was recruited by General William J. Donovan to join the foreign intelligence service under development in Washington—later to be known as the Office of Strategic Services—as an information officer working under the playwright Robert E. Sherwood.

FROM BAD TO HEARST. Edmond Taylor was still at the helm in the *Chicago Tribune*'s Paris bureau when William L. Shirer made an inglorious return to the city. Life in a small coastal village on the Costa Brava had been idyllic but failed to open the way to the literary life. Magazine articles and stories Shirer turned out for income were routinely rejected, and he had no better luck catching on as a book reviewer. His only choice, he realized, was to go back to newspapering. He tried all his contacts in America and abroad, but the lone job offer came from Eric Hawkins in Paris. "Our money is gone," Shirer noted in his diary. "Day after tomorrow I must go back to work. We had not thought much about it. A wire came. An offer. A bad offer from the Paris *Herald*. But it will keep the wolf away until I can get something better."

The winter of 1934 was dismal, and Shirer dismally returned to where he had begun nearly a decade before, a well-traveled foreign correspondent reduced to filling a chair on the rim of the *Herald*'s copy desk. His pride suffered but he was grateful to be working at all, and Paris was still enchanting. A new and rancorous political atmosphere, however, pervaded the city, leading to street rioting by fascist groups bent on overthrowing the Third Republic. Soon Shirer was switched from the deskwork to reporting, and during the winter and spring he chronicled increasingly lawless events—

events, he came to believe, that revealed a growing inability of the French government to react forcefully. At the same time Nazi power was darkly gathering in Germany and Austria.

In August Shirer was in the *Herald* office when a phone call came from Arno Dosch-Fleurot, the correspondent who had done front-line reporting in World War I for the *New York World* and was now with Hearst's Universal Service news agency, offering him a job with the agency in Berlin. Dazed by the sudden swing of fortune, Shirer fled the office, crossed Rue de Berri to the bar of the Hôtel California, and celebrated with a double cognac. He was "going from bad to Hearst"—as the pun came to him—but for journalists with any organization Berlin was a central location of the time.

In the city he happily settled into the routine of the job. During the day he combed German newspapers and periodicals for ideas and in the evenings worked late before telephoning stories to either Paris or London for transmission to New York. Long talk sessions followed at the Taverne, a restaurant with a corner reserved for British, French, and American correspondents. Regulars among the American group were two young assistants from the United Press bureau, Howard K. Smith and Richard Helms, one to become a prominent broadcaster, the other head of the Central Intelligence Agency. Another familiar figure was a young embassy secretary who wrote short stories and was pondering a career translating Russian classics, George F. Kennan.

Shirer himself was rebitten by the fiction bug and finished the draft of a novel about India based on his time there with the *Chicago Tribune*. A literary agent in New York was hopeful, but the novel was never published—fortunately, Shirer decided later, since his invented characters were wooden and the figure of Gandhi was better treated in nonfiction. (Although she did not include Shirer in the group, Martha Foley thought such fellow correspondents during his Vienna days as John Gunther and Dorothy Thompson lacked a natural feel for fiction because they "saw *things*, not people.") It would be 1980 before *Gandhi—A Memoir* appeared.

After the Universal Service disbanded in 1937, Shirer stayed on with Hearst's wire service, the INS, as number two man in its Berlin bureau. Let go from that as well after a short while, he once again found himself wholly without job prospects. Earlier he had tried and failed to catch on as a correspondent with the *New York Times* and the *Chicago Daily News*; the best course seemed a return to America and a hunt for ordinary newspaper work, assuming he could raise the money for ship passage.

At this low point Shirer opened a telegram from Salzburg which had arrived and been set aside a few minutes before the INS wire about his lost position: CAN YOU MEET ME ADLONE 8/27 FOR DINNER . . . MURROW COLUMBIA BROADCASTING. He had only a dim awareness of London-based Edward R. Murrow, and assumed the dinner invitation was merely a routine brain-picking session by a visiting bigwig. As for CBS, his only connection had been a fifteen-minute broadcast, arranged by the network's Berlin representative, about German response to the *Hindenburg* explosion, an ordeal that left him certain he was not cut out for radio.

At dinner in the Berlin hotel Murrow told Shirer he was looking for an experienced foreign correspondent to head a CBS office on the continent and work under his direction in London. He could pay what Shirer made with the Hearst organization: $125 a week. The matter was settled on the spot, with the qualifier that William S. Paley, the network owner, would have to pass on Shirer's voice in a test broadcast.

An agonizing delay followed the test before Murrow phoned from London:

"The bastards in New York finally came through."
"Yes?"
"They think you're terrific!"
"Really?"
"When can you start?"
"Any time you want."

"Shall we say October first?"

"Okay."

VIENNA AGAIN. Shirer would be based in Vienna, which pleased him despite the fact such companions of earlier days as John Gunther, Whit Burnett, and Martha Foley had departed. Pleasing as well was his imposing title, Continental Representative of the Columbia Broadcasting System. Disillusionment set in when he learned that, despite the test broadcast, he would not speak on the air. Nor would Murrow. In CBS's view, having their own people read the news smacked of editorializing, so newspaper correspondents would be brought to a studio to read the scripts. Feeling let down by Murrow and Paley—he had been hired, after all, because he was an experienced correspondent—Shirer told himself he would stay with radio only until he could get back to newspaper work.

CBS changed policy when German troops entered Austria in 1938. With his wife in a hospital after an emergency cesarean delivery of a daughter, Shirer flew to London while Murrow took his place in Vienna. In a fifteen-minute broadcast on March 12, 1938, Shirer gave an eyewitness account of the invasion—his first CBS broadcast in his new position and, as he noted, "the first time CBS had ever allowed one of its own staff to go on the air and report the news firsthand." A call to Shirer from the CBS news director in New York, Paul White, followed: "We want a European roundup tonight. One a.m. your time. We want you and some member of Parliament from London, Ed Murrow from Vienna, and we want you to line up American newspaper correspondents in Berlin, Paris and Rome. The show will run thirty minutes. Can you and Murrow do it?" With no idea if they could, Shirer said yes.

The mismatched pair—Murrow darkly handsome and elegantly turned out, Shirer short, wispy-haired, rumpled—went to work, rounding up correspondents available on a Sunday and with clearance from their home offices while stitching together a network of telephone lines and shortwave transmitters, Shirer thankful for his adequate French, German, and Italian in dealing with directors of European broadcasting systems. The correspondents chosen were Edgar Mowrer of the *Chicago Daily News* in Paris, and Frank Gervasi in Rome and Pierre Huss in Berlin, both with INS. At the last minute the phone connection could not be arranged with Rome and Gervasi dictated his report to a stenographer for Shirer to read on the air.

Shirer thought the roundup went well enough, given the brevity of preparation and the technological complexity of live hookups. New York was enthusiastic. "So much so," Paul White informed Shirer, "that we want another one tomorrow night—tonight, your time. Can you do it?" A tired Shirer again said yes. Neither Shirer nor Murrow realized it at the time, but they had created on the fly a format that would become a staple of radio and eventually television news broadcasting.

BERLIN DIARY. Shirer was Murrow's man positioned in Berlin when he learned the shocking news that Webb Miller had died in a fall from a railway car near London. Miller had been the United Press bureau chief in Paris and then its European head, based in London. On many assignments Shirer and the older correspondent had crossed paths, and Shirer had used Miller as one of the newsmen reading his CBS radio scripts. The shy, unassuming Miller seemed to him one of the most distinguished of American reporters abroad—and he had only recently published another in the string of popular memoirs by foreign correspondents, *I Found No Peace.* Dying the way he had, after more than two decades covering wars and often under fire, seemed wholly wrong—the feeling only intensified by stories in the German press claiming the correspondent had been murdered by the British secret service.

Shirer's spirits were raised, however, by the presence in Berlin of Ralph Barnes, an old friend from early Paris newspaper days and now the *New York Herald Tribune*'s Berlin correspondent after assignments in Rome, London, and Moscow. Their reunion would last only briefly. For a dispatch he filed suggesting possible future Russian-German conflict, Barnes was ordered out of the country, joining a list of earlier forced departures that included Dorothy Thompson and Edgar Mowrer. The true reason for the dismissal, Shirer speculated, was Nazi irritation with *Herald Tribune* editorial policy and the paper's insistence on maintaining strongly independent correspondents in Berlin. "Ralph and I had a farewell walk in the Tiergarten this afternoon," Shirer recorded in his diary, "he naturally depressed and not quite realizing that his going was a proof that he had more integrity than any of us who are allowed to stay."

Any thought Shirer had of returning to newspaper work had been abandoned. He continued to report from Berlin for CBS until, late in 1940, German censorship made it impossible to continue and he left for Lisbon and ship passage home. Just ahead, in 1941, was publication of his first book, *Berlin Diary: The Journal of a Foreign Correspondent, 1934–1941*, a chronicle of newspaper and radio work that linked Shirer with Sheean and Gunther in the procession of best-sellers, all within a six-year period, by Midwesterners turned foreign correspondents. (Later, in his memoirs, Shirer would write: "I think we all felt that luck had smiled on us when our early books, Jimmy's *Personal History* in 1935, John's *Inside Europe* in 1936, and my *Berlin Diary* in 1941 made the best-seller lists and gave us financial independence at least for a while.") Yet in the future was the vast success of Shirer's *The Rise and Fall of the Third Reich*.

FIELD MARSHAL. Ralph Barnes was not so fortunate. In late 1940 he was based in Cairo and reporting on the British army in the Middle East and North Africa when Italian forces invaded Greece. Immediately he joined other correspondents on a British warship and made his way to Athens. Among correspondents already present in the city was Leland Stowe, Barnes's *Herald Tribune* bureau chief in Paris a decade earlier.

"No bureau chief," Stowe said of that time, "ever had a more eager and indefatigable assistant than he, nor a more loyal friend." Barnes had demonstrated all his qualities in 1929 when he teamed with Stowe in reporting on a war reparations conference in Paris that culminated in a plan put forward by the head of the American delegation, Owen D. Young, for creation of an international bank to handle reparations payments. Barnes and Stowe had worked longer and harder than the competition, pooling their material but writing independently, Barnes for the Paris *Herald* and Stowe for the *New York Herald Tribune*.

A major scoop had fallen into their laps when a member of the Japanese delegation, ardently cultivated by Barnes and Stowe, passed them a copy of the plan with the stipulation that the document be returned that night and the source kept confidential. The two correspondents had hurriedly typed a copy and the following day the text had appeared in both the Paris and New York papers. For his work in the *Herald Tribune* Stowe had received a Pulitzer Prize in 1930—following Paul Scott Mowrer as the second recipient of the correspondence award and the second given to a Paris-based journalist. Barnes had received only praise. "A great deal of credit," Stowe would appropriately note, "also belonged to Ralph Barnes."

Now, in Athens, Barnes was a widely respected correspondent known among colleagues as the "Field Marshal" for his broad knowledge and doggedly persistent reporting. Stowe had moved on to the *Chicago Daily News*, working under Paul Mowrer in Chicago after Wilbur Forrest, who had become an executive with the *Herald Tribune*, turned down his request to go overseas as a war correspondent on grounds that, at thirty-nine, Stowe was too old. Over the years Barnes and Stowe had had many friendly meetings, and Barnes would recall about a book he hoped to write that in 1936— after he had flown to New York as one of the correspondents on the maiden voyage of the *Hindenburg*—"Lee Stowe took me to see Knopf, the publisher, about my 'book' on *Under Three Dictatorships*." In Athens, however, the two were competitors.

The Greek military refused to allow correspondents into the battle zone, so Barnes and others talked the British into allowing them on Royal Air Force night bombing raids over Italian supply areas. Lots were drawn to see who would go on the flights, and Barnes went the second night. Stowe later wrote of Barnes stuffing apples in the pockets of his greatcoat—a British private's coat of which he was deeply proud—and fretting that during the flight he would be unable to smoke for six hours or more.

The RAF plane he was aboard crashed on a mountainside in Yugoslavia, far off course in fog and rain, killing all aboard. While gathering Barnes's belongings from his hotel room, Stowe found the correspondent had been doing some typically hefty reading, T. E. Lawrence's *Seven Pillars of Wisdom*. He sent off a dispatch about Barnes's death, painful to write, and later found himself recalling with sad irony an unpublished novel he had written in 1930, when Barnes was his assistant in the *Herald Tribune*'s Paris bureau. The central figure in the story had been a correspondent who covered an imagined Italian invasion of Yugoslavia and perished of pneumonia in the mountains of Albania.

CHAPTER FIVE

A Smart Little Magazine

"I'll walk you to the other side of the street,"
he said, "and then we'll meet at the door."
"No, we oughtn't even to sit together.
I'm a countess—laugh it off but anything
I do will be in that damn 'Boulevardier.'"
—F. SCOTT FITZGERALD,
"News of Paris—Fifteen Years Ago"

THE LIGHTER SIDE. Jed Kiley opens a memoir of his friendship with Hemingway with a quick-paced account of running into a muscular young man in a Paris bar and wondering where they had met before. Possibly it was in a nightclub the entrepreneur-writer owns in Montmartre, but otherwise he is unable to place his barmate. Given his thick wrists and strong hands, he might be a Left Bank sculptor; certainly he is an American, holding his drink in the death-grip of someone who has escaped Prohibition. When the young man says, "Been reading your stuff in *The Boulevardier*," Kiley takes him to be a fan.

The Boulevardier, Kiley explains, is a "smart little magazine" he and Erskine Gwynne are producing from an office on the Champs-Elysées, and he is its "top writer." "They used to read my stuff in *The Boulevardier*," he goes on, "and then came up the Hill [to Montmartre] to meet the author. You might say I was literary in the day-time and mercenary at night. I liked to talk about my stuff too." So, in the bar, he asks if the young man likes his stuff.

"No," he said.
"Oh," I said. "What are you doing here [in Paris] besides
    drinking?"
"Writing," he said.
"Writing what?" I said.
"A book," he said.
"Oh," I said.

Eventually the young man introduces himself—"The name's Hemingway"—and with that Kiley realizes he has not seen his fellow Chicagoan since World War I when both were ambulance drivers in Europe. Their bar talk turns from Hemingway's interest in boxing to his ambition as a writer, and Kiley imagines he can be of some help: "You know how it is when you run into a guy from your own home town. Might start by running something for him in *The Boulevardier*. You could see he could use the prestige. If he can write like he can drink . . . I'll take him in my stable."

The barroom encounter is not a chance meeting, it becomes clear, when Hemingway produces "a few crumpled sheets of yellow paper written in lead pencil" and hands them to Kiley. "Here's a low kidney punch for that throwaway of yours," he says. "Don't change a word." The characterization of the magazine is rude and Hemingway arrogant in demanding his piece be printed as written; Kiley nonetheless holds his fire: "But I didn't say anything. Just stuck the thing in my pocket without reading it. Might need it for wrapping up a parcel some day. I was still sore about that crack he had made about the magazine. Better change the subject, I thought. One more drink and I'd be telling him what he could do with his wrapping paper."

Jed Kiley's account of his meeting with Ernest Hemingway, if not his entire memoir, smacks of fiction, yet *The Boulevardier* was a genuine Paris-American publication, Erskine Gwynne was its founder and Kiley among its leading writers, and the young Hemingway was a onetime contributor. Rather than Hemingway's dismissive throwaway, the magazine—as the Paris *Tribune* noted in a "Who's Who Abroad" profile of Gwynne in 1927, the year the magazine began publishing—was an ambitious journalistic venture "devoted to the lighter side of life in Paris." More precisely, it was a straightforward Paris imitation of *The New Yorker*—always coyly referred to as "our contemporary"—that, unlike its model, seldom sought to be anything more than a local publication of humor and entertainment.

MAGAZINES FOR FRANCE. Earlier in the interwar period, two American magazines, radically unlike in style and audience but with content that appealed beyond national borders, had followed a different course by producing from Paris versions of their publications for French readers. Bernarr Macfadden's confessional magazine *True Story*, a pulp publication when it appeared in 1919 but so successful it converted to slick paper, had a circulation of more than two million by the mid-twenties and on into the depression. Abroad it was published not only in a French edition but in Britain, Germany, Sweden, and Holland under arrangements with host-country publishers that required three-quarters of each issue come from the American edition.

Condé Nast's sophisticated bimonthly fashion magazine *Vogue* was limited to French and British editions (and a failed German effort) that featured more resident content and editorial control while also developing into long-running foreign successes. Before World War I *Vogue*'s American issue had modest distribution in Britain and on the continent, but with wartime shipping disruptions the idea was hatched for an edition produced in Britain, with fashion material from the American *Vogue* supplemented with local copy and thereby capitalizing on British advertising. British *Vogue* was not an overnight success, nor was the editorial operation smooth when the veteran American editor Edna Woolman Chase came from New York to London to oversee the British staff; yet with the end of the war and improvement in the business climate Condé Nast was sufficiently encouraged to develop a second foreign edition in France. The first French *Vogue* appeared on June 15, 1920, printed in London and distributed in France by the French firm Hachette, using the same fashion contents as New York and London and a small amount of locally created material. A year later, with printing now in Paris, the magazine had circulation—as Edna Chase, who also oversaw the French edition, boasted—"never before attained on the continent by a class publication."

In 1923 a key figure joined the magazine's Paris staff. During World War I Chicago-born Main Bocher was a sergeant major with the American Expeditionary Forces, working in intelligence since he spoke French and German. With the war's end he meant to pursue a career as an opera singer but ended up—another talent—sketching fashions for *Harper's Bazaar* before joining French *Vogue* at a salary of $15,000 a year. What the magazine wanted was not his drawing ability so much as what was considered a nearly infallible eye for fashion styles, and soon the short, sturdy Bocher found himself the magazine's resident editor despite the limitation of never having written a word for publication. His gift, said Janet Flanner in a magazine profile, was "an uncommon flair for picking, at the collections, the Paris dresses and styles which the fashionable women of Paris and America would, within a month or so, winnow out and select for themselves, thus making the seasonal mode."

Bocher found the work of running the editorial operation confining and the handsome salary, raised to $25,000, limiting, and so in 1929 he left *Vogue* to set up in Paris his own dressmaking business in the Avenue George V. Under the compressed name of Mainbocher and with financial backing of three American women he was an immediate success, helped along with his innovation of the strapless evening gown and publicity that followed after he designed the wedding trousseau of Wallis Simpson for her marriage in 1937. When he closed down with the outbreak of war in 1939 and returned to America, a citizen still after some two decades in France, his firm was a leader among the fiercely competitive Parisian houses of couture.

It was during Bocher's tenure as editor of French *Vogue* that Pauline Pfeiffer became a staff member. From a wealthy landowning family in Piggott, Arkansas, she had spent the war years studying journalism at the University of Missouri and took her first newspaper job on the night desk of the *Cleveland Star*. After time on the *New York Daily Telegraph* she switched to magazine work and fashion reporting for *Vanity Fair*, the stylish monthly that Condé Nast bought in 1913 and, in 1937, would subsume into *Vogue*. When she arrived in Paris with her younger sister, Virginia, some assumed the trim, chic, thirtyish Pauline was husband hunting; if so, she was also serious about her magazine job, with the opportunity to work in Paris clearly a step up for a fashion writer.

Early in 1925 Pauline met Ernest Hemingway and his wife in the Paris apartment of Harold Loeb and Kitty Cannell. A clandestine affair followed while Hemingway worked on final revisions of *The Sun Also Rises* and writing *The Torrents of Spring* and Pauline attended a succession of fashion shows and wrote up her raw notes for the magazine. When Pauline returned to Arkansas as her part of an enforced separation from Hemingway demanded by his wife, *Vogue* asked her to consider a period of temporary work in the New York office. "They don't know that I am marrying out of all that," she responded in a letter to Hemingway. "I said I didn't think I could do this. But they said they would write me to Piggott." She did, nonetheless, consider the offer to the extent of asking Hemingway what he thought about her negotiating for a salary of $100 a week from the magazine. As it turned out, the job offer came to nothing, disappointing neither Pauline nor Hemingway. After his Paris divorce from his wife in January 1927, the way was open for his marriage to Pauline that May in a Catholic church a short distance from his new wife's elegant Right Bank apartment.

COMET TALES. Several years passed between *Vogue*'s appearance as an American magazine for the fashionable French and the initial number of *The Boulevardier* as an American magazine for fashionable Paris-Americans—yet almost at once the small-niche publication spawned a local rival. Following *The Boulevardier*'s inaugural issue in March 1927, the *Paris Comet* began publishing as an "Anglo-American Fortnightly," operated and edited by Mildred Kearney from offices just off the Place de L'Opéra at 19 Rue Louis-le-Grand.

Early issues paid passing homage to *The New Yorker* with an opening news-notes section signed "Comet Watchers," cartoons, London and New York letters, and articles about London theater and current fashions. The *Comet* was also modestly literary in its interests, carrying accounts of Theodore Dreiser's brief stopover in Paris and Ludwig Lewisohn's expatriate life in the city; a report by Oliver B. Sayler on "Three Great American Novels" (by Willa Cather, James Branch Cabell, and Floyd Dell); and scattered book notices that included a must-read recommendation for Hemingway's new collection of stories, *Men Without Women*.

A few original poems and stories made their way into the magazine's pages, including work by the young Lillian Hellman, whose husband, the writer and editor Arthur Kober, came from New York to work on the *Comet* staff as the magazine was starting up. In later years Hellman dismissed her stories, none carrying her name, as "very lady-writer stuff," meaning "the kind of stories where the man puts his fork down and the woman knows it's all over." After some six months in Paris and elsewhere in Europe Hellman returned home alone, with Kober—who published one article under his name in the magazine, a leisurely profile of the Hollywood film director Rex Ingram—leaving the *Comet* and following soon thereafter.

Few Paris-American journalists were named writers in the magazine, and local journalistic matters drew little notice in its pages. Harold Stearns, then with the Paris *Tribune*, made a lone appearance with "Racing in November," a report on French devotion to the turf season, and Leland Stowe of the *New York Herald Tribune* bureau contributed a brief piece called "Paris Is a City Where . . ." ("Newspapers are terribly dull because there's only a small robbery once a week—and the bandits never shoot the policemen!"). An item in the news-notes section showered praise on the "work of the newspaper boys" in covering the rakish American Legion convention that had preoccupied the city a month earlier:

> The Paris American dailies acquitted themselves in a manner that must have won the admiration of editors at home. The *Herald* issued a special supplement and the *Chicago Tribune* revived the *Stars and Stripes*. The entire staffs of both papers worked day and night on the Legion "story." Most accounts were exceptionally well handled and edited.
>
> The bureaus, too, came in for their share of work. The *New York Times*, I hear, had sixteen men on the job, including Lincoln Eyre, Berlin correspondent, and Walter Duranty, Moscow correspondent. The convention, from all appearances, was the biggest "story" since the war in point of work.

The praise came from the hand of "Americanus," the *nom de plume* also attached to a continuing column of Parisian impressions called "Why I Like Paris." The column eventually inspired an essay contest for readers in America—in house ads the *Comet* promoted itself as the only American magazine published in Europe with wide circulation in the United States—on why, from male and female points of view, they wished to visit the city. The *Comet* published some of the contributions, and in the late summer of 1929 the two winners— California man, New Jersey woman—arrived in France for a month-and-a-half stay that, as the magazine announced, culminated in a "Gala-Soirée" in the ballroom of Hôtel George V. The contest was apparently judged so successful that it led to another for French readers of a cooperating evening newspaper on why they wanted to visit the United States, with the winners receiving expense-paid tours from coast to coast.

In time the *Paris Comet* dropped its billing as an Anglo-American publication, switched to a monthly schedule, and developed a more streamlined Art Deco look. Its opening section took on a new name, "Tales of the Comet," while still given over to such fluffy matters as reporting that the Left Bank game of guessing the originals of the characters in Hemingway's *The Sun Also Rises* had long since given way to similar sport with André Gide's *The Counterfeiters*. Beginning its third year of publication in January 1929, the magazine paused to thank its readers, take notice of its history, and set out its conception of itself:

> The first number of Paris Comet appeared on the Boulevards of Paris the week of Lindbergh's arrival.
>
> The present one finds the Glorious Augustus [Lindbergh's middle name] about to deal the heaviest possible blow to the millions of his heaving and sighing female fans [by his marriage to Anne Morrow]. We are still frightfully young.
>
> We are still ready and willing to attempt things forbidden by the wise experts and grave authorities.
>
> Our favorite story still remains the one dealing with the brilliant banker who advised Mr. Ford in 1903 that "nothing could beat the horse". . .

A house ad in the same issue went on to catalog what readers would continue discovering in its pages:

> Breezy bits of gossip, more ear-tingling than the kind you hear over the cups. . . . Pungent patter of Mayfair, snappy stories of Paris that will be more than twice-told. . . . Sophisticated chatter impertinently put . . . a whack at this idol and a boot in the back of that dignified but dumb deity. . . . The latest in fashion and the fashions of the latest. . . . All this "under the covers."

In fact, beyond an occasional sprightly item in its opening section there was little in the magazine that was pungent, irreverent, or revealing. As it developed, the *Paris Comet* came to resemble not *The*

New Yorker so much as a scaled-down version of *Town & Country*—a magazine of fashion and furnishings, of the rich and prominent at play at beaches and racetracks. Kathleen Cannell—the Kitty Cannell who had been Harold Loeb's lover and, as she unhappily saw herself, the model for Frances Clyne, Robert Cohn's mistress in *The Sun Also Rises*—became the magazine's fashion editor, the lone section editor named on the masthead, while writing breezy travel articles as well as lengthy fashion reports. Profiles appeared about wealthy sportsmen, business tycoons, society hostesses, and political figures, usually accompanied by flattering formal photographs. A notable exception among the usual run of photos was a striking full-page portrait by Berenice Abbott of Sylvia Beach, one that lacked an accompanying article but bore a caption reading "An American Publisher in Exile." Equally arresting were self-portraits by Abbott and Man Ray.

Late in 1929, the depression taking a toll with advertisers, the *Comet* dropped back from a peak of eighty pages and began appearing in combined monthly issues. In December 1929 "Tales of the Comet" led off, under a heading "Dies Irae," with a bleak account of Parisian reaction to the collapse of the American stock market—and a charge leveled at one of the local messengers. The Paris edition of the *London Daily Mail* had done "its damned best to spread the panic," claimed *Tales*, with a seven-column headline proclaiming "New York is a City of Gloom and Suicide" and a story noting the grim possibility of grass growing on Fifth Avenue. With the January–February 1931 issue the *Comet* became a casualty itself—a sudden demise but one the rival *Boulevardier* was in no hurry to record. Said the magazine, with mock solemnity, in its May 1931 issue:

> It is with the same resignation that we have to admit that the *Paris Comet* (mentioned for the first time in these columns), a magazine that had appeared at first regularly, then at bright intervals, gave up what ghost of a chance it had three months ago. Amen.

The "same resignation" was a reference to a news-notes item in January 1930 when *The Boulevardier* remarked that the Paris *Herald* had run a page-one account of the death of the *Paris Times*—a surprising news story only in that it broke the "long established tradition of our local Anglo-American daily press of never mentioning the name of any other English-language daily." "It must have broken the *Herald*'s heart to mention this," the item added, "but the medicine was apparently taken bravely."

ITS VERY OWN MAGAZINE. "There was a time," said the Paris *Tribune* in its profile of Erksine Gwynne, when the publisher of *The Boulevardier* was known as "The Playboy of Paris," this despite the insistence of close friends that he was a serious, hardworking fellow. The British writer Sisley Huddleston simply had it that Gwynne was a "curious combination of social lion and business man." Born in Paris and raised in luxury as a member of the Vanderbilt family, he had worked in a French munitions factory in World War I and later joined the American army. Following the war he took a reporting job on the *San Francisco Bulletin* that was followed by an around-the-world cruise. Back in Europe, he returned to journalism as a correspondent for the *New York American* before, at age twenty-eight, bankrolling *The Boulevardier*.

The masthead of the initial thirty-two-page issue listed Gwynne as publisher and editorial offices at 65–67 Avenue des Champs-Elysées but named no editor. An opening statement, signed "The Editor," declared that "at last the Anglo-American colony in Paris has its own, its very own magazine" that would feature "the best authors, the best cartoonists." Readers should not, the statement went on, be misled by the magazine's title to think

you will be treated to anecdotes about the Boulevards.
Nothing of the sort. We all know that the Boulevards no

longer have their own charm. BUT, when they were "à la
mode," they created a type of man that we all know about.

The earlier boulevardier was a perpetual fun seeker who demanded
of society only wine, women, and song. In contrast,

> your Boulevardier is much nicer to society . . . noblesse
> oblige. He will not tell one tenth of what he really knows. He
> is a kindly soul and does not intend to hurt anybody.

In the event, however, that readers thought the figure "not gossipy
enough," they should inform the magazine.

> We know several women hereabouts to whom we could refer
> you, and who could tell you all you want to hear about many
> other people, and more.

The issue's whimsical cover drawing, turned out by the painter
Gilbert White, depicted a satyr firing an arrow into the rear of a figure who appeared more a hapless than kindly wanderer of the
boulevards. The magazine noted in "Boulevard Brainwork," an
opening piece again signed "The Editor," that "whatever trash we
may choose to write inside, the Boulevardier's exterior cover will always be a chef d'oeuvre." The rest of the thin issue was made up of
drawings, cartoons, light satirical pieces, a column by Hector the
Horse called "My Column" (soon, and happily, to fade from the
magazine), a listing of theater and music events in Paris ("Things
you need not see but will"), and a lengthy article about Cannes
signed with Erskine Gwynne's initials.

Another long piece, "My Daily Life and Work" by "Bonita
Mustardini," was described as an "Intimate story of how the Duce
spends his twenty-four hours. As told to Signor Jed Kiley, Special
Correspondent of The Boulevardier." Kiley would become one of
the magazine's most familiar humorists and invariably in the same
broad, over-the-top manner. The third issue would feature
"Ladies Prefer Argentines" by "Senor Jed Kiley de Chili"; in the

fourth would appear "Little Morphine Annie" by "James Whit-comb Kiley."

OUR STAR CONTRIBUTOR. After the University of Wisconsin, Jed Kiley had worked as a newspaperman in Chicago before landing in France as an American Field Service ambulance driver. He served in the army when America joined the war, and following the armistice had a short stay on the staff of the Paris *Herald*. The job ended suddenly, as Eric Hawkins of the paper recalled, when Kiley was assigned to cover a luncheon talk by the American ambassador at the American Club of Paris. By the time the ambassador rose to speak, Kiley was "sailing the seas of that euphoria which only good Beaujolais can induce" and failed to listen; all he caught was a re-mark comparing the French leader Clemenceau to Joan of Arc. Un-fortunately the remark was uttered by the club's president; when Kiley's story attributed it to the ambassador, who objected, Kiley was fired but given a week's pay.

He used the money to turn businessman, promoting dances de-spite a postwar Parisian prohibition of such events at night. The profits that followed were plowed into an ice cream business, a mis-taken venture that went under when the French failed to see the point of consuming ice cream in winter. Kiley returned to the en-tertainment business with Le Palermo, a popular nightclub in Rue Fontaine in Montmartre that introduced black jazz groups and blues singers and attracted such notable customers as the Prince of Wales and Erskine Gywnne. An item in John A. Maar's long-running nightlife column "Out!" in *The Boulevardier* of October 1927 re-ported that Kiley, "our star contributor," was joining a former Uni-versity of Michigan athlete in opening a new club, this one across the river in Montparnasse. "Jed says that he is running out of ideas for his writing," the column continued, "and wants to get back in the old game to get some local color."

Although the College Inn in Rue Vavin became another successful nightspot—with American collegiate décor and Kiley's partner, Jimmy Cossitt, as a formidable bouncer—Kiley kept his connection with the magazine. In the Paris *Tribune* Alex Small, a columnist not given to casual compliments but possibly with tongue in cheek on this occasion, offered the opinion that "the only writer I have met in Montparnasse whose collected works I feel I might read with pleasure is Jed Kiley." *The Boulevardier* of June 1929—the year in which Kiley also began appearing on the masthead as an associate editor—carried one of his better sketches, "The Boat Train Girl," in which a winsome young woman claims to have lost her boat ticket and the narrator foolishly gives her money. In the end, a rich American named Freddy Gotstock is equally taken by the girl and taken in by the scam.

Shortly thereafter, in November 1929, the magazine reported that Kiley had been lured to Hollywood for screenwriting at a dazzling "five hundred Smackers a week." As Kiley himself would put it in his memoir of Hemingway, "Universal Pictures had seen a story of mine in *The Boulevardier* and had come over five-thousand miles to sign me up." A year after the Hollywood departure, Wambly Bald reported in his "La Vie de Bohème" column in the *Tribune* that Kiley was "not very hot in the scenario business" and might return to Paris where he had written "very good stories for *The Boulevardier*." (Bald mentioned in the column Kiley's "famous crack" that "the way to change your girl is to change your town." Bald himself demurred, thinking the better way was simply to "ask her permission," and offered an example: "Tell her: 'Sunset, into the limbo you must go.'")

THE QUARTER'S BOSWELL. With *The Boulevardier*'s fourth issue in June 1927, Arthur Moss appeared on the masthead as the magazine's editor, though judging by the writing style of editorial statements and the "Boulevard Brainwork" column he was at the helm from the start. In a Paris guidebook published in 1926, Basil Woon—a former Paris-based Hearst correspondent and a *Boulevardier* contributor whose name rivaled only Wambly Bald's in improbability—saluted Moss as the Boswell of the Latin Quarter. Certainly Moss was among the Quarter's better-informed figures as well as a fluent journalistic writer and experienced editor.

Through the twenties Moss was married to the *Tribune*'s theater critic Florence Gilliam, and together they founded in Paris in 1921 the short-lived journal *Gargoyle*, considered the first English-language arts-and-letters review to appear in Europe between the wars. The pair had met the year before in Greenwich Village, where the small, ebullient Moss—known variously among Paris acquaintances as Arthur Mouse and Li'l Abner—who had attended Cornell and worked on upstate New York newspapers was editing a magazine called *The Quill*. Gilliam, a graduate of Ohio State University, left a teaching job to become the managing editor and in 1921 accompanied Moss to Paris, where they were quickly drawn into Montparnasse café life and soon editing *Gargoyle* from their tiny apartment. The magazine, Gilliam later observed, seemed a natural outgrowth of the "multinational exchange of ideas and tastes" that she and Moss experienced in the cafés.

Moss wrote book reviews and humor pieces for *Gargoyle* while Gilliam covered theaters and concerts. Among American contributors were Malcolm Cowley, Hart Crane, Robert Coates, Matthew Josephson, Sinclair Lewis, and John Reed. In 1922, out of funds, they shut down the magazine and took up freelancing for American publications, with Gilliam specializing in the Paris theater and Moss, among other things, writing cooking articles for New York newspapers and collaborating with Hiler Harzberg, a painter and owner of the popular Left Bank nightclub Le Jockey, on an illustrated book about clowns. Another job for the two included typing menus in a Swedish restaurant—where diners who glimpsed Gilliam at work assumed she was writing a novel—in return for daily meals.

Freelancing brought in money only when pieces appeared, so Gilliam and Moss turned to the Paris-American newspapers for steady-paying work. During the twenties Moss was a columnist for the *Herald* and the *Paris Times*, and Gilliam contributed work to all three. On *The Boulevardier* they were again united when, in the magazine's second year, Gilliam began writing the theater column called "And So to the Theatre." Moss presumably wrote the magazine's opening news-notes section, with the heading "Boulevard Brainwork" evolving into "If Talk We Must . . .," a loose assembly of short takes about people and events. The above item about the death of the *Paris Comet* was more or less typical, as was an observation in "Boulevard Brainwork" of July 1927 about Lindbergh's departure from Paris after his epic flight:

> Now Lindbergh has left us—leaving behind him a trail of admirers. To the French he is one of the few Americans who have come to Paris without wanting to visit the haunts of fun of the capital, to chase little girls around the Boulevards or to win the beer drinking contests.

THE *TRIBUNE* CONNECTION. From the Paris *Tribune* Moss drew columnists for the magazine in addition to Gilliam. Irving Schwerké's "Words and Music" became a regular feature while Harold Stearns, who first appeared with articles about jockeys and the return of the Paris racing season, turned out "The Turf," an occasional column in the manner of his *Town & Country* letters rather than the track tout Peter Pickem. In the nicely titled "The Left-Over Bank," Wambly Bald contributed a version of his offbeat *Tribune* work, with the column also written by other hands in other styles. From the *Paris Times* came George Rehm with a sporting column treating the high-end sports of golf, tennis, polo, and yachting. Among other Paris-American newsmen appearing in the magazine were Theodore Pratt, Hérol Egan, Lawrence Blochman, Leland Stowe, and Willis Steell.

A culture column in the magazine joining those of Gilliam and Schwerké was Van Dyke Black's "art with a small a," and there were attempts at modest book columns in "Read 'Em N' Weep" signed by M (presumably Moss)—where *Benjamin Franklin of Paris, 1776–1785,* a narrative history published in 1928 by the *Herald*'s Willis Steell, was among works mentioned—and later "Books Will Be Books," signed Casual Reader. There was also further imitation of *The New Yorker* in the "New York Letter" and "London Letter" columns.

But for *The Boulevardier* culture criticism and letters from abroad were essentially secondary matters. So was short fiction. The second issue in April 1927 featured Michael Arlen's two-page story "The Girl from Chicago," and the following issue carried a single-page story from Noel Coward—both name-value exceptions in a magazine whose main offerings were amusing and satirical short articles together with gleanings of local gossip found in "If Talk We Must . . ." and the regular column "Ritz Alley." Here, in its core milieu—which Florence Gilliam characterized as Ritz Bar more than Left Bank—the magazine's featured contributors included Freddy Muller and Sylvia Lyon together with the editorial hierarchy of Moss, Kiley, and Gwynne.

THE REAL. . . . Nearly as well known at the time as Michael Arlen and Noel Coward was Louis Bromfield, a young Midwestern novelist who had won the Pulitzer Prize for fiction in 1926 and, the year before, headed off to Paris. Bromfield had first come to Europe in 1917, leaving journalism study at Columbia University to join the ambulance service and, attached to the French army, eventually receiving the Croix de Guerre for his work on the western front. He was back in New York with jobs as a reporter and editor when his first novel, *The Green Bay Tree*, was published in 1924. His European return, intended as a vacation, turned into a long exile, first in Paris and then as a flourishing country squire in the village of Senlis, ending only in 1938 with the imminent German invasion—and at a time when Bromfield was heavily involved in relief efforts for American wounded in the Spanish Civil War. Janet Flanner was among Bromfield's guests in Senlis for Sunday luncheons featuring, as she recorded, "extraordinary bouquets he concocted in perfect imitations of the flower paintings by the sixteenth-century painter Brueghel." She added that "Louis had the greenest thumb and maintained the finest flower garden of any American in the Ile-de-France territory, except Mrs. Edith Wharton, whose white garden was celebrated."

In *The Boulevardier* of September 1927 Bromfield's "The Real French" was an unusually solemn contribution that sought to enlighten, as the title had it, on what the French were truly like. Bromfield first dismissed the views of American Francophiles who were either bores or substituted French types for actual Frenchmen. Then—after setting out his credentials by telling of spending the war years with the French army living in dunghills, dugouts, and châteaux—he substituted his belief that the cook, chambermaid, and chauffeur of his own amply staffed household were "the realest of the *real* French."

Weighty as it was for a lighthearted magazine like *The Boulevardier*, "The Real French" was harmless magazine fare yet provoked Hemingway to the "low kidney punch" of Kiley's memoir. Behind his swift reaction was more, though, than simply Bromfield's article. Bromfield was a Paris-American acquaintance who had generously read the manuscript of Hemingway's parody of Sherwood Anderson in *The Torrents of Spring* and had recommended Hemingway to the publisher Alfred Harcourt. In a letter to Scott Fitzgerald, Hemingway acknowledged that Bromfield in his efforts had been "damned decent." A little over a year later—"The Real French" not yet in print but with it seemingly in mind—gratitude had turned to heavy-handed mockery of Bromfield's literary pretensions. He was, Fitzgerald was now informed, a writer whose next work will likely include

> a decayed old new england preacher named Cabot Cabot Cabot and naturally he talks only with God—to rhyme with Cod. But sooner or later I can see that the decayed French aristocracy will come into the book and they will all be named the Marquis Deidre de Chanel and will be people whom Louis Bromfield the most brilliant and utterly master of his craft of all the younger generation of decayed french aristocracy novelists will have studied first hand himself at the Ritz and Ciros—doubtless at great expense to his friends.

Hemingway's "The Real Spaniard" in *The Boulevardier* of October 1927 carried a needless editor's note: "We have a vague idea that Mr. Hemingway intended this article as a follow-up to the essay of Louis Bromfield on 'The Real French' that appeared in The Boulevardier last month." The connection between the two pieces was impossible to miss. The author in Hemingway's parody had spent the war attached to the Spanish army and, like Bromfield, had slept in "dunghills and châteaux and the like, but to me the Spanish never seemed real. . . . They seemed like cathedrals." Also like Bromfield, his search for the authentic Spaniard had ended at home, though in the company of his wife rather than among servants: "'You are the real Spaniard,' my wife said softly and as I looked into her eyes and saw the truth gleaming there, I knew that my search too, like that of good old Brommy for the real French, had ended in the home."

The parody neatly matched the magazine's manner, and Hemingway was a prize name for its pages. Whether the article was wholly his, however, is in question. Jed Kiley reports in his memoir that when he showed the manuscript to Erskine Gwynne, the publisher "read it, hit the ceiling, and grabbed a big blue pencil":

> "Where does he write, on restroom walls?" he roared. I looked over his shoulder and there were two four-letter

words. They were words that you heard around the office all
the time. But you didn't see them.

"Well," I said, "he spelled them correctly, didn't he?"

Gwynne turned over the manuscript to Arthur Moss, who after
reading it asked, "Where's the rest of it?"

"That's all he gave me," I said. I read it myself. It's an unfinished
symphony, I thought. But maybe he wants it like that.

I said aloud, "It's the latest style in literature and—" I
added, "he comes from my home town."

"OK," Moss said. "Write an ending to it and we'll run it
on page forty-two."

"Not me," I said. "Promised I wouldn't change a word."

"You don't have to change a word," Arthur said. "Just add
a paragraph. I'll take the rap for you if he squawks. We go to
press in an hour and we can't print it that way. The story
stinks and you know it."

So Kiley wrote the final paragraph, ghosting Hemingway's "style a
little and it turned out swell. The story wasn't bad at all with my
ending. Then we ran a little blurb about his book. That ought to
please him, I thought."

Of course, Hemingway was not pleased either with the blurb or
Kiley's ending. The magazine was barely on the newsstands when
he "came roaring into the office with fire in his eye." The diminu-
tive Moss, as good as his word, took the rap:

"Pipe down, big boy," he said. "I'm the editor and I rewrote
your story for the better. What are you going to do about it?"
Ernest looked like he couldn't believe his ears. He bent over
to get a better look.

"Stand up and I'll show you," he said.

"I am standing up," Arthur said, and he really was.

That broke the spell. Ernest stuck out a big hand. I knew he would.

"Shake, brother," he said. "You got guts."

It makes for a good yarn, but a possibly more reliable version of the aftermath of the editing of "The Real Spaniard" came from Moss many years later. He maintained the article was filled with obscenities that had to be removed; when they were, an angry Hemingway told him, "If you were my size I'd knock your block off." Moss replied: "If I were your size maybe I'd knock your block off." At once Hemingway's mood switched and he invited Moss to have a drink.

NEWSPAPERS AS SUBJECTS. Paris-American newspapers provided *The Boulevardier* with occasional subject matter as well as contributors—due in part, perhaps, to the fact that the three papers publishing at the time regularly advertised in its pages, joining such glossy regulars as Elizabeth Arden, Jean Patou perfumes, Chrysler cars, and Chesterfield cigarettes. A Willis Steell article reviewed the career of the Paris *Herald*'s James Gordon Bennett, Jr., and a "Left-Over Bank" column reported on a literary tussle in which Elliot Paul took Sisley Huddleston to task in print. "Then arose Monsieur Alex Small," commented the magazine, "who wrote an article approving, on the whole, of the Paulian diatribe, but pointing out, not without reason, that it was a case of unlimbering a howitzer to kill a sparrow."

In the "Talk" item mentioned above taking note of the passing of the *Paris Times*, the magazine also offered an explanation for the paper's failure—and the earlier failure of the *Paris Evening Telegram*. The problem was that afternoon papers everywhere depend on homeward-bound readers on subways and suburban trains, and not enough Paris-American workers traveled that way. As for American tourists—"the restless visiting throng"—they were not the "carpet slipper type that reads an evening paper before the fire." Afternoon papers had the advantage of availability on the Riviera the following morning, "but who ever got up in the morning on the Riviera?"

In June 1929 *The Boulevardier* carried a full-page house ad featuring a photo of Alex Small and reprinting his favorable mention of the magazine in his *Tribune* column of April 19. Small had pointed out, correctly, that the magazine was showing month-by-month improvement but faced a difficult editorial situation: "They cannot be too imitative of *The New Yorker*, and yet it is precisely something of that sort which they must put out." Other tricky matters arose from the magazine's need to be both Parisian and American, leaving it with a small audience and an equally limited pool of contributors. After listing some good things in the current issue, Small concluded with faint praise: "Whilst you are about it, you should never forget to read in The Boulevardier the house advertisements. They are fully as amusing as the best of the articles."

And the best of the cartoons, he might have added. As with "our contemporary," many *Boulevardier* readers likely thumbed to them first—and found there, among other things, more attention to the Paris-American press. A full-page drawing in December 1928 was titled "Impressions of Leading Paris Clubs (By one who has never been a member) No. 5.—The Anglo-American Press Association." The figures identified in the drawing included Bill Bird of the Consolidated Press, Hank Wales of the *Chicago Tribune*, Laurence Hills of the Paris *Herald*, Edwin James of the *New York Times*, and Arno Dosch-Fleurot, then with Hearst's Universal Service. In June 1929 a two-page drawing by the artist Pandl caricatured thirty-one Anglo-American "Gentlemen of the Press"—among them, as identified in the caption, Bird, Wales, Harold Stearns, Sparrow Robertson of the Paris *Herald*, Sam Dashiel of the United Press, and (indicated as "G" and "K") Erskine Gwynne and Jed Kiley of *The Boulevardier*. "Paris Times boys," the caption added, "are among the missing" in the drawing.

For those drawing the cartoons, however, the magazine had limited appeal as a market. Shortly after she arrived in Paris at the end of the twenties, Carol Weld sold Moss some of her drawings of American life in the city, receiving what she called the magazine's "habitual insignificant rates." When she noticed that Paris newspapermen, also badly paid, nevertheless seemed to eat more regularly than Paris artists, Weld began taking courses to improve her language skills and applied for work on the *Tribune*. She was still reporting for the paper and eating regularly when it shut down in 1934.

GWYNNE ALONE. The Anglo-American Press Association cartoon was drawn by Sylvia Lyon, an able cartoonist as well as a versatile contributor of humor and verse. In September 1928 Lyon was listed on the masthead as an associate editor, and a year later dropped yet continuing as a contributor. With the November 1929 issue Jed Kiley was off to Hollywood and his name removed from the masthead. With the July 1931 issue Arthur Moss's name was gone and Erskine Gwynne listed as both editor and publisher.

In the dual roles, Gwynne's career was brief. Through 1931 the magazine had shrunk in size, falling back from a high period of eighty pages to the thirty-two of its initial issue. With the January number of the new year, just as Wambly Bald in the Paris *Tribune* was touting it as a "stimulating monthly rag that appeals to so many Americans," *The Boulevardier* ceased publishing.

The death ended Gwynne's magazine career but not an interest in seeing his own work in print. In 1936 he produced his only book, a light romantic novel called *Paris Pandemonium*. During the same period he began turning out a series of sound-alike columns in the Paris *Herald*—"Around the Town," "Around the Riviera," "Around the Resorts," "On the Normandy Coast"—that in their display of detail about celebrities and smart society recalled the untroubled days of the twenties. Until nearly the moment German forces swept into Poland in 1939, Gwynne went about cheerfully informing readers of the posh world he still traveled in—one of elephants entertaining at Lady Mendl's party; of guests at the Etienne de Beaumont ball, all dressed as characters from Racine, forced inside due to rain; of members of the Yale Glee Club speaking French far better than run-of-the-mill American tourists.

CHAPTER SIX

Countless Reams of Stuff

. . . send along about a thousand words,
along the lines outlined, as soon as you can.
—JANE GRANT TO JANET FLANNER,
1925

WRITING HOME. In his letter of introduction to Lewis Galantière in Paris in 1921, Sherwood Anderson portrayed his Chicago protégé, Ernest Hemingway, as a "quite wonderful newspaper man" who despite having "practically given up newspaper work for the last year" had now "got an assignment to do European letters for some Toronto newspaper for whom he formerly worked." Possibly only a slip of the pen caused Anderson to characterize the work sending Hemingway abroad for the *Star* as letters rather than the feature articles he had been hired to produce. On the other hand, Anderson may have been trying to clarify the puzzling matter of a young writer who had nearly abandoned newspaper work taking on a newspaper assignment abroad to write what was not ordinary newswriting—and doing "European letters" was a readily graspable way of putting it.

Galantière, a former Chicago newspaperman now working in Paris with the American section of the International Chamber of

Commerce, would help Hemingway and his wife find their first apartment in the city, as previously he had helped Anderson. Galantière also had literary interests, and during Hemingway's time in Paris contributed a "Reviews and Reflections" column to the Paris *Tribune*'s Sunday magazine under the name Louis Gay. Surely he was aware that occasional letters from Europe for American publications—or, far better, a regular letters column for a newspaper or magazine—was a tried-and-true way of helping underwrite an expatriate's Paris days. He himself had reversed the ordinary geography of transit by writing the "New York Literary Letter," a Paris-eye view of American book activity, for a 1924 issue of Ford Madox Ford's *transatlantic review*. (Later that same year Hemingway would produce the journal's New York letter, mentioning therein Galantière's critical work in the *Tribune* and the unrelated fact he was about to marry a Miss Butler of Chicago.)

As writing tasks, publishable letters were scarcely more demanding than scribbling a few pages of local color for friends or family back home—or so they could temptingly seem. That the illustrious Henry James had been a spectacular Paris failure at them was a cautionary tale presumably few exiles knew, or would have pondered if they had. Late in 1875, shifting his base of operations from New York to Paris, James struck a deal with he New York *Tribune* for a series of Paris letters—at $20 a letter—that he intended to dash off partially to cover living expenses while working on a new serial novel he was calling *The American*. In November 1875 his first contribution appeared, identified as a "Letter from Henry James, Jr." who was "a regular correspondent of the *Tribune*."

When James read the letter in print—"I have often thought," went the numbing first sentence, "that some very entertaining remarks might be made under the title of 'Paris Revisited'—remarks that would find an echo in many an American heart"—it even registered with him how wide of the mark the letter was as newspaper writing. But with the second letter he faced a more acute, and baffling, problem: with all of Paris before him—as he was soon lamenting in private letters to his family—"there has been a painful dearth of topics to write about." "I can think of nothing to put into the *Tribune*: it is quite appalling." Nonetheless he soldiered on, writing in all twenty letters for the paper at a twice-a-month pace until finally begging off with the *Tribune*'s merciful agreement. In a letter to the paper's editor and publisher, Whitelaw Reid, James concluded that, while he understood the "'newsy' and gossipy" nature of newspaper fare, "I can't produce it—I don't know how and I couldn't learn how."

James's letters would have been better suited, as Whitelaw Reid had indicated to him, for a magazine rather than a newspaper. Especially fitting would have been the pages of a journal like the *Dial*, where Ezra Pound's "The Island of Paris: A Letter," a racy survey of new French writing, appeared in 1920—or those of the *transatlantic review*, where in 1924 Hemingway in the casual, fragmented "Pamplona Letter" alerted readers to his enthusiasm for Spanish bullfighting and his present disdain for newspaper work ("It is only by never writing the way I write in a newspaper office . . . that I make you believe that I can write"). The problem was that publication in magazines and journals of this sort brought in little or nothing in fees, and James had been writing strictly for money. For a writer with Hemingway's golden touch, on the other hand, publication in Ford's journal eventually led to real money when he was recruited by Arnold Gingrich to contribute outdoor pieces to *Esquire*, the men's magazine he founded in 1933.

Gingrich had the "Pamplona Letter" in mind for the style of informal compositions he wanted—work that was not "a major effort involving gestation and labor pains." Hemingway was willing to pitch in to that extent but pointed out that for "a non-commercial publication published in the interest of letters" he expected no money, whereas for commercial magazines like *Esquire* he expected "the top rate they have ever paid anybody. This makes them love and appreciate your stuff and realize what a fine writer you are." Gingrich accepted the distinction and offered to pay the solid depression-era fee of $250 per article. Among the nearly monthly letters Hemingway supplied to *Esquire* during the thirties while he was living in Key West and Havana, one was called simply "A Paris Letter," a gloomy stringing together of memories of a previous fall in Montana, the absence in Paris of old friends, a Renoir exhibition, French boxing, a mention of the Paris *Herald*'s Sparrow Robertson, a call for America to remain free of any future European war, and a closing hymn to the autumnal beauty of the city.

HOW THE FRENCH ORDER THINGS. In his letter introducing Hemingway to Lewis Galantière, Sherwood Anderson had added about Hemingway that "he is not like Stearns, and his wife is charming." He left the brusque distinction unexplained beyond, in the next sentence, noting that Hemingway and his wife would "settle down to live in Paris, and [I] am sure you will find them great playmates." Stearns might well have been a questionable companion at play, but after his Paris arrival in 1921 he too would settle into expatriate life and, just months after Anderson's letter to Galantière, match Hemingway's feature-story output for the *Toronto Star* by entering a productive three-year phase of sending home Paris letters for regular publication. Like Hemingway and unlike Henry James, he had no difficulty turning up material.

Wisely, Stearns bypassed newspapers as a fit home for his work and went straight to a magazine, the glossy society publication *Town & Country*. In later years he would acknowledge that *Town & Country* was "the type of magazine for which one would think I ought to be the last person in the world to be selected as a correspondent." But at the time the job came his way—again with the help of the sculptor Jo Davidson, who was acquainted with the magazine's editor—his long unstable period was still ahead. About him yet was the aura of the Harvard graduate and promising intellectual whose move to Paris was in the vanguard of the general exodus of the restless and talented across the Atlantic. The Harold Stearns of the time was a perfectly reasonable choice as Paris correspondent of a high-toned American magazine.

Stearns's "Our Paris Letter" ran in *Town & Country* from March 1922 through September 1925, ordinarily appearing once a month for the bimonthly publication and joining other regular letters columns from London and Washington. Now and then Stearns cobbled together a column of odds and ends, but his typical approach was to develop at length a single subject and then fill out his allotted space with brief items.

"Strangely enough the most interesting events of the Paris year thus far have been political conferences," the initial column began, opening a topic he repeatedly turned to—the endless wrangling about the tangled political and economic affairs of postwar Europe. He began a column on February 1, 1923, by noting that, the holidays over, Paris and the world had to get back to the very serious business that "once again war clouds are gathering menacingly over all of Europe." On April 15, 1923, he examined the political game of "finding the goat" for postwar policies gone wrong, concluding that at the moment Britain was "it."

Important as political matters were, they made for heavy going, and Stearns switched late in his opening column to literary concerns by observing "there is no excitement about literature in Paris at the present moment, except among the English-speaking residents." The excitement had to do with publication of Joyce's long-awaited *Ulysses*, with Stearns confessing that "I have not read the book yet, merely snatches from it, but I solemnly intend to do so, when I fully recover my health." Frequently Stearns injected himself into the column, often about health concerns, but he seldom touched upon his reading and only occasionally took up the cultural interests of the expatriate community.

His third column on May 15, 1922, was a dense discussion of the new and the old in the arts. "One had a sharp sense that, like any work of art," he reported about a concert of music by Arnold Schönberg, "a great deal had to be brought to it, that the demands were heavy, perhaps capricious. For the concert ended only in what can be called a squeak." A subsequent exhibition of a hundred years of French painting similarly revealed a development from "charm" toward "concentration, abstraction, unfettered vitality, even harshness." Joyce's *Ulysses* was in the same "style of the *dernier cri* in painting and music." Elsewhere in the column Stearns described the present cultural movement as one from "old-world charm" to "new-world intensity," and wondered if it was possible to harmonize the two. Paris and the French suggested a way, he decided in a quick and unconvincing stroke, since they are "alive to the new currents (in the arts they usually originate in France)" while at the same time "they know that the amiable and the charming shall inherit the earth, and that this is as true of art as of people."

For Stearns, the French way of ordering life was always different and always admirable—and always, at bottom, for the same reason: the French preferred what was real; their national attitudes were rooted more exactly in the human condition. A column drew on the annual summer invasion of Paris by young, independent, spirited, college-educated American women. The attractions of the type were fleeting, and Stearns leaned toward the traditional French view that women become interesting only as they matured and married. Another column wondered whether Americans should send their children to study in Paris, thereby tasting true freedom for the first time. If there were weak spots in their characters, Paris would find them; control had to be self-control, for the city provided no other. So if parents wished to know what their children were made of, in Paris they would learn in short order. French parents, of course, always preferred to know the truth about such matters, however unpleasant.

Just as cultural matters appeared infrequently in "Our Paris Letter," so too did mention of Paris-American journalism. Stearns noted in a 1923 column that people back home thought Paris correspondents had a cushy job, while the truth was that Paris was the most "exasperating" of major news centers if "one has a remote resemblance to an intellectual conscience." To cover all the city's news possibilities the ideal correspondent had to be "extraordinarily endowed" with three or four languages, broad knowledge of European history, an understanding of finance and trade, skill at "back-stairs methods of obtaining information," and a willingness to work fourteen hours a day, Sundays included.

An earlier column examined the French press in Paris, admittedly corrupt by American standards but colorful, amusing, and given to furious personal attacks. "Flaying alive," Stearns pointed out, "is a mild sport compared to some of the campaigns waged against individuals in the Paris press." This in turn partly explained the great number of Paris papers. Any important figure, it was half-seriously claimed, needed three papers at his command—one to wage attacks himself, a second for defense against attacks, a third to laugh at the other two.

Following a gap among the monthly columns early in 1924, Stearns explained that he had been ill, which led to an account of private Paris hospitals where he encountered again the genuine human understanding of the French. Another gap early in 1925 was explained in a column with the multiple dateline "Havana, Tucson, San Francisco, New York, Paris." He had returned to America for the first time in four years, he reported, but now was contentedly back in Paris, free "from the tension we so elaborately heap upon ourselves at home, as if it were a duty to be hysterical."

Looking back on "Our Paris Letter," Stearns believed he had been "something of a success on the job" in that he avoided the expected material of a magazine like *Town & Country* in favor of "subjects you might normally expect, in those days, to see discussed with preternatural seriousness in *The New Republic* or *The Nation*." This was roughly true of his political columns, if not the columns as a whole. In any case, the "work was fun; it was easy; and at the then rate of exchange it paid well." Best of all, it had taken only two or three days of work a month at a time when, still in his balanced period, he was juggling full-time work on the *Herald* and occasional dispatches for the *Baltimore Sun*.

APOLOGIA. With the end of his *Town & Country* connection, the Great Exile began his turf column in the *Tribune* and was finished with Paris letters—with one inglorious exception. In 1928 Scott Fitzgerald blundered into a misadventure of trying to come to his aid after running into Stearns in Paris and—as Fitzgerald confided in a letter to Hemingway—"feeling drunk and Christ-like," suggested to him the subject of an article, "'Why I go on being poor in Paris,' and told him to write it as an informal letter to me and I'd sell it." The letter form possibly came to mind because of Fitzgerald's awareness of Stearns's columns in *Town & Country*. In the April 15, 1922, issue carrying one of Stearns's Paris letters, William Curtis had reviewed at length Fitzgerald's *The Beautiful and Damned* and pronounced it a certain best-seller.

Stearns wrote the letter Fitzgerald proposed and Fitzgerald placed it in *Scribner's Magazine*, where it appeared as "Apologia of an Expatriate" in March 1929. The $100 fee left Stearns grumbling. "Now Harold writes me," a chastened Fitzgerald informed Hemingway, "that $100 isn't very much (as a matter of fact, it isn't much of a letter either) and exhibits such general dissatisfaction that I think he thinks I held out on him. You've got to be careful who you do favors for—within a year you'll probably hear a story that what started him on his downward path was my conscienceless theft of his royalties."

In the letter Stearns had returned to his now threadbare argument about lack of freedom in the land of the free:

> But the point is, in the United States you are not free. You are in prison, even if you don't happen to have spirit enough to be in jail. It is seldom you that gets a creative joy out of being part of a vital current; it is usually you who are cracked on the head and hounded and badgered at every turn by currents that are often much too vital for comfort. The practical difference is enormous.

For illustration he offered the matter of drinking—his. In America during Prohibition he got drunk as often as possible, and when he arrived in Europe he simply carried on. But after a time—"perhaps two years," he calculated—his drinking moderated. His taste for hard liquor and cocktails vanished altogether, as did getting drunk: "There was no longer any point in getting drunk—when you could do it any time you wanted." In other words, in Europe he was free to drink or not, as he never was at home.

A LITERARY LOT. During the period Harold Stearns's Paris letters were running in *Town & Country*, the magazine in May 1922 carried a photo of a striking oil painting of Janet Flanner by Neysa McMein, with Flanner identified as "an Indianapolis newspaper woman" yet looking more like a glamorous socialite posed with a ritual book in her hand. It was an odd foreshadowing of her future career, for just three years later Flanner would become another Paris-American writer of letters for a magazine—and one who would leave Stearns and all others in her distant wake. For nearly fifty years Paris letters were both the staple commodity of her lucrative writing career and a relaxed, commonplace form she elevated to stylish higher journalism.

The same year the photo appeared, Flanner left for Europe on the final leg of the customary journey of literary-minded Midwesterners eager to be elsewhere: Chicago, Greenwich Village, Paris. From a prosperous Indianapolis family, her Chicago days included two years at the University of Chicago before returning home and a brief period on the *Indianapolis Star* writing about the arts and movies. In 1918, newly married, she was off to New York and an intense period of writing poems and stories she was unable to sell. One of her many new writer and artist friends of the time (Neysa McMein, said to be the most celebrated woman in New York in the twenties and thirties, was among the latter) was Jane Grant, a *New York Times* reporter who would soon marry Harold Ross, a former *Stars and Stripes* editor in Paris now looking to make his way in magazines.

In New York Flanner also met and fell in love with Solita Solano, an experienced journalist who had moved from Boston to become drama editor of the *New York Tribune*. Despite the importance of her new job, the dark, attractive, worldly Solano saw herself as only marking time in newspaper work until she succeeded as a fiction writer. When Heywood Broun rejoined the *Tribune* after World War I and she was demoted to reporting, she left for a press agent's job that was better paying but a journalistic step downward. At the same time Flanner's marriage was disintegrating—she would eventually be divorced—and she could neither find work nor sell her stories.

When Solano got an assignment to Constantinople from *National Geographic*, the two women left New York in 1921 with a plan to support themselves in Europe with freelance writing and Flanner's small inheritance. In later years Flanner would point to her Midwestern background as a principal stimulus to flight: "I think if I had been born in a prettier part of the country than I was born in, which was flat and corn land, I wouldn't have been so eager to appreciate the beauties of Paris and Europe. I came from pure aesthetic selfishness and on a tiny, tiny income. Which is what gave the freedom to live here, as Ernest [Hemingway] says, on almost less than less."

After European travel Flanner and Solano settled in Paris in the fall of 1922, taking a large room for less than a dollar a day in a small hotel at 36 Rue Bonaparte near the church of St-Germain-des-Prés, their address for the next sixteen years, and quickly fell in with the quarter's writing community of poets and novelists. "We were a literary lot," said Flanner of her new acquaintances. "Each of us aspired to become a famous writer as soon as possible." Both Flanner and Solano had novels under way, and in 1924 Solano published *The Uncertain Feast*, the first of a trio of novels she produced over three years. In the Paris *Tribune* Eugene Jolas promoted her as one of the "highly gifted American writers who live in France" and praised her prose style as that of a "poet of emotional crises."

Flanner's first and only novel, *The Cubical City*, appeared two years after Solano's initial book, but by then her writing had already turned in a new and unexpected direction. "Writing fiction is not my gift," she later acknowledged. "Writing is but not writing fiction." She had kept up correspondence in New York with Jane Grant, now married to Harold Ross and helping him find writers for *The New Yorker*, the new magazine he had just launched. A regular Paris letter was a particular interest of Ross—"the magazine had always," quipped A. J. Liebling, "considered London and Paris, although not Newark or Chicago, within its sphere of inaction"—and Grant remembered "gay and attractive" letters Flanner had sent her from the city. In June 1925 she wrote offering the thirty-three-year-old Flanner a job as *The New Yorker*'s Paris correspondent.

A writer previously lined up for the position, Grant explained, lacked adequate knowledge of Paris, so she was looking to Flanner as her "great white hope." She knew the city, and Grant was certain she could grasp what Ross wanted, which was

> anecdotal and incidental stuff on places familiar to Americans
> and on people of note whether they are Americans or
> internationally prominent—dope on fields of the arts and a
> little on fashions, although he does not want the latter treated
> technically; there should be lots of chat about people seen
> about and in it all he wants a definite personality injected.

She was confident Flanner could handle the letter, Grant added, so she was writing to ask her to "give it a try, if the idea interests you, and send along about a thousand words, along the lines outlined, as soon as you can. Ross wants it about every other week and for it he will pay $40 per."

In its first year *The New Yorker* had run through a procession of Parisian articles in what seemed a work-in-progress effort to settle on a satisfying and repeatable format. "Nous, Etrangers à Paris" on May 9, 1925, led the way—a lightly assembled piece advising Americans to make the journey abroad in the coming summer because

Paris promised to be gay and prices reasonable. It noted as well that young Paris-American literary hopefuls still flourished "as vigorously as when the Transatlantic Review first saw the light of day," with only a single writer highlighted by name: "Up to the present only one writer of real merit, Mr. Ernest Hemingway, has been revealed, and as a book of his short stories is to be published in New York in the autumn, he may possibly be read and criticized by other circles than the *Dial*." The article was signed with the initials H.E.S.—as it happened, those of Harold E. Stearns, who before his Paris period had been editor of the *Dial*. The article appeared just as Stearns was winding down his Paris letter for *Town & Country*, but he would have been an unlikely candidate for carrying on in *The New Yorker*. His gloomy coverage of French politics—as a Flanner biographer described his work—was not what Ross had in mind for his bright and airy new magazine.

The following month came "Summer in the City of Light," signed by Ralph Barton, a mildly amusing effort at capturing the lucrative chaos of the annual tourist invasion. A week later the magazine turned to "From Paris," a sober effort by Argus, and on September 26 offered its first "Paris Letter," signed with the uninspired name Top Hat and for the first time using the straightforward device of someone writing home about the city—in this instance, about its interseasonal return to itself in the absence of American tourists.

GENÊT. The money Ross offered Flanner was good—$35 a letter rather than $40—and publication in the magazine allowed her to keep a long-distance association with her New York friends. Her initial "Paris Letter" appeared on October 10, 1925, with a dateline of September 25 and with the *nom de correspondance* Genet tacked on the end, a Ross inspiration (the continuing title "Letter from Paris" would appear later, as would Genêt with the circumflex). The magazine's editing left the impression the letter was a carryover from

Top Hat's Paris Letter two weeks earlier. "Paris has not chosen to alter much in the last two weeks; that is, so far as the externals are concerned," reported Flanner of the departing tourists. "It is a breathing spell, as we said." Despite the editorial "we" of the opening, within the first paragraph the "I" emerged: "The last word as I write is that anyone who thinks anyone of consequence is back in town yet is a yokel." The second letter, on October 24, would pick up where she had left off—in the first person: "I have observed a curious phenomenon lately which I put down to a bad dinner I had last week; but the thing has come up again and so I must mention it. . . ."

Flanner credited *The New Yorker*'s editing over the years with tightening her onrushing style and shaping the column into a distinct type of foreign correspondence that, in the evolving style of the magazine, was both personal and detached, amused in tone, often archly mannered, drawn to the surprising metaphor. "I don't want to know what you think about what goes on in Paris," was the only directive Ross gave her. "I want to know what the French think." In practice this meant not getting out and about among the French so much as ransacking local newspapers for material (at the time, Flanner remembered, there were eight daily secular papers in Paris) and rewriting it, as Jane Grant had said Ross wanted, with a definite personality injected. A personal edge in her work came naturally; she "instinctively leaned," as she put it, "toward comments with a critical edge, indeed a double edge, if possible"—work with a "certain personal aspect or slant of the writer's mind." (Gardner Botsford, who after World War II was Flanner's editor at *The New Yorker*, called her "completely unbuttoned and impressionistic" as a writer. "Her words would pour out as from an open faucet, yet every Flanner sentence was instantly identifiable as her own." He added: "She was a great one for rewriting, or trying to rewrite, a piece after turning it in—not, I always felt, because she had detected a flaw in it but because she didn't know how to turn off the faucet.")

The initial number of *transition* in 1927, wrote Flanner, contained "if not a feast, some good food for thought," and the "tastiest plate" within was not the opening pages of Joyce's "Work in Progress," a contribution written "in the most extreme jabber-wocky." Lindbergh was "a young tourist" whose airplane had "swung through the sky" before landing and provoked such "pretti-ness of French journalism" the following morning as "'He has a heart of steel in the body of a bird. He is a carrier pigeon.'" Although he is not "amorously identified with the tale," she remarked of *The Sun Also Rises*, "it should be safe to say that Donald Ogden Stewart is taken to be the stuffed-bird-loving Bill." With the appearance of Sherwood Anderson's *Winesburg, Ohio* in French translation, it ap-peared to Flanner that the "Chicago, Indiana, Ohio twang of verity is what the sophisticated Parisian brain wants."

Flanner's work routine sent her, after pulling material from newspapers and personally covering events that caught her atten-tion, into seclusion in her hotel room for long bouts of two-fingered typing amid clouds of smoke of ever-present cigarettes. Solita Solano aided with typing and editing and by reading material aloud while Flanner worked. The finished copy was posted from the Gare St. Lazare to a boat train for a New York–bound ship, with Flanner rarely having any response from *The New Yorker* before seeing her work in print. (In an advance in speed if not reliability, immediately after World War II Flanner's copy was transmitted to New York by cable. Often garbled—once the Paris letter arrived as twenty-six pages of the letter O—the material had to be laboriously traced back to Paris for correction.)

While she clung still to a view of her magazine work as a means of earning a living while working on a second novel, increasingly Flanner took pleasure in *The New Yorker* and association with its growing stable of skilled writers. At the urging of the editors she be-gan contributing other pieces, including appreciative Parisian pro-files of Isadora Duncan, Edith Wharton, and the American ambassador to France William Bullitt. The Wharton profile, "Dearest Edith," appeared in 1929, earning Flanner a fee of $165 and, for the first time in *The New Yorker*, her own name on her work. Later, in "Tourist," she carefully retraced the murder of the American dancer Jean De Koven by the handsome German criminal Eugene Weidmann, the notorious crime that had claimed Eric Sevareid's attention in the Paris *Herald*. Flanner's account mentioned the paper but not the reporter—and added a significant detail about Weidmann's death by guillotine. His executioner, nervous since this was only his "third performance," insisted it should take place at Greenwich time rather than at dawn, causing the execution, contrary to custom, to take place "in broad daylight." Weidmann, added Flanner, "met his end bravely. That is to say he shut his eyes when he saw the guillotine and walked to his death like a somnambulist."

As she did additional work for the magazine, becoming in effect its general correspondent in Paris, and freelance writing for other magazines, Flanner's hopes for fiction dwindled even though she published some stories and considered translations and a work of history. Her career was now firmly settled in journalism—she had become, as she said, a "gentleman of the press in skirts"—and imaginative writing remained at best a distant yearning. In the final number of *The Little Review* published in Paris in May 1929, the journal that had been born in Chicago in 1914 sent out a ten-point questionnaire to a variety of prominent figures, among them T. S. Eliot, William Carlos Williams, and Ford Madox Ford as well as Flanner and Solita Solano. "I should like to have been a writer—to have been Sterne or any of the Brontes," Flanner wrote in response to what she would most like to be. "I should like to be a writer—to be even Hemingway since he is better at being Hemingway than any of the other Hemingways." With another question—What things do you really dislike?—she reverted to the reality of her fact-writing career: "I dislike fiction as a theory and usually as a practice."

With the thirties Flanner edged her Paris letter into politics while at the same time *The New Yorker* was stretching her work to include the "Letter from London" (later, in 1939, taken over for long duration by Mollie Panter-Downes) and major profiles of Britain's

Queen Mary and Germany's Hitler (about whom, Flanner noted, there were editorial questions when the article was written in 1935 as to whether for American readers he was worth ten thousand words) as well as coverage of the Berlin Olympics and the abdication of Edward VIII. She had, nonetheless, little confidence in her mastery of newsgathering as traditionally practiced, once confessing in a letter to Solita Solano her sense of abject failure at "huntsmans reporting." Fortunately, what *The New Yorker* primarily wanted from her and she richly supplied was not news but news in context—framed, enlivened, stylized.

HOME AND BACK. As the decade wore on and war loomed, Flanner grew anxious to return home. She raised the possibility with the magazine but editors wanted her stationed in France. For the time being she remained, doing added writing and organizing a collection of her articles that would be published in 1940 as *An American in Paris: Profile of an Interlude Between Two Wars*. But shortly after Britain and France declared war on Germany in September 1939, Flanner and Solano fled to Bordeaux and ship passage home. The ostensible reason was the illness of Flanner's mother and *The New Yorker* granting her a three-month leave of absence; but the magazine had repeated its wish that she remain in France, and the overriding reason was that she was too fearful to remain in Europe at war.

The New Yorker immediately replaced her with A. J. Liebling, delighted to return to the city he knew and loved while claiming surprise at a "reporter coming away from a story just as it broke." He made clear that he "knew very little about Lady Mendl, Elsa Maxwell, Mainbocher and Worth the dressmakers, Mr. and Mrs. Charles Bedaux, or a number of other leading characters in Genêt's Paris dispatches," but this hardly mattered "since it seemed probable that they would lam anyway." The implication, that Flanner had lammed as well, left her replacement free to treat the quite different material of what he called the "reactions to war of ordinary French people."

The assignment had come about, so Liebling claimed, because of barroom assurance he had given St. Clair McKelway, then the magazine's managing editor, about his deep knowledge of the French. Harold Ross went along with the assignment and the writing focus on ordinary people yet cautioned, "But for God's sake keep away from low-life." Once in Paris, Liebling established his credentials as a more or less typical correspondent by joining the Anglo-American Press Association and at least once a week showing up at the Hôtel Continental for official press briefings.

After the fall of the city he trailed the French government on its flights to Tours and Bordeaux. Later, as a war correspondent, he would file pieces for *The New Yorker* from London and North Africa and eventually follow the fighting—as he would title a book—on *The Road Back to Paris.* "There is an old proverb," he wrote therein, "that a girl may sleep with one man without being a trollop, but let a man cover one little war and he is a war correspondent. I belong to the one-war category." The war he covered was not a little affair but Liebling kept to an avowed narrow focus in his reporting, avoiding high-level politics and grand strategy in favor of direct, dense accounts of war's up-close reality. (His usual attire in battle zones was in keeping with the absence of the showy in his reporting. "Other correspondents," said *The New Yorker*'s Gardner Botsford, who had encountered Liebling during the fighting in France, "generally tried to look more military and warlike than any soldier—parachutists' boots, aviators' scarves, tankers' jackets—but Liebling was not one to make believe. He was a correspondent, not a solider, and he looked it.")

Meanwhile, back in New York, Janet Flanner continued during the war to write for *The New Yorker.* Then, late in 1944, she flew to London as one of the magazine's war correspondents. Soon thereafter, five years after leaving, she was back in France and Genêt's "Letter from Paris" back in the magazine on December 15, 1944. In it "your correspondent," as she referred to herself, calmly resumed her work without pausing to mention she had ever been away.

PARIS FLAPNOODLE. In "Why I Like Paris," an article in the December 1927 *Paris Comet*, "Americanus" lamented the illusory "flapnoodle" about the city appearing endlessly in American publications—the fanciful, recycled stories of year-around rain, absence of fish in the Seine, the impossibility of finding a decent cup of coffee. With their unhappy effect of trivializing the great city, the stories were the work of the horde of Paris-Americans living off per-piece writing for the back-home market. "How many writers freelancing here for publications back home nobody knows," sighed Americanus.

> I have heard that almost every large American newspaper receives a so-called letter from Paris, to say nothing of countless reams of stuff that the magazines use. It is often said here humorously that most of the stuff is found and written within a shadow of the Dôme café.
>
> However this may be, there is no denying that an awful lot of flapnoodle finds its way to Main Street every month.

James Thurber, speculating from Columbus, Ohio, before his move to France in 1925, confidently assumed the production of freelance flapnoodle from Europe would pay his way while he concentrated on fiction writing. ". . . Then I hies me to Paris, France," he wrote a friend,

> whence I shall ship many a glowing story of affairs European, French, English and etc. Free-lancing over there is soft—few newspapermen in peace time go into it—few want to—fewer can—fewer yet know anything about it—and me, well, I gotta big drag with Embassy and other officials there, know the ropes and should get over big. In the interim between

contracts or stories, I shall write many bits of inconsequent
verse, short stories, and my great American novel, of course.

Contrary to Thurber's hopeful view, peacetime newspapermen *did*
get into freelancing as well as other sorts of outside writing tasks,
usually out of pressing need of adding to meager paychecks.
Thurber became one of them. While working nights on the copy
desk of the Paris *Tribune*, he spent days spinning out articles for the
back-home market—among them the magazine sections of the
Kansas City Star and the *New York Herald* as well as the humble
pages of the *Detroit Athletic Club News*. His top publication was a
humorous piece in *Harper's Magazine*, "A Sock on the Jaw—French
Style," upholding the American method of settling arguments with
the fist. The $90 payment arrived just in time for Thurber and his
wife to settle their rent at a Left Bank hotel.

But to live entirely as a freelancer—defined by Waverley Root
as "a journalist who sells his gleanings to anybody and, he hopes,
everybody"—was a different matter. It demanded unstinting appli-
cation at the writing desk, a discipline all the more daunting given
the seductive pleasures of Paris, together with the up-to-date market savvy needed to give editors what they wanted. In time, those
who attempted the freelance route usually found themselves forced
into some sort of salaried journalistic work.

When the work could be found. For women especially, openings were always few and far between, and markedly so on Paris-
American newspapers where desk skills of expanding cables,
editing and rewriting, and headline writing were in most demand.
The *Herald's* Martha Foley was a rare woman accepted into the
typically male preserve of the copy desk. Such newspaper jobs as
there were for women were ordinarily in the specialized areas of
writing about society or fashion or, as with Florence Gilliam on
theater, some area of the arts.

For Rosemary Carr the specialty was haute couture. After finishing the University of Chicago she became the Paris *Tribune's* fashion

editor and occasional reporter in 1920. Vincent Sheean, who had first met her in Chicago, found her a beauty, but it was a young poet and fiction writer who caught her eye, Stephen Vincent Benét, ostensibly studying at the Sorbonne on a graduate fellowship from Yale. They met in November 1920 and were married a year later in Chicago. After a period in New York where Rosemary worked for *Vogue*, they returned to Paris in 1926 and, over the next three years while living in suburban Neuilly, Benét finished and published *John Brown's Body*, the long poetic work that made his name, while Rosemary wrote the Paris letter for *Town & Country* that earlier had been turned out by Harold Stearns.

Irene Corbally Kuhn was Rosemary Carr's successor as the *Tribune*'s fashion specialist, the only woman then on the staff. With no experience, Kuhn had to learn quickly, which turned out easier than expected since Paris fashion houses, eager to inform American readers of their offerings, gave her full access to working areas and showrooms—and provided sizable discounts on clothing she managed to buy while living on what she called "one undernourished salary check to the next."

The *Tribune* also used Kuhn for the tracking of prominent guests arriving at the hotels, and in her designer attire she felt passably at ease in the elegant lobbies of the Ritz, the Crillon, and the George V. What she wrote were mostly routine notes for the social columns, but now and then her interviews turned memorable, as when Charlie Chaplin invited her to join him for a morning stroll along the Champs-Elysées. Memorable in a different way, as a small feat of undercover reporting, was working with a French writer on *Le Matin* to determine if Americans in Paris were typically overcharged—a customary complaint—by hotels, restaurants, and shops. The two made their rounds of the same places independently, the Frenchwoman speaking perfect Parisian French and Kuhn only English. They learned that in all cases save one—a milliner's shop were Kuhn was offered a few francs off on a hat just tried on by the Frenchwoman—prices were the same, with parallel stories reporting the findings running in both papers, no doubt to the righteous pleasure of local advertisers.

All-purpose women reporters and feature writers—like Rosemary Carr and Irene Corbally Kuhn on occasion and Rosamond Cole of the *Herald* and Carol Weld of the *Tribune* regularly—remained uncommon on Paris-American newspapers, and a self-styled gentleman of the press in skirts like *The New Yorker*'s Janet Flanner was unique. On Paris-American magazines, positions were equally unlikely since few existed. Nearly always, the better choice for a woman was to begin as a freelance contributor to newspapers and magazines, sending out an assembly line of Paris flapnoodle—and hope that a job offering steady wages ultimately came her way.

STRAY JOURNALIST IN PARIS. When Ida Tarbell blazed a trail to Paris in 1891 she had no hope of catching on with the *Herald*, the lone Paris-American paper of the day, or with any other news organization. Thirty-three, with little writing experience and only a reading knowledge of French, she nonetheless was betting she could turn up enough Parisian feature material and interested American newspapers willing to print it to support herself wholly as a freelance journalist. In her spare time, such as it was, she would work on a long-range project of a life of Madame Roland.

Accompanied by three friends sharing food and rent, she settled into rooms in the Latin Quarter near the Musés de Cluny, immersed herself in the life of the city, and sent off inquiries to six American newspapers. Three said they would consider her work, the *Chicago Tribune* among them, and after several weeks came her first payment for an accepted article—$5. A two-thousand-word article mailed off to the newspaper syndicate of S. S. McClure brought her double the amount and an encouraging expression of interest in seeing more of her work. She produced more, some merely cribbed translations from French papers, and some were accepted—"enough," said Tarbell, "to make me feel that this might be a stable and prosperous market for short and timely articles."

Eventually the McClure syndicate began suggesting articles, which brought in $2 to $12 each, and translations of short stories, which paid a dollar or less. Tarbell had found a steady market, becoming in effect the syndicate's Paris representative, but the stern requirement was relentless effort and, after her friends returned home, a lonely, hand-to-mouth existence. She ordinarily began work at eight in the morning and seldom ended before midnight, writing in longhand and making such careful final copies that in the McClure office in New York it was assumed she was a spinster schoolteacher.

In the summer of 1892 the bustling proprietor of the syndicate, Sam McClure, appeared in Paris and told Tarbell that for a new magazine he was starting he wanted from her a series of articles on leading French and English scientists. For a "stray journalist in Paris," as Tarbell described herself, it was a crucial breakthrough at a difficult period. An economic downturn in America had shrunk the freelance market, and even when articles were accepted payment was sluggish. The breakthrough became all the greater when, the articles written, a delighted McClure lured Tarbell to New York as a staff fact writer for *McClure's Magazine* and set her to work on a biography of Napoleon. Still to come was her biography of Madame Roland, a two-volume study of Lincoln, and her monumental history of the Standard Oil Company.

In January 1919, World War I just ended, Tarbell briefly returned to France for the *Red Cross Magazine*, filling an assignment from John S. Phillips, her former editor at *McClure's*, to gather material on the organization's postwar efforts. In Paris she found Americans swarming the city, so much so that walking to the Red Cross headquarters on Rue de Rivoli seemed like passing along government buildings of Washington. She was dressed in a military-style Red Cross uniform, and American soldiers on leave stopped her with requests for shopping help with gifts to take back home. She visited her old Left Bank living area and later traveled about the country, struck by devastation, neglect, and the deaths of old friends but heartened by what she called the "slow redemption of the mutilated land."

Her magazine work required at least an article a month and attendance at the Versailles peace conference. She endured the swirl of formal sessions and press conferences and kept up with commentaries in the British, French, and American newspapers, her own views of the conference swinging between a sense of utter bedlam and guarded optimism. In the summer of the year she again left France behind, now to fill a contract for an American speaking tour on the Chautauqua circuit explaining to suspicious audiences what if anything had taken place at Versailles.

SCOOPING THE WORLD. Not long after Ida Tarbell left Paris, Dorothy Thompson arrived—and found notably less rewarding work grinding out publicity for the American Red Cross. To finance her transatlantic crossing and an intended journey through Europe to Russia, she had tried for a bank loan with a confident announcement that "Miss Thompson has ascertained that she can make herself self-supporting . . . through correspondence for American newspapers, provided she can borrow sufficient money to secure her expenses, pending delivery of her articles." The loan was not forthcoming, nor was she able to line up assignments from editors; for the journey she had only the companionship of a close friend, Barbara De Porte, and the shared ambition to start out as journalists and eventually become fiction writers. In June 1920 the two pooled their savings and booked passage to England.

Thompson was twenty-seven, and the only writing she had done were newspaper pieces growing out of work for the suffrage movement and a social-work group. During ship passage she fell in with a group of Zionist leaders on their way to a London conference, a fortunate connection as it turned out. When Thompson and De Porte called at the London office of the International News Service they used the encounter—and De Porte's Russian-Jewish background—to talk their way into an assignment covering the conference, their initiation into the procedures of operating as string correspondents in Europe.

Shortly thereafter, during a trip to Ireland searching for relatives, Thompson stumbled into a scoop when she interviewed a leader of an Irish rebellion just before he was sent to prison and began a hunger strike that ended in his death. She had no sense of the interview's value, the last conducted with the leader, but in London the INS bureau chief did. "Sit down at a typewriter, girl, and write out those notes!" he commanded. The interview made front pages of newspapers around America and got Thompson an INS assignment for a series of reports about Austria—a thrilling prospect that vanished when the news service changed its mind.

From London, Thompson and De Porte moved on to Paris, took rooms in a hotel on the Boulevard Raspail, and supported themselves by writing for the Red Cross at a penny a line. The time remaining was used to scout out material for freelance articles and produce a stream of inadequate fiction. When De Porte suddenly decided to marry, Thompson, like Ida Tarbell before her, was on her own in Paris, lonely, despising her fellow Red Cross workers, questioning whether she was capable of anything better than hack writing. "The whole place is cluttered up with almost successful people," she bemoaned in a diary.

> Scenario writers, magazine writers, photographers. They
> know their job well. Do it. Make a 'good living.' But oh, their
> shallowness. Appalling! . . . Every night I come back to my
> little room on the top floor of this absurd hotel, where never
> an American stayed before. I write, but what I write is so thin.
> . . . Oh, why, why haven't I talent?

A ray of hope in her life was a new friend, one who matched her writing ambition yet already had a record of achievement. Rose

Wilder Lane had worked on newspapers in Kansas City and San Francisco and published popular biographies of Henry Ford, Jack London, and Herbert Hoover when she arrived in Paris in 1920 with a salaried job in the publicity department of the Red Cross. She also had an arrangement with the *San Francisco Bulletin* for a series of articles drawn from travels in Europe—and her Red Cross work allowed her to produce freelance articles for the American market while living on her salary as long as she made some mention of the organization. She was thirty-four when she met the tall, vigorous, rosy-faced Thompson in 1921, beginning a friendship that endured despite Lane's return to America just two years later with the phasing out of her Red Cross job. She would return to Europe for more work with the Red Cross, this time in Albania, followed by a long career in America as a ghostwriter, popular fiction writer for the *Saturday Evening Post* and other magazines, and the revision and rewriting of the popular *Little House* books of her mother, Laura Ingalls Wilder.

"Rose, you can *write*," Thompson had encouraged Lane in a letter about the shared miseries of their Paris publicity work and freelance writing. "When I think of you piddling around on Red Cross newsletters and articles and short stories and translations, I should like to shake you." Despite misgivings about her talent, Thompson could write as well, as Paul Scott Mowrer recognized when he read an article on Russian refugees in Paris she had sold for $20 to the *Philadelphia Public Ledger*. The *Chicago Daily News* bureau chief invited her to dinner and—struck by her appearance, brains, and fierce will—suggested that, given the overwhelming crowd of journalists in Paris, she would be better off looking for a position in another city. Vienna was a possibility.

"You haven't got a correspondent in Vienna," Thompson pointed out when she called on Wythe Williams, head of the *Public Ledger*'s Paris office. He told her there was no need since the paper's Berlin correspondent covered Central Europe; besides, Vienna was a "second-string" city in postwar shambles. Undeterred, Thompson pushed her case, and finally Williams caved in to the extent of allowing her to introduce herself as the paper's Vienna correspondent but with pay coming only for pieces it chose to publish and with no prospect of advancement.

Although she ascribed the position to little more than a belief that "people will always give you a job if there is no risk involved," Thompson readily accepted. Already she had found work writing for the Red Cross in Budapest, a job she handled from Vienna by shuttling back and forth and that brought in money until she established herself as a correspondent. War-depleted Vienna of 1921 was grim, but she began work with a series of light features on coffee and music and other staples of the city's life. As her confidence in the German language increased ("Those who heard her speak German in her later years," recalled Vincent Sheean, "can have no idea of the fluency with which she handled it in the 1920s"), so did the range and depth of her subjects.

An exclusive came when Thompson interviewed the Hapsburg emperor Karl I—a newsworthy figure since he was trying at the time to reclaim the Hungarian throne—after getting inside his castle while outfitted in a Red Cross nurse's uniform and masquerading as a medical assistant attending to his pregnant wife. "It scooped the world, of course, that story," she said later. "The only interview with Karl. The other correspondents were—well, you can imagine."

THE ONLY WOMAN NEWSPAPERMAN. After a time the *Public Ledger*'s Paris office decided Thompson's piece-rate stories from Vienna were so numerous they could save money by giving her a regular position. Installed as the paper's Central Europe representative with a Vienna office, a salary of $50 a week, and an expense account, she was the first woman to operate a significant foreign news bureau. "I had nine countries to cover," Thompson said of her work, "over an enormous territory, each one of them with a different history and problems. I had no assistance, not even a secretary." What she did possess was a model of how a foreign correspondent should operate in the *Chicago Tribune*'s intrepid Floyd Gibbons—"Floyd's notion of journalism was confined to being wherever anything was likely to happen," she said with admiration, "and to dramatize the occurrence to the hilt"—together with her own verve and intelligence.

In 1924 the *Public Ledger*'s foreign service merged with the *New York Evening News*, giving Thompson a larger American audience for her work. The following year her career took another leap forward when the *Ledger* made her its permanent correspondent in Berlin—a major posting that put her in friendly but serious competition with such accomplished newsmen as Edgar Ansel Mowrer, H. R. Knickerbocker, and George Seldes. She was more than up to the job. In what was meant as a supreme compliment from one correspondent to another, Seldes, the *Chicago Tribune*'s man in Berlin, saluted Thompson's ability by ranking her "the only woman newspaperman."

Within some six months of her arrival in Berlin, however, a significant rival for the title emerged when Sigrid Schultz, Seldes's longtime assistant, replaced him in the *Tribune*'s bureau. Born in Chicago, Schultz had returned to Europe with her artist parents before World War I, had been educated in France and Germany, and in 1919 had been hired by the *Tribune*'s Berlin bureau because of her facility with English and German. In 1926 she became the bureau chief and soon distinguished herself as an early and clear-eyed observer of German military ambition. She gained a shrewd insider view of current trends through the tool of frequent dinner parties at her apartment, and as one of her guests Thompson was introduced to leading German writers, artists, and political figures. Among those in politics she came to know some "very important fellows . . . long before the Nazis came into power and when nobody thought that they ever would."

Sigrid Schultz would remain a stalwart presence in Berlin as war began, masking her identity with the name John Dickson in some *Tribune* reports to prevent ejection as a correspondent. For Dorothy

Thompson, on the other hand, European reporting had long since proven too small a stage. "This isn't enough for me," she confided to a friend in the late twenties. "It's not what I really want. I'm nothing in my own country. I want to be something there—something no other woman has been yet." Following a series of articles written in Russia during the tenth anniversary of the revolution, she left her Berlin post—replaced with H. R. Knickerbocker—and moved on to marriage to Sinclair Lewis and return to America.

In August 1934, back in Europe and writing now as a magazine journalist, Thompson was abruptly expelled from the Third Reich for "numerous anti-German publications," the first such action against an American correspondent and another fortuitous development in her career. She was now certified at home and abroad as a major voice in opposition to Hitler—and out from under the shadow of her Nobel laureate husband. Just in the future was the major stage she craved as a widely syndicated columnist on world affairs for the *New York Herald Tribune*, a regular writer for *Ladies' Home Journal*, and a radio broadcaster commanding a national following.

KNIGHT WORK. Just as a woman correspondent heading up a foreign news bureau was exceptional, so was one at the other end of the journalistic spectrum—the less than glamorous setting of a wire-service office, another generally all-male stronghold through the interwar years. Mary Knight, who appeared in Paris a decade after Dorothy Thompson, managed to land such a job with the United Press and, out of desperate need, cling to it. When she finally determined to look for something different, it was the service that refused to let go, recognizing it had on its hands a present-day Nellie Bly.

After a genteel but impoverished Southern upbringing that left her hungry for independence and adventure, Knight in the fall of 1929 left Atlanta behind for New York. A temporary job with *Good Housekeeping* was followed by work with Butterick Publishing Company reading manuscripts for the young women's magazine *Romance*. When the magazine folded she found a $40-a-week job on Hearst's *New York American* writing an existing advertising column, "About New York with Peggy," that required she also sell the ads. As she described it, the work was "pretty silly—specialty shops, beauty parlors, places where superfluous hair can be removed by multiple electrolysis, corset shops, luggage stores—every little hole in the wall is grist to my mill. I hate the selling part but the writing is easy."

Europe was on her mind, and even after her salary was raised to $50 a week she was unable to resist, nor could she when the *American* offered a compelling depression-period increase to $60 to stay on. A cattle boat took her abroad together with a borrowed Ford roadster, and when she reached England she set off on a three-thousand-mile tour. Driving around the continent followed, and only when she returned to Paris was she ready to begin a settled stay.

Knight found a room at a club for American college women on Rue de Chevreuse, returned the Ford to America, and began hunting for work in journalism. She assumed it would be an easy task: "If I made the rounds of all the English speaking concerns—newspaper offices and agencies—someone would take me on." The reality was otherwise. At the *New York Times* the bureau chief advised her that if she stayed in Paris more than six or eight months the city's hold would be so strong she would never leave. He also suggested she try the United Press. There the bureau chief, Ralph Heinzen, told her he had nothing but to keep checking back.

Knight worked at her French and waited for something to develop. When she had nearly reached the end of her financial rope, she placed a classified ad in the *Herald*: "American college graduate seeks whole or part-time work, preferably newspaper or literary connection." The work that resulted was a comic mixup when she found herself as a governess-servant for a haughty Frenchwoman in a château near Tours. Back in Paris, her pride battered and down to her last forty francs, she went back to Ralph Heinzen at the UP.

"Well," he told her, "how would you like to start here at $25 a week?" He added: "I warn you, it is a doubtful experiment, with your lack of experience, but . . . we'll see. It may be easier to teach you than to unlearn you."

Knight's first assignment was one Heinzen was eager to get off his own hands—the typical journalistic task for a woman of a daily 250-word "Paris Styles" fashion article together with a longer fashion piece for the Sunday papers. He advised Knight not to take the "fashion racket" too seriously and try seeing its humorous side, but however approached it turned out to be the hardest journalistic work she had attempted. After she covered her first fashion collection, Heinzen flung her copy in a wastebasket: "We can't use stuff like that. It's the dresses you are sent to describe, not the furniture and the flunkies and how the people in the audience look!" With two fingers he batted out a new story from what little she could remember of the outfits paraded past her.

Covering glittering fashion shows could be taxing, with as many as five or six a day during the high season, and Knight's work period stretching to the early morning hours. To preserve her sanity, as Heinzen put it, he assigned her to the perennial stories of Parisian suicides and sent her on a round of butcher shops for figures on the amount of horse meat passing over the counters. He also allowed her to do some interviewing. "In this way," said Knight, "I kept my equilibrium and learned to become a full-fledged staff reporter."

Her full-fledged status, however, did not extend to the basic work of the office—the generally exclusive male duty of interviewing important figures, writing spot news stories for the wire, firing off cables. Knight's introduction to it came on a Sunday in October when a new British dirigible, a vast airship built for service between England and India, crashed and burned in France with fifty-four passengers aboard. When news of the disaster reached the office, Heinzen rushed a reporter to the scene of the crash and ordered Knight to work at the desk under his direction, handling a phone line to London as details of the crash came in from stringers and eventu-

ally the reporter on the spot. When the long day was over messages
were wired to the bureau from London and New York: CONGRATU-
LATIONS CLEARED GOOD FOUR MINUTE BEAT CAUGHT ALL AF-
TERNOONERS WHICH WIDELY BANNERHEADING UP BREAK.

Another step up with the wire service came in the spring of 1931
when Heinzen sent Knight to cover a murder trial in Nice. Never
before had she been out of town on assignment, never on the Riviera, and never had she traveled first class. The trial involved a celebrated crime of passion in which an American, Charlotte
Nixon-Nirdlinger, a former beauty queen of St. Louis, had shot her
husband to protect her two small children. If found guilty, Nixon-
Nirdlinger could die by the guillotine.

In Paris, Knight had already shown a talent for scheming her
way into interviews with such notable figures as Madame Curie and
Mahatma Gandhi. In Nice she talked a jailer into allowing her to
see the imprisoned woman in her cell, getting a bylined UP exclusive that was printed around the world. Then during the trial in
which the former beauty queen was found innocent, Knight, with
the aid of a UP colleague vacationing on the Riviera and a direct
phone line to Paris, scooped her fellow reporters, all men, with
news of the verdict. She had bested the Associated Press by a
healthy sixteen minutes, she learned later, the International News
Service by a whopping thirty-five.

FLAGPOLE SITTING. When the president of France, Paul Doumer,
was assassinated shortly after taking office, Knight was present at the
execution of his killer. When she had asked Heinzen to assign her to
the guillotining, he was puzzled by her interest yet agreed; but to
French authorities, a press pass to a woman to cover an execution
was out of the question. So Knight, from irritation as much as enterprise, outfitted herself in men's clothing, pushed her short bobbed
hair under a billed cap, went out to La Santé Prison, worked her way
through the crowd, and when police were distracted bolted into the

small group of accredited reporters. She had a closeup view when the "widow's kiss" did its efficient work.

Back in the office in her usual attire, Heinzen overheard Knight casually telling another reporter she had managed to see the execution. He strode to her desk and in firm terms told her to get to work: ". . . you have the gall to call yourself a newspaperwoman and sit there with a front page story sewed up in your mug, doing not a God damn thing about it! Hell, Mary, haven't you learned *any*thing! Christ alive, snap to it and let's get going!"

Knight's story, with its how-a-woman-did-it angle, drew wide attention, so much so that in 1932 Knight was sent to America for two weeks to promote the UP among newspaper editors and publishers and retell her story on radio shows, before clubs, and in journalism schools. Nothing she did later, including talking her way into an exclusive interview with Anne Morrow Lindbergh when she and her husband visited Paris, drew as much attention as what she came to think of as her "one moment of unintentional flagpole sitting."

After five years in Paris an urge to move on came over her, now to see the Orient, but Heinzen would hear no talk about her leaving the UP bureau. When through an acquaintance she was offered a writing job in Hong Kong, she decided to accept. Furious with her, Heinzen insisted she keep some connection with the wire service. The New York office agreed, and in 1935 Knight was off to Hong Kong with an agreement to write for the UP weekly mailed-in articles about shopping around the world and to work as a string correspondent. In the wire service's language, she was "merely furloughing" in the Orient.

When she finally returned to America, coming by ship from Japan, Knight found a UP message awaiting her in San Francisco: HAVE KNIGHT PROCEED HOLLYWOOD INTERVIEW STARS AND TRY CRASH MOVIES AS EXTRA GIRL MORE INSTRUCTIONS LATER. Similar flagpole-sitting assignments would follow: ARRANGE KNIGHT FLY NEWYORKWARDS AS AIR STEWARDESS FOR SERIES QUOTE LIFE IN CLOUDS UNQUOTE.

In New York, Knight's reputation as a participatory journalist had grown to the extent that the UP loaned her to the *World-Telegram* for a series of articles about life and work as a nurse in Bellevue Hospital. Not long thereafter, the young woman who less than a decade earlier had been forced to meekly appeal for work with a classified ad in the Paris *Herald* was in position to write a book about her experiences as a wire-service correspondent. "One makes the guess," a *New York Times* reviewer ended a glowing account of *On My Own*, published in 1939, "that the lecture platform is not far away in Miss Knight's future."

WITH THE BOYS. A key springboard for Mary Knight, Paris was only a useful starting point for Martha Gellhorn. "I wanted to go everywhere and see everything," she said of herself, echoing Dorothy Thompson's early goals, "and I meant to write my way." No one city could contain her relentless ambition, nor would she make the familiar transition of stray journalists from Ida Tarbell onward to routine, regular-paycheck work. In every sense of the word, Martha Gellhorn remained a determined freelancer.

She came to Paris the same year as Knight, the spring of 1930, with a pair of suitcases, a typewriter, and $75. Slender, blonde, stylish, she had parted company with Bryn Mawr after her junior year with a plan to parlay a brief period of newspaper work into similar work abroad. A summer job in New York reading galleys for the *New Republic*, where she also published her first article ("Rudy Vallee: God's Gift to Us Girls"), was followed by a cub reporter's position with the *Albany Times Union*, one she abandoned after six months. After a trying sojourn with her well-off family in St. Louis and a failed attempt to catch on with the local *Post-Dispatch*, Gellhorn announced she was off for Paris. She was twenty-one.

Paris was not new to her—she had visited the city on holidays—but now she was looking for work, beginning the search at the high end by calling at the *New York Times* and innocently informing the bureau chief she was ready to begin as a foreign correspondent. He declined the offer. There is no record she called on the two Paris-American newspapers of the time; instead she found a place—after odd jobs that included writing copy for an advertising agency—with the United Press, taking down material phoned in by stringers and writing a few stories of her own.

The wire-service job came to a sudden end when Gellhorn complained to a superior that a visiting figure with ties to the agency had made a pass at her in a taxi. Later, in a short story, she wrote of a young woman fired by an editor because of the poor quality of her writing and later feeling "her pride, her complete assurance, wilt." She tries, nonetheless, for a brave front: "No money. Jobs hard to get. What the hell." Gellhorn's own response to the job loss was to back away from journalism, move to a cheap pension on the French Mediterranean, start a novel.

After a few weeks she was back in Paris, continuing with her novel and, in real life, meeting the son of a political figure who was also one of France's most important journalists. Bertrand de Jouvenel, urbane, English-speaking, five years older than Gellhorn, married, was following in his father's footsteps as a journalist and author. A passionate affair followed while Gellhorn worked on her novel and arranged with the *St. Louis Post-Dispatch* for two lengthy articles about prominent women delegates at the League of Nations assembly in Geneva. She shrugged off the newspaper work as a bit of harmless whoring, though it was far less so than occasional fashion articles she dashed off for funds. For her future career as a correspondent, a benefit of her time in Geneva was meeting journalists covering the assembly and finding herself accepted into their elite ranks.

After Geneva and a period with de Jouvenel in Italy, Gellhorn returned to America, pregnant. Following an abortion she took up more freelance writing for the *Post-Dispatch*. The heated affair with de Jouvenel was far from over, and in the summer of 1932 Gellhorn returned to Europe, eventually locating work as a general editorial helper on French *Vogue* while sending back articles to American magazines and carrying on with her novel. When she again returned to America in the summer of 1934, the affair had finally run its course.

Gellhorn's novel, with an epigraph from *A Farewell to Arms*, was published that year as *What Mad Pursuit*, and a volume of stories, *The Trouble I've Seen*, followed two years later. The latter work was widely acclaimed, with Dorothy Thompson giving it lengthy treatment in the *New York Herald Tribune* and the *Saturday Review of Literature* running a cover photograph of the glamorous author. Gellhorn continued to write and publish fiction, but her future work was primarily as a freelance magazine journalist. In the company of Hemingway—whom she met while in Key West, his home at the time, and who would soon make her his third wife—she established her credentials as a full-fledged war correspondent with stories about the Spanish Civil War for *Collier's* that avoided battlefields and military maneuvers in favor of moving behind-the-front accounts of the wounded and the displaced.

Reporting from wartime Spain was hazardous, but just before arriving in the country Gellhorn endured a fashion assignment from *Vogue's* American edition that had perils of its own. Needing money for ship passage to Europe, she agreed to write an article on the "Beauty Problems of the Middle-Aged Woman" that involved undergoing an experimental skin treatment meant to peel away old skin, leaving fresh beneath. Years later she confided to a friend that, while far from middle-aged at the time, the treatment had ruined her skin yet transported her to Spain. "Me, I am going to Spain with the boys," she wrote a friend as she boarded a ship. "I don't know who the boys are, but I'm going with them."

With the D-day invasion of World War II Gellhorn shipped out with the boys again. She managed to be among the correspondents transported to Normandy by stowing away on a hospital ship that crossed the Channel to anchor off Omaha Beach and briefly went ashore with ambulance teams before the ship returned to England filled with the wounded. Hemingway, a *Collier's* correspondent during the war as well, was in effect Gellhorn's European chief. As magazines were in theory limited to a single correspondent at the front, he chose himself for the position and Gellhorn was left with using unofficial means to cover the fighting across Europe—a clash of journalistic and literary egos that doomed all the more a marriage already in shambles.

When Paris was liberated, Gellhorn made a hazardous journey there from the war in Italy, eager to learn the fate of friends in the city during the occupation. She found Hemingway ensconced in the Hôtel Ritz as a conquering hero; staying on the same floor was a reporter for *Time* magazine, Mary Welsh, soon to become wife number four. Gellhorn wrote stories about a Paris that struck her as curiously unchanged by war, had them passed by Allied censors, and was on her way, pursuing the war into Belgium and Germany—true still to her early aim of going everywhere, seeing everything, and writing her way.

CHAPTER SEVEN

Stories of Paris

Here in Paris I have done more deep,
serious thinking about writing than
ever before in my life. Certain things are
beginning to clarify in my mind.
I think I know the direction I want to take.
—HENRY MILLER,
Letters to Emil

A SEPARATE CHAPTER. When Alex Small mused in the Paris *Tribune* in 1934 about a future "separate chapter" on Paris-American journalism, he presumably had in mind a factual account—a full, wide-ranging work of research and recollection of the sort he might well have turned out himself. But most of his fellow journalists of the interwar years, if they gave thought to their work as subject matter, seemed more likely to recast it as imaginative writing. In plotting to escape news work for the literary life they typically meant to follow Hemingway's way: through stories and novels rather than the sober plodding of fact writing. That sort of sturdy work—in memoirs, autobiographies, histories—could come later if at all.

As it happened, few ink-stained exiles carried on with the pursuit of fiction, let alone drew in stories and novels on their experiences as Paris-American journalists. Most seem to have reluctantly

[253]

traced the career of James Thurber after he joined the Paris *Tribune* in 1925 following his unsuccessful bout of fiction writing in a Normandy farmhouse: "It didn't work out because I got tired of the characters at the end of five thousand words, and bade them and novel-writing farewell forever." The exiles who eventually turned their hand to broad accounts of their Paris days mostly did so in factual recollections—and insofar as attempts were made at Small's separate chapter, they were largely here, in varied works by Samuel Putnam, Al Laney, Eric Hawkins, Harold Stearns, Waverley Root, Harold Ettlinger, and others.

Still, it remains true—as noted in the prologue—that two enduring novels of the expatriate period, Hemingway's *The Sun Also Rises* and Henry Miller's *Tropic of Cancer*, came from Paris journalists who in their fiction made use of their working days. Another pair of journalists who did, Ned Calmer in a central way and Elliot Paul only marginally, shared with Miller the connection of once laboring as Small's colleagues on the *Tribune*. The books the three produced, however, could hardly have been more unlike in manner and public reception. Placed together, the Paris accounts of Miller, Calmer, and Paul take up narrow space on the unburdened shelf of renderings of the life and times of expatriate journalism. They afford nonetheless a glimple—in the favored form of fiction or, with Paul, near-fiction—into Paris days as journalists themselves chose to treat them. They comprise the imagination's modest contribution to Small's separate chapter.

The same year Alex Small's remarks appeared in the *Tribune*, Henry Miller put his newspaper work on prominent display in *Tropic of Cancer*, the bawdy, then-scandalous autobiographical novel published in Paris by Obelisk Press in an edition of some one thousand copies. Miller's period as a *Tribune* proofreader and occasional freelance contributor was brief and attracted little notice from other newsmen. But as George Wickes observed in *Americans in Paris*, "the impressions of that time remained among the most vivid of his Paris years." Transferred to the novel, the impressions gave Miller characters and actions that occupied a central place in the book's onrushing sections—and, through emphatic contrast with fellow proofreader Wambly Bald, helped define his fictional persona as a down-and-out American who in expatriate Paris wrote his way to happiness and art.

While newspaper work in *Tropic of Cancer* is part of the story, in Ned Calmer's *All the Summer Days* it is the whole story. The novel had its germ in a short story, "Paris Interlude," published the same year as Miller's novel. After Calmer's slight, humorous yarn about a fictional newspaper called the *Paris American* appeared in Whit Burnett and Martha Foley's *STORY* magazine (under the name he then used, Edgar Calmer), nearly three decades passed before it reemerged as a full-blown realistic novel about the paper. Unlike *Tropic of Cancer*, which after its unheralded Paris beginning went on to lasting life and critical respect, *All the Summer Days* remained an entertaining minor novel yet one with the distinction of providing the most detailed portrait of Paris-American journalism in fiction.

Of all Paris journalists, Elliot Paul seemed the most likely candidate to write such a fictional portrait. The expatriate journalist, biographer, and editor Samuel Putnam even thought he could have been "the historian of the exile decade" had he wished. Certainly Paul had the background for a big Paris book of whatever type: work on the *Tribune* and *Herald*; editing of *transition*; wide and varied acquaintance with writers and artists; and the fact he was a published writer before arriving in Paris. The little he actually wrote about Paris days in fiction, however, had virtually nothing to do with Paris-American journalism. And what became in 1942 his major Paris work, *The Last Time I Saw Paris*, a memoir that leaned heavily in the direction of imaginative writing, had only slightly more to say about journalism while offering a highly private account of the exile experience. In his fiction and near-fiction about Paris, what Paul wrote—as Putnam said about his memoir—were unusual and charming stories that, as he might well have intended, confounded expectations.

Ultimately, *The Last Time I Saw Paris* had a fate that must have confounded Paul as well. The book sold well, got generally good reviews, and film rights were sold to Hollywood. But only the book's title made it to the screen, tacked on to a 1954 Van Johnson–Elizabeth Taylor film loosely based on Scott Fitzgerald's classic story of expatriate remorse, "Babylon Revisited." In the film, Fitzgerald's contrite businessman, Charlie Wales, becomes a former *Stars and Stripes* journalist now working with a news agency.

(Kay Boyle's review in the *Nation* was a scathing exception to the favorable reception of Paul's book—and given its film future, a telling one in its reference to Paul's "Hollywood conception" of Parisian life. Boyle applauded Paul's decision to present a French rather than American Paris—and refrain from tired anecdotes about Joyce, Hemingway, Picasso, and Gertrude Stein—but found the book as a whole "careless and touristic." Despite affection for his lengthy cast of characters, she thought Paul sketched them in the manner of a "clever make-up man, and their true substance has nowhere been set down." The result was a "Hollywood conception of a typical little-street-in-Paris scene," the characters "so picturesque and so quaint that they end by being grotesque.")

ON THE EDGE OF THINGS. Henry Miller marked his start as a genuine writer with a short story about a prostitute that Samuel Putnam accepted for publication in his Paris-based *New Review*—and Peter Neagoe reprinted in his anthology *Americans Abroad* together with work by Hemingway, Pound, and Dos Passos. Putnam had come to Paris in 1927 following study at the University of Chicago, various newspaper jobs in the city, and work writing art and literary criticism for the *Chicago Evening Post*. The latter caught the eye of H. L. Mencken, who suggested an article on the fading of the city's once-bright literary renaissance. The outraged local feeling that followed the appearance of Putnam's "Chicago: An Obituary" in the *American Mercury* of August 1926 brought to the *Evening Post* one day Henry Blake Fuller, the old and distinguished author of *The Cliff-Dwellers*, *With the Procession*, and other Chicago novels. "I have been following you," Fuller informed Putnam, "and I've come to offer you some unasked-for advice. I think I know what is troubling you, and my advice is: Go to Paris, young man, go to Paris. You may have to come back as I did, but at least. . . ."

Putnam took the advice when the publisher Pascal Covici agreed to underwrite a study of Rabelais. In Paris with his wife and child, Putnam ground out the rest of his living with an art letter for the *Chicago Daily News* and a weekly letter for the *New York Sun*. Eventually he made his scholarly mark with the Rabelais biography and gained literary standing as associate editor of Edward Titus's *This Quarter* and subsequently founder of the *New Review*, a journal that in its editorial statement said its purpose was to provide "international *reportage* for the arts, the higher journalism of ideas."

Before accepting a short article on the filmmaker Luis Buñuel and then "Mademoiselle Claude" for his journal, Putnam had given little thought to Miller as a writer. The thin, balding, late-expatriate at age thirty-nine seemed to him "merely someone on the edge of things. Very few suspected that he was interested in writing, much less that he himself wrote." What was known was that Miller worked nights as a proofreader for the Paris *Tribune* and, the paper put to bed, held forth at various Montparnasse drinking spots on his view of life. "Briefly stated," said Putnam, "it was to the effect that prostitutes are about the only pure beings to be found in a world of reeking garbage." Occasionally someone would mutter in weary response, "For Christ's sake, Hank, why don't you write a book? It ought to be a goddamned classic, or maybe even a best-seller."

Putnam's view of Miller changed dramatically after he saw "Mademoiselle Claude." He not only included the story in the third number of the *New Review* but left the entire issue for Miller and fellow *Tribune* proofreader Alfred Perlès to see through the press while he was away on a trip to New York. Miller and Perlès used the opportunity to revamp the issue, replacing accepted work with material of their own, thwarted only—in Putnam's version of what took place—when his wife discovered the changes and salvaged the issue, including Miller's story (and, whether from Putnam's hand or from Miller-Perlès, fiction by Perlès, Wambly Bald, and James T. Farrell; a poem by Samuel Beckett; a photo of a painting by Don Brown, a Paris *Tribune* artist and reporter; and an article by Robert L. Stern, at the time city editor of the *Tribune*). Putnam later passed off the incident as merely *pour le sport*. As an episode in *Tropic of Cancer*, it became an occasion for characteristic raw humor, with the editor the hapless victim.

Putnam appears in the novel as Marlowe, a drunken scholar, translator, and review editor encountered at the Dôme. Despite his ability to read Old French and his fine translations, even the local prostitutes fail to understand his spoken French. When time comes to pay for drinks, Marlowe has varied strategies of avoiding the bill, and when Carl (Alfred Perlès) calls him on them, he counters with catty gossip about Carl losing his proofreading job. After they leave the bar together, Marlowe, "touched now by Carl's helplessness" at the thought of being out of work, asks Carl and Miller to take over his review while he is away. When Marlowe falls into inebriated sleep, there is a get-even exchange between Carl and Miller:

"Listen, Joe [Miller], we'll take him up on it. We'll take his lousy review over and we'll fuck him good and proper."

"What do you mean by that?"

"Why we'll throw out all the other contributors and we'll fill it with our own shit—that's what!"

"Yeah, but what kind of shit?"

"Any kind . . . he won't be able to do anything about it. We'll fuck him good and proper. One good number and after that the magazine'll be finished. Are you game, Joe?"

PUNCTUATE THE CALAMITIES. Marlowe is a passing figure in the novel. Central to the book are the trio of companions Miller recreated from his *Tribune* days—Miller himself as Miller, Alfred Perlès as Carl, Wambly Bald as Van Norden—and the talk and adventures following their nightly shifts on the paper. Miller's fictional *Tribune* job has its beginning one evening at the Coupole in the company of Van Norden when the pair learn from a drunken newspaperman ("one of the upstairs guys" on the editorial staff) that a proofreader, an Englishman named Peckover, has fallen down the elevator shaft and is not expected to live. "There's only one good aspect to it," Van Norden tells Miller. "You may get his job. And if you have any luck, maybe you'll fall down the elevator shaft and break your neck too. We'll buy you a nice wreath, I promise you that."

Miller does in fact land the proofreading job after Peckover's death ("After sucking the boss's ass for a whole week—it's the thing to do here. . . .") and finds the downstairs work surprisingly satisfying. The "slick guys upstairs" send down reports of the "hard facts of life"—"no joy, no misery passes unnoticed"—and all he is required to do is "punctuate the calamities." The work is even therapeutic. Under the avalanche of news he feels inoculated from catastrophe, absolutely secure:

> Seated at my little niche all the poisons which the world gives
> off each day pass through my hands. Not even a fingernail
> gets stained. I am absolutely immune. I am even better off
> than a laboratory attendant, because there are no bad odors
> here, just the smell of lead burning. The world can blow up—
> I'll be here just the same to put in a comma or a semicolon. I
> may even touch a little overtime, for with an event like that
> there's bound to be a final edition.

Miller's contentment baffles his fellow basement workers. They have pride and ambition while he insists he has neither, and so is able to relish work in which all that matters is getting the words spelled right. His pleasure in finding such a comforting occupation seems, even to him, incredible: "How could I have foreseen, in America, with all those firecrackers they put up your ass to give you

pep and courage, that the ideal position for a man of my tempera-
ment was to look for orthographic mistakes?" Among the perplexed
proofreaders are Carl and Van Norden, who each night Miller
instructs—in one of the book's bravura passages—about work that
even has about it aspects of a new religion:

> A world without hope, but no despair. It's as though I had
> been converted to a new religion, as though I were making an
> annual novena every night to Our Lady of Solace. I can't
> imagine what there would be to gain if I were made editor of
> the paper, or even President of the United States. I'm up a
> blind alley, and it's cosy and comfortable. With a piece of
> copy in my hand I listen to the music around me, the hum
> and drone of voices, the tinkle of the linotype machines, as if
> there were a thousand silver bracelets passing through a
> wringer; now and then a rat scurries past our feet or a
> cockroach descends the wall in front of us, moving gingerly
> on his delicate legs. The events of the day are slid under your
> nose, quietly, unostentatiously, with, now and then, a by-line
> to mark the presence of a human hand, an ego, a touch of
> vanity. The procession passes serenely, like a cortege entering
> the cemetery gates. The paper under the copy desk is so thick
> that it almost feels like a carpet with a soft nap. Under Van
> Norden's desk it is stained with brown juice. Around eleven
> o'clock the peanut vendor arrives, a half-wit of an Armenian
> who is also content with his lot in life.

Satisfying though it is, the proofreading job requires concentration, and Miller has to cut down on his alcohol intake since "it's
hard to read proof when you're not all there." He allows that "you
can be brilliant sometimes, when you're drunk, but brilliance is out
of place in the proofreading department." As a result, he has to keep
his intellectual light hid beneath a bushel. A letter from "one of the
big moguls upstairs" remarks sarcastically on his intelligence and
hints he must toe the line in his lowly place as a proofreader. There-

after he rarely speaks a polysyllabic word and plays the "high-grade moron, which is what they wanted of us." He even flatters his boss by now and then inquiring about the meaning of a word:

> He liked that. He was a sort of dictionary and timetable, that guy. No matter how much beer he guzzled during the break— and he made his own private breaks too, seeing as how he was running the show—you could never trip him up on a date or a definition. He was born to the job.

Still, Miller cannot entirely hide from the boss the fact that he knows too much: "It leaked out now and then, despite all the pre-cautions I took."

Work finished, Miller, Carl, and Van Norden walk from the Right Bank newspaper office to Montparnasse, and their early-morning talk leads to a digression about Monsieur Paul's, Miller's name for Gillotte's as "the *bistro* across the way" from the *Tribune* office. Here a backroom is reserved for newsmen who eat on credit:

> It is a pleasant little room with sawdust on the floor and flies in season and out. When I say that it is reserved for the newspapermen I don't mean to imply that we eat in privacy; on the contrary, it means that we have the privilege of associating with the whores and pimps who form the more substantial element of Monsieur Paul's clientele.

The association, adds Miller, suits the men from the paper well enough since they are always on the lookout for girls, yet it leaves them appearing miserable when they must sit beside a pimp who, "despite the little hardships of his profession, lives a life of luxury by comparison" with their own.

The digression—a recurring mode in a work given over, as Anaïs Nin wrote in a preface to the novel's first edition, to the "pure flux and rotation of events" with only "an obedience to flow"—leads to reflection on the varieties of Parisian pimps and prostitutes and, at length, praise for the vivid, old-fashioned art of Matisse that evokes "the pastoral days of wine and fornication": "Even as the world falls apart the Paris that belongs to Matisse shudders with bright, grasping orgasms, the air itself is steady with stagnant sperm, the trees tangled like hair."

THE ANTI-ARTIST. Matisse is the life-affirming artist who takes full advantage of the grand display of Paris. Van Norden is his opposite, the anti-artist, a jaded newsman for whom everything is invariably wrong: "No matter what he does or where he goes things are out of joint. Either it's the fucking country or the fucking job, or else it's some fucking cunt who's put him on the blink." Van Norden's soliloquies on the walks home are obsessively about sexual conquest, at which he is accomplished yet dissatisfied. The sex is mechanical, devoid of human passion. Miller provides an analogy with newspaper production: sex for Van Norden is "like a machine throwing out newspapers, millions and billions of them every day, and the front page is loaded with catastrophes, with riots, murders, explosions, collisions, but he doesn't feel anything."

His life narrowed rather than extended by Paris, Van Norden is unable to begin the big book he says he wants to write. The book must be absolutely original, so he reads one author after another yet has scorn for what they accomplished: "And forgetting completely that he has not written as much as a chapter he talks about them condescendingly, quite as though there existed a shelf of books bearing his name, books which everyone is familiar with and the titles of which it is therefore superfluous to mention."

Van Norden is his fellow proofreader and nightly companion, but the Miller of *Tropic of Cancer* is linked with Matisse as an authentic artist. While Van Norden is locked within ("He has only to say 'my book' and immediately the world shrinks to the private dimensions of Van Norden and Co."), unable to begin his great work, Miller faces outward, a Whitmanesque singer embracing the "cancer of time," a writer who actually writes. On his book's opening page he declares himself "the happiest man alive" since "a year ago, six months ago, I thought that I was an artist. I no longer think about it, I *am*."

(Alfred Perlès was content enough with his treatment in the novel to, two decades after its appearance, publish a book about his enduring friendship with Miller. Wambly Bald, not surprisingly, held a long grudge. He insisted he invented raw sexual episodes just to shock Miller and had no idea they would turn up in his book. "It took me years to stop hating Henry Miller for what he wrote about me as Van Norden," he said in 1974. "But, what the hell? I now bow to his storytelling genius." Miller, the novel written but not yet published, held to his portrayal of Bald. "Glad I did him up brown in the book," he said in a letter. "He's a real character, uninteresting as a human being—just a *character*. If that guy could ever bring himself to write, what a book he would give!")

GENEROUS SOULS. As Miller has it in *Tropic of Cancer*, his proof-reading job ends not from his intelligence leaking out but from a skinflint business decision. "One of the big muck-a-mucks from the other side of the water had decided to make economies," and Miller is one of the staff members let go. (Later, after anonymous hack writing and a grim teaching episode in Dijon, Miller learns from Carl of an upstairs vacancy and returns to the paper, though in the book nothing is related about the new job.) Back on the street again, his prospects are not, as far as meals go, overly bleak. Around Montparnasse he can still pretend he is working, making it easier to bum meals, and at Monsieur Paul's his credit holds for a week or two. Also he is skilled at leaning on friends.

In a letter while working on *Tropic of Cancer*, Miller reported that "the food problem I've solved fairly well. I get a warm meal every night by rotating among my friends. Fred [Alfred Perlès] gives me breakfast about three in the afternoon. Cigarettes come as a matter of course. But a room! Shit, there's the rub!" Moved to the novel, the scheme begins with Miller writing letters to a dozen friends: "Would you let me have dinner with you once a week? Tell me what day is most convenient for you?" As it turns out, the letters "worked like a charm. I was not only fed . . . I was feasted. Every night I went home drunk. They couldn't do enough for me, these generous once-a-week souls." Such is his long-term success in lining up food and drink that he can cross off old hosts from the list in favor of new and better ones.

In actuality, among the generous souls with meals were Ned Calmer and his wife. "Ned Calmer has a baby," said Miller in the letter about the couple's inability to likewise assist with his room problem, "and besides the maid wants a place to sleep." Later, a friendship with Hemingway cast Ned Calmer on the receiving end of generosity. In Paris following his African safari recounted in *Green Hills of Africa*, Hemingway met and liked the young newspaperman who had a first novel, *Beyond the Street*, about to appear from Harcourt, Brace. Hemingway served as godfather for the baptism of the Calmers' daughter and following the ceremony hosted a family lunch. When he learned Calmer could not afford ship fare to New York for his book's publication, he wrote a check for $350 that provided passage for the family. Two years later, when Calmer wrote about repaying what he considered a loan, Hemingway told him to consider it a gift and offered to send more funds if needed.

WHEN PARIS WAS PARIS. Ned Calmer had come to Paris from the University of Virginia in 1927, caught on as a *Tribune* reporter, contributed to early issues of *transition*, and later moved over to the *Herald*. After his American return in 1934 for his novel's publication, he took a job in New York as an editor with the French news service Havas. Eventually he turned to a career in broadcasting with CBS news in New York, and during World War II was a member of Edward R. Murrow's dashing team of European correspondents.

Throughout his years as a broadcaster, which ended with his retirement in 1967, Calmer continued to write and publish fiction.

In "Paris Interlude," Calmer's early use of Paris-American journalism as fictional material, a reporter, John Hagen, comes to Paris in 1925—a time "when Paris was Paris and not the other end of the longest gangway in the world"—and is hired by the *Paris American*. (A Paris paper called the *American* had been an early and brief competitor of James Gordon Bennett's *Herald*.) His short, happy career on the paper lasts just fourteen days but long enough for Hagen to weave a legendary trail of alcoholic ineptitude. The culmination comes when he writes an account of the Prince of Wales beating a boy's brains out during a visit to an orphanage outside Paris and the story, evading copy editors and proofreaders, appears in print.

Obviously modeled on the much-recalled career of Spencer Bull of *Tribune* and *Herald* notoriety, Hagen failed to reappear as a character when Calmer returned for his fourth novel to the *Paris American* in *All the Summer Days* in 1961, though the mischievous tale about the prince did. And again the paper, an amalgam of the *Tribune* and *Herald*, is center stage as the workplace that brings together the story's main figures. A listing of eighteen of them at the start is a breakdown of the paper's entire staff, running from the publisher and managing editor to reporters, copyreaders, rewrite men, various editors, and a copy boy.

In a brief prologue, the narrator, Alex Gardner, now an instructor in political science at an American college, returns to the postwar Paris he originally came to in 1925 and the paper he worked on as a proofreader and copyreader. In the office there is dim memory of him as one of the paper's old-timers. A staff member still with the paper who knew him well, Glenn Perry, happens to be away on assignment.

With this, the novel switches in a sustained flashback to the summer of 1927 and Gardner's recollection of Perry's arrival in Paris, fresh from a newspaper job in Cincinnati and eager for a position on the *Paris American*. Perry's first sight of the office, with workers crammed together getting out the eight-page paper, fires his enthusiasm all the more. Although the paper itself is mediocre at best—the toy of a Pittsburgh millionaire looking for international prestige, it consistently loses money but continues to appear six days a week to a regular readership of 25,000—it provides the means for living in Paris. "Radiantly drunk" with the city, Perry draws Alex Gardner's memory back to his own innocent days of arrival before he wearied of both the paper and Paris.

The *Paris American* employs two types of newspapermen, says Gardner, who equally pay "as little attention to the job as possible. Who cared about the daily news? Politicians were fools, economics a bore. And a boss was meant to be laughed at or ignored." One lot are transients who "come abroad on a lark, pick up a job for a meal ticket, stay a year or so, and then go back. And call themselves *Paris American* men forever after." The other is a small, hard-core group who "came and stayed, for one reason or other, by accident, out of some necessity in themselves, or whatever."

The story's main characters are hard-core types. Roger Austin, who joined the staff after ambulance service in World War I, is a pipe-smoking music lover who reviews the arts, writes a column of Latin Quarter notes, and seems wise and cosmopolitan. When Gardner came to the paper, Austin was the man he modeled himself on. Don Holmes, among the would-be novelists on the staff, left the *Brooklyn Eagle* to write a novel after well-regarded publications in the *Dial* and *transatlantic review*. Ware Kendall, the paper's attractive society editor by way of Vassar, tries to hide her poetry writing from the staff while frustrating them with her sexual indifference. The puzzled Gardner remarks that the unlikely "fact appeared to be that, Paris or no Paris, Ware Kendall was a virgin, and determined to stay that way."

The characters are set in motion in three main locales: the newspaper office, the café, the hotel. The office is a dingy second-floor room with copyreaders around the rim of a central table and reporters and rewrite men at desks on either side. The décor is mostly battered typewriters, empty beer bottles, and cigarette butts. On the street level below is the composing room, and in the basement the ancient presses which, running at night, shake the building like the engine room of a steamer. La Vieille's is the staff hangout, providing food, drink, and fortnightly credit, "as essential to life as the city room and the hotel." A new recruit on the paper is informed that the place is exactly "twenty-nine steps in a straight lines from the front door" of the *Paris American*—"a few more if you have to be assisted by some kind friend." The Edmond Rostand et d'Auvergne, a hotel first inhabited by Roger Austin, shelters nearly the entire staff and provides a measure of concealment for sexual liaisons.

Historical events are drawn into the story—coverage of Lindbergh's landing provides the most hectic days anyone on the news staff can remember, with the crash landing of Richard E. Byrd's plane in the Normandy surf a close second—and there are Paris sightings of Elliot Paul, Harold Stearns, Eugene Jolas, and Ernest Hemingway, the last said to have the look of a bashful college boy. Within the office the reporter Spencer Adams is an enthusiastic journalist with the dogged style of Ralph Barnes of the *Herald*. Another reporter, Harry Fullerton, is a tireless womanizer in the mold (as cast by Henry Miller) of the *Tribune*'s Wambly Bald. The publisher, Henry Potter, gained his position in the fortuitous manner of the *Herald*'s Laurence Hills and oversees the *Paris American* in the same tightfisted manner.

A rumor the money-losing paper will shut down causes panic in the office and prompts Spencer Adams to lecture staff members on their journalistic failings:

> "What are you all worrying about? It would do you good to
> be fired, every one of you. You've all had it too easy. Now
> you'll have to get jobs on real newspapers somewhere else. . . .
> The *Paris American* has been dying for years. It's doubtful if it
> ever lived. It was never worth anything. None of the foreign

papers in Paris is worth anything. It's been a lazy living, that's all, and now it comes to an end. . . . Not one of you is worth any more than this paper you've been working on. No wonder it's no good. The men who make it don't care a snap about anything or anybody in the world. You're all a lost generation. Gertrude Stein said it."

The paper survives the scare, and the staff return to the routines of work and after-hours revels that Adams succinctly summarizes: "All any of you live by is eating, drinking and sex."

Adams is presented as naive and censorious, yet his portrayal of both the newspaper and the staff is essentially the narrator's as well. A new copyreader, Gilmore, stoutly defends the paper—and Paris—but immediately undercuts the defense in a way that confirms Adams's indictment:

"I like Paris. Paris is lovely. And the longer I stay the better I like it. What's wrong with Paris? The *American*'s all right, too. In fact I might go so far as to say you guys are the best bunch I ever worked with. But even if you weren't I'd stay on as long as Ben [the paper's managing editor] let me. You want to know why? It isn't the easy work, or the grub. . . . But the big thing, boys, and I don't care who knows it, is I've got my French girl."

The paper has only infrequent moments of journalistic zeal and manifests scant interest in Parisian literary and artistic life. Notable cultural figures are largely objects of satire. When Alex Gardner sees the *transition* crowd at the Dôme, he notes Eugene Jolas is among them, "proclaiming the Revolution of the Word in three languages—speaking all three poorly." Ezra Pound is said to "chant praises of himself."

As for Paris as a creative stimulus, there is little it provides the staff beyond abundant opportunity for indulging in Adams's trilogy of eating, drinking, and sex. Don Holmes, the promising writer, sinks to writing pornography for added money, is hospitalized with acute alcoholism, and eventually is sent back to New York by the American Aid Society. Roger Austin cruelly abandons a woman who has come to love him, Don Holmes's former wife Sarah—his apparent inner calm and self-sufficiency now understood by the narrator as selfishness—and withdraws from his colleagues and from Paris. Austin remains in the city during World War II and ends his days as a reclusive figure with a minor job in the American Library. Only the poetess, Ware Kendall, sustains her literary dreams by eventually publishing four novels.

WILLFUL KIDS. In the novel's brief epilogue Ned Calmer extends Spencer Adams's indictment of the *Paris American* to a sober—and, from the angle of the becalmed, self-satisfied early 1960s of his novel's period of publication, familiar—assessment of the expatriate period generally. Glenn Perry, reunited with Alex Gardner, says the paper's present staff is now colorless but made up of "responsible newspapermen." He has become one himself, as Gardner has become a "responsible teacher." The expatriate past now stands in opposition as a period of reckless irresponsibility, or as Gardner reflects, a time in which they were all "willful kids" with a "self-conscious amorality thinly overlaid on the hidden Protestant American conscience. The general reliance on alcohol to sidestep the problem of life. The promiscuity of it all . . . and how the confluence of time and place proved disastrous to so many of us." In the novel's closing scene, the irresponsible past is laid to rest with an even heavier hand when Perry meets Sarah, the unfortunate woman abandoned by Don Holmes and Roger Austin but now agreeably married to Alex Gardner.

In the sharply differing mood of their endings, *All the Summer Days* recalls Scott Fitzgerald's "Babylon Revisited," published thirty years earlier. In the story Charlie Wales, now a somber and solvent widower, returns to Paris to reclaim the young daughter he loves, but when his wild years in the city accidentally resurface his unfor-giving sister-in-law and her husband refuse to grant him custody. At the end Charlie tries to convince himself that "they couldn't make him pay forever"; certainly his dead wife "wouldn't have wanted him to be so alone." Yet this surely is his fate. Changed though he may be, what happened in Paris will haunt his lonely future. At the end of *All the Summer Days*, on the other hand, nothing about the Parisian past endures save for the briefly rekindled friendship be-tween Alex Gardner and Glenn Perry, united in rejection of a time now understood as reckless summer indulgence. That easily, with-out hint of ambivalence, Paris is wiped away and Gardner, devoted wife at his side, is assured of future bliss.

(The final assessment of the expatriate experience by his fic-tional characters was not Ned Calmer's last word on the subject. In 1979, nearly two decades after the publication of *All the Summer Days*, he recreated in a nostalgic journal article about Elliot Paul his own introduction to Paris-American newspaper work—a moment suffused with the same golden glow that enveloped Glenn Perry's first view of *Paris American* men at work:

> I was standing in the door to the city room, looking inside as
> though I'd just discovered the kingdom of heaven on earth
> and was having my first sight of the Lord's most favored
> creatures. There were a dozen of them in a tiny, crowded
> space, loud with talk and typewriters, and they were busy
> getting out the little eight-page daily that gave them their
> chance to live in Paris in the Nineteen Twenties. Nothing
> much was going on in the world that long-ago May evening.
> . . . But to the enchanted man in the doorway, these people
> could have been putting together the news story of the
> century.

Over the newsroom hung a cloud of illuminated smoke like that above a boxing ring. Beneath were copyreaders around a big table and rewrite men and reporters at desks on either side:

Several had their hats on. The thinnest sported a pair of cowboy boots, the fattest a loud jacket. Two wore beards. And one of them was Elliot Paul. At that moment he happened to look up, guessed me at once for the newspaperman I longed above all else to be, and gave me his gentle satyr's smile of understanding and encouragement. It was the beginning of a 30-year relationship of master and student.)

THE ORDINARY FRENCH. *A Narrow Street*, the unadorned British title of Elliot Paul's Paris memoir (with an opening chapter called "A Narrow Street at Dawn"), is a vastly better fit than *The Last Time I Saw Paris*, the sentimental lines lifted from the Jerome Kern–Oscar Hammerstein tune. What Paul celebrates is not the nostalgic Paris of visiting or expatriate Americans implied in the American title but, quite literally, a confined passageway of the ordinary French. Adam Gopnik, in a contemporary anthology of Paris-American writing, remarks that the Lost Generation was not lost enough in that it was always clear where its members were: "at a bar, alongside other Americans." Joseph Freeman, a Paris *Tribune* staff member at the start of the twenties, observed of his fellow newsmen's myopic ways that "we saw France, Europe, the world through the newspapers which we read and rehashed. It was hackwork, the symbol of which was our boss Floyd Gibbons who, after years in Paris, could not read French." Elliot Paul spent his share of time bending elbows with his countrymen and engaged at newspaper hackwork, but, a rarity in the Paris-American colony, he also knew well and cared deeply for the city of the French.

Paul's memoir has its roots, however, in a curious five-year departure from Paris. Samuel Putnam, as a first, exploratory step to his return to America, had joined in a journey of Paris-weary fellow expatriates to literary and artistic hideaways either "somewhere in the provinces" of France or in more distant "runaway" colonies. Paul may have been looking for a similar retreat when he vanished from his job on the Paris *Herald* late in 1931 and turned up in the village of Santa Eulalia del Rio on the Spanish island of Ibiza. Paris friends were familiar with his penchant for sudden departures—"he had an element not of mystery," Gertrude Stein said of him, "but of evanescence"—but this most recent one came at an odd time. Since leaving his editorial work with *transition* and joining the *Herald*, Paul had experienced a productive period of fiction writing, turning out two novels and a pair of novellas in a space of two years. This departure, moreover, would take him farther afield and last longer than usual.

To Robert Sage, a co-worker both on the *Tribune* and *Herald* as well as *transition*, Paul was a gregarious figure, "rotund and be-whiskered and as mischievous as a Katzenjammer Kid," quick to entertain with accordion or piano and lead forays to favorite bars and restaurants. Maria Jolas, who worked closely with Paul in the early days of *transition*, said that, "with ready laughter and ready wit . . . his presence added zest to any gathering." To Waverley Root, Paul was an "easygoing, well-mannered extrovert" who "made an avuncular impression—imperturbable, blessed with a quiet sense of humor, a man who never seemed to lose his temper." Nonetheless, one close observer of Paul's career suggests his Spanish sojourn was prompted by a breakdown caused by severe depression and an accompanying bout of writer's block.

Paul remained on Ibiza until 1936, publishing nothing and apparently writing little but undergoing what he called "the most soul-stirring adventure of my disorderly life." With Nationalist troops advancing on the Republican-controlled island at the start of the Spanish Civil War, he fled with his wife and son, and thereafter, living between France and America, rapidly produced in *The Life and Death of a Spanish Town* a report of his Ibiza days. For the rest of his life, which included in the forties time as a Hollywood screenwriter, work flowed regularly from Paul's typewriter. At the time of his death in Providence, Rhode Island, in 1958 he had published some thirty books.

ISLAND WAR. In his first work of nonfiction—meaning a blend of memory and reporting overlaid with invention—Paul developed the manner he would use when he turned to his Paris material. The opening sets the purpose and tone of the book: he will show how the coming of the Spanish war shattered the peaceful world of the inhabitants of Santa Eulalia, whose lives he had shared on intimate terms. He will write of them objectively yet with open affection and a measure of guilt for having left them behind:

> I loved them and their animals and the shadows of the trees
> that fell upon their houses. They divided their last pesetas and
> red wine and beans and gay spirit with me. I got away, and
> they did not. Their land is dying. Mine is not. This book is a
> debt I owe them.

Structurally the book comes in two nearly equal parts, the first given over to the villagers and the measured pace of village life— with end papers providing a sketch of the town with buildings identified and a frontispiece listing characters—the second to a detailed account of the coming of war to the island over a brief period from July 14 to September 15, 1936.

The opening section is vividly personal, yet Paul himself is a shadowy presence. He has come to the village "to find tranquillity," but beyond this the reader learns little about him beyond his ability as a musician who plays the accordion and piano in a small orchestra performing at village functions. In the latter section, when he returns to the island with a new wife and her five-year-old son, he mentions he has passed through Paris, where a few newspaper friends suspected trouble might be awaiting him in Spain but had not mentioned it, erroneously assuming he was already aware of the threat. One of them, Dick Glenn of the *Herald*, is singled out as equally in the dark and planning on spending his vacation with Paul in Santa Eulalia.

Paul's newspaper connection surfaces again following an impromptu welcome-back party in which he is both guest of honor and orchestra leader, and the village exhausts its supply of fireworks in celebration. The gaiety is short-lived. When airplanes drop newspapers from Valencia on Ibiza, Paul reads a copy carefully and concludes it carries crude propaganda for the Republican cause. His friends among the Republicans are jubilant and he does nothing to discourage them despite, "having worked in print factories where similar bilge had been manufactured (with special reference to the *New York Herald* in Paris), I was discouraged and depressed." Shortly thereafter he plays the *Marseillaise* in a joyous street march while, certain the situation is in fact worsening for the Republican cause, feeling "as if I was at the throttle of some huge engine in a dream."

When a German destroyer appears in the harbor, Paul requests passage as a neutral, and he and his wife and son are taken on board. In a brief postscript, dated June 14, 1937, he tells of the developing war, with Nationalist planes bombing the port towns of the island, and of his inability to get news of friends left behind. The book ends on a note of rhetorical defiance in the face of otherwise bitter loss: "It was a privilege to be associated with such courageous, high-minded men and women, and their enemies will do well to be afraid of them as long as they are above ground."

Helped along by a surge of American interest in the Spanish war, *The Life and Death of a Spanish Town* became Paul's first commercial success. He would not immediately, however, return to its winning formula. His next books were a pair of traditional novels followed in 1939 by an eccentric mystery novel, a first venture in genre fiction and a first use of Paris material. Paul later located the origin of the novel in his response to Spanish refugees streaming across the border into France—a shameful sight from which "your author turned his head away. He was ten days in an alcohol tomb in the legendary city called Rouen, and when born again with something or other missing he started tapping self-defensively a tale called *The Mysterious Mickey Finn*."

THE GREAT LOAFER. Paul's sleuth in the tale, the Montparnasse lounger Homer Evans, is a man of several parts—handsome, well off, and skilled at writing and painting, yet after publishing a short monograph and painting one portrait he has disdained the pursuit of either form. Of the arts, music interests him most, and he spends each January and February in Morocco attending to Arab musicians playing their repetitive melodies, thereafter returning to Paris for the remainder of the concert season. Although Homer Evans strains the imagination, as does the plot Paul puts him through, Samuel Putnam pointed out his basis in a real Parisian figure, Homer Bevans, who had been an engineer, a flautist with the New York Philharmonic, and a sculptor before concentrating with lasting attention on his highball glass. (In his text to an 1947 book of Paris photographs by Fritz Henle, Paul relates a story that involves breakfasting one morning on the terrace of the Closerie des Lilas in the company of Homer Bevans and the writer Hendrik Willem Van Loon.)

Wambly Bald, in his "The Left-Over Bank" column for *The Boulevardier* magazine in December 1931, reported Bevans's return home after eight expatriate years and added a lighthearted tribute to the sculptor "whose work no one had ever seen":

> The moral tone of the colony receives another shock with the
> news that Homer Bevans has gone back to America. More
> than one element here will miss the phlegmatic giant whose
> wit and genuine insouciance have won for him the coveted
> distinction of being known as 'The dean of the exiles.'

Described by Bald as a huge, bland figure with melancholy eyes and a thick mustache who dressed in black and typically was seen wandering in and out of favorite bars, Bevans "seldom said anything, but when he did it was worth remembering. Homer could set a whole bar on fire with a spontaneous crack that seldom failed to merit the envy of the higher brows."

Samuel Putnam's view was darker: Bevans was among Montparnasse's tragic characters, a fine life wasted. In Elliot Paul's hands as Homer Evans he is merely a charming oddity and purposeful idler. He contentedly identifies himself to his slow-to-develop love interest, Miriam Leonard, an earnest young schoolteacher from Montana, as "the great loafer":

> "That's what I want to be. I have written a book and painted a portrait, only to prove to myself that I don't have to loaf if I don't want to. But that's what I want to do. I like it. I hate activity and bustle. I don't want to carry on the torch of civilization."

The story's setting, Paul announces in an author's note, is Montparnasse "in the heyday of the American occupation . . . in the postwar years." He makes background use of beloved personal haunts, and famous figures of his acquaintance come on stage for token appearances, as in one particularly witty passage:

> James Joyce was making the sixth revision of page two thousand and forty of his *magnum opus* called "Work in Progress"; Harold Stearns was sitting at the Sélect bar, murmuring that murders were unusual, therefore banal, consequently uninteresting; Gertrude Stein and Alice Toklas were drinking brandy and soda, Gertrude the brandy and Alice the soda; Ernest Hemingway was in the Bois thinking what he would do if the Bois was Wyoming, the swans were wild ducks, and he had a gun.

In another passage Harold Stearns is seen in a bar "drinking with the usual appropriate seriousness and thinking about the Atlantic Ocean because it was between him and prohibition in the United States." Apart from the references to Hemingway and Stearns, Paris-American journalism is represented only by an invented Paris *Herald* reporter, Tom Jackson, who at one point explains to Evans that he was assigned to cover a banquet of French artists despite knowing less about painting than anyone in the office because "if there's a kick about the story, the management can say: 'It was the reporter's fault. He didn't know his job. We'll fire him.'"

FINDING PARIS. *The Mysterious Mickey Finn* opens with Homer Evans lounging on the terrace of the Dôme, as would *Hugger-Mugger in the Louvre*, the second of Paul's Paris-based mysteries (others take place in the far-flung locales of Montana, Boston, and Hollywood), the loafer now incongruously turned detective. According to Samuel Putnam, Paul himself was "seldom seen around the Dôme but belonged rather to the *transition* group of the Place de l'Odéon quarter; he was one American who mingled with the French and had a passionate desire to know them." The passion, glimpsed in the French figures in the Evans stories, receives full display in *The Last Time I Saw Paris*, Paul's return to nonfiction in the manner of *Spanish Town*. Once more there is tight focus on the ordinary citizens of a limited locale, now the compressed Rue de la Huchette just off the Boulevard St. Michel, and especially the Hôtel du Caveau at No. 5, where Paul lived off and on for eighteen years. "There I found Paris—and France," he proclaims, as previously he had found Santa Eulalia and Spain.

Again Paul supplies an endpaper sketch of the locale (in *Mickey Finn* a map is included as a reader's guide), with buildings named and street numbers given, and again he opens the book with a list of the characters who densely populate the account. Among them he moves on familiar terms as "Heliot," the local approximation of Elliot, yet he himself is a narrative center more than a distinctive presence. The reader is well into the book before learning that Paul worked on the Paris *Tribune*, halfway before learning that his press connection got him tickets to state funerals and other important functions.

His time on *transition* is only suggested in an engaging story of binding into two volumes the first twelve issues of the journal—or as Paul playfully identifies them, "twelve monthly copies of a modern magazine, containing among other baffling items several plates or reproductions of paintings by contemporary experimental artists"—from the period in which he and Eugene Jolas worked together as co-editors. After much discussion, Paul reaches an agreement with Monsieur Dorlan, the unhurried local bookbinder, who in his shop labors from seven in the morning to midnight in the company of two pale apprentices, the three speaking only with customers while at work. The bound books are to be ready on April 1, but when Paul passes the shop he sees through the window the magazines still stacked in a dusty corner where Dorlan has placed them. "Delicacy," he writes, prevents him from "prodding the conscientious old man," and so months pass, then a year while Paul is away in America. At length, the job finished, the bill amounts only to fifty francs—about two dollars—for each bound volume.

Paul separates his Parisian memories into the twenties, the thirties, and a final section on the immediate run-up to World War II. With the middle section he reveals more about himself. A close confidant calls him a man of letters, and there is mention of such friends as Leland Stowe, the Paris correspondent of the *New York Herald Tribune*, and the wife of Ralph Jules Frantz, who first met the former managing editor of the Paris *Tribune* at Paul's hotel. "The same moon shone over Ibiza," Paul recalls of his period of exile on the Spanish island, "in the days when life there was wonderful and free, and letters from my friends in Paris lent moonlight to my thoughts of them and of my little street and what we were all coming to."

His eventual return to Paris is greeted, as was his return in *Spanish Town*, with an impromptu celebration in which he plays the accordion and finally passes out from drink and is carried to an overnight bed in a hotel room ordinarily reserved for hurried trysts. Once again the gaiety is short-lived. With part three of the book—called "The Death of a Nation" in parallel with *Death of a Spanish Town*—the sorrow of war descends, both in news of fighting in Spain and the coming French struggle with Germany.

Just before war is declared following the German invasion of Poland, the French owner of a shortwave radio station transmitting to Britain and America in English and French asks Paul to fill in as broadcaster. His task one evening is to follow a French soprano with a reading of an essay on Racine, a performance he doubts audiences in London and New York find of breathless interest. He suggests a future improvement: "I volunteered to write a daily description of Paris under stress of war, nothing censorable or informatory to the enemy, but local color that would keep the customers awake." When no one at the station has time to respond to his offer, nothing more is heard of it.

With war, newspapermen Paul had known in Paris reappear in the city as correspondents, among them William L. Shirer and Jay Allen, and pay their respects to the memory of happier times at the Hôtel du Caveau. Literary notables who were once guests in the hotel or had visited Paul there are recalled (Ernest Hemingway, Scott Fitzgerald, Robert Coates, James T. Farrell, e. e. cummings), as are former Paris-American journalists (David Darrah, Virgil Geddes, Waverley Root, Irving Schwerké, Wolfe Kaufman, Jack Pickering, Kenneth Stewart, Bettina Bedwell, Bravig Imbs, Louis Atlas, Ned Calmer, James Thurber, Whit Burnett, Martha Foley, Harold Stearns). Yet at the book's close it is the ordinary citizens of Rue de la Huchette, those unable or unwilling to flee the advancing German war machine, that Paul returns to. For them the war means the "end of a world in which Paris was supreme, in which France was alive, in which there was a breath of freedom." Now oil fouls their city's air, soot the rain. Now its buildings are empty, its pavements bare.

About how and when he himself fled their desolate street, Paul makes no mention.

EPILOGUE

Curtain Fall

*There was a tightening in my throat as I put
on my hat, locked the office door and walked
out into blacked-out Paris. There wasn't a
farewell to be said, and while I could never
convince myself that this was the end of the
Paris Herald, many others felt that way.*
—ERIC HAWKINS,
Hawkins of the Paris Herald

DEPARTURE. The final Paris *Herald* wartime edition carried a single
byline, Walter B. Kerr's. In a long and personal report he wrote
poignantly of the mass exodus from and through the city of people
carrying "everything from a loaf of bread and a bottle of wine for
the evening meal to mattresses, chairs, clothing, bird cages, dogs
and cats":

> These people are taking with them things they could never
> use and the stuff is weighing them down. I have seen old men
> and women carrying baggage that would tire a strong man
> after a while.
>
> The number of push carts is as astonishing as it is tragic.
> But you cannot push a cart all the way to Bordeaux or
> wherever it is they are going.

I don't know what they will do for doctors and nurses on the way. Perhaps first-aid stations have been organized in every village. I hope so or the suffering will be unbearable.

Many newsmen would similarly flee to Bordeaux, the temporary location of the French government after the initial move to Tours, and subsequently make their escape from France or continue their journey through Spain to neutral Portugal. Kerr would be among those leaving from Lisbon, but for the time being he remained in Paris—a city, as he noted in the *Herald* story, rapidly becoming a faint shadow of itself:

> Almost every office has closed. Hundreds of cafés and restaurants have been shut tight. Fouquet's went out of business yesterday afternoon. Hotels are closing fast, the Plaza Athénée today and the Crillon tonight or tomorrow. Small bistrots have shut down.

Following prep school at Andover, the depression had forced Kerr to drop out of Yale, class of 1934, after a year and begin a newspaper career, first in his native Syracuse and then with the *New York Herald Tribune*. Promoted to the paper's Paris bureau as an assistant to John Elliott, the young correspondent was shuttled about to crisis points in Europe, and in the depths of the winter of 1939–1940 he was the *Herald Tribune*'s man in Finland covering the Russo-Finnish War. Back in Paris in the spring, he found himself among a small number of American correspondents on hand to witness the fall of the city.

Some *Herald* staff members who had seen the paper through its last days were stranded in Paris and, with the occupation, interned. Others scattered. By roundabout means Eric Hawkins reached country property he had long owned in Nérac in the Bordeaux region. Robert Sage joined his French wife in Brittany. With a fake Italian identity card, Vincent Bugeja vanished into the French hinterland. B. J. Kospoth's fate was uncertain, with one report saying he tried to gain diplomatic immunity but ended up in a German concentration camp, while another placed him as an officer in the Germany navy. The paper's prominent Mailbag poet, Pauline Avery Crawford, remained in Paris through the occupation and, due to her physical infirmity, was spared internment when America joined the war.

From Walter Kerr's desk in the *Herald* building, Eric Sevareid had typed his final CBS broadcast from Paris, making it known the city had been abandoned to the Germans while using oblique phrasing that passed the censor. Then, together with Edmond Taylor, the *Chicago Tribune*'s former Paris bureau chief and now Thomas Grandin's replacement with the CBS radio group, he left by car for Bordeaux. Earlier Sevareid's wife, who had just given birth to twin boys, had left the city by ship for America. From Bordeaux Sevareid and Taylor sent out broadcasts from a distant radio transmitter they had discovered until German troops were within miles of the location, then with Taylor's wife found passage on an overloaded ship for a perilous voyage to England. "We've all been in a sweat about you people," a relieved Edward R. Murrow said when Sevareid phoned him in London. "You know, you and Taylor have pulled off one of the greatest broadcasting feats there ever was. Come on to London—there's work to be done here."

The *Herald Tribune* Paris bureau chief John Elliott, broken ankle in a plaster cast following a driving accident while returning from an inspection tour of the front, fled Paris in the company of A. J. Liebling of *The New Yorker* and Waverley Root, now with the Mutual Broadcasting System. After four years with the United Press in Paris upon leaving the *Tribune*, Root had been fired for a story filed in January 1938 forecasting the date of the Nazi invasion and annexation of Austria—a story that resulted in German newspapers dropping the wire service. His prediction of the Anschluss turned out to be off by two days. After Root was fired, with $1,000 compensation from the UP, the German papers resumed the service. For the remainder of 1938 Root joined the *Time-Life* bureau in Paris before turning to broadcasting.

ARMISTICE. Root's aged Citroën bore the three newsmen south from Paris on roads, as Liebling recorded, "gorged with what was possibly the strangest assortment of vehicles in history," including a farm tractor hitched to a large trailer flying the American flag and with a sign reading "This trailer is the property of an American citizen." In Orléans no beds were available, and a night was spent shoehorned together in the car. "Every time I dozed," said Root, "my elbow would hit the horn. At 4 a.m. there was an air raid siren. Joe [Liebling] said, 'Good. I hope they blast this place. I'd like to see it.' I said, 'You'll have to get out, then. This car's going to Tours.'"

When they reached the town the newsmen realized it was too near Paris and too lacking in accommodations for the French government to remain, though they themselves found agreeable rooms outside the city in a small roadhouse on the Loire. When they left with the government for Bordeaux they paused for a night in Barbezieux, where Liebling talked the owner of an auto garage into lodging with a story of Elliott's grave wounding at the front and the likelihood his leg, if cramped in the Citroën overnight, would be lastingly deformed. The garageman and his wife provided three mattresses for their dining room floor and would accept no money in return.

When the newsmen arrived in Bordeaux, Liebling pronounced the city "the worst of all." Beds for sleeping were impossible except for the wealthy; restaurants were jammed with heavy-jowled men who "spent all afternoon over their meals, ordering sequences of famous claret vintages as if they were on a *tour gastronomique* instead of being parties to a catastrophe"; the city's air was thick with a noxious odor, "heavy and unhealthy like the smell of tuberoses," that stemmed from what the newsmen understood was the betrayal of the French people by the French government in accepting defeat without an all-out struggle.

Following the armistice with Germany on June 22, 1940, John Elliott left Bordeaux to cover the rump French regime in unoccupied Vichy. Waverley Root made his final broadcast for the Mutual Broadcasting System on the day of the armistice, then with A. J.

Liebling left Bordeaux for St. Jean de Luz, the town near the Spanish border where his wife and infant daughter had been waiting since spring. Soon thereafter Root and his family were on their way to Lisbon and passage to New York, as was Liebling, who recalled a strangely calm, sunlit interlude in the Portuguese capital, "one of the few remaining comfortable cities left in Europe," while awaiting a flight home arranged by *The New Yorker* on a Pan American Clipper.

OCCUPATION. Walter Kerr lingered in Paris, hoping to file reports on life under the occupation, but when three days after entering the city the Germans transported a group of American correspondents from Berlin, keeping tight rein on what they saw and reported, there seemed little point in his presence. Among the Berlin group were two former Paris *Herald* staff members, Ralph Barnes, now Kerr's colleague as a *Herald Tribune* correspondent, and William L. Shirer of CBS news.

"It was no fun for me," Shirer recorded in his diary. "When we drove into Paris, down the familiar streets, I had an ache in the pit of my stomach and I wished I had not come." The June weather was idyllic, but the city's shops and cafés were eerily shuttered while military vehicles roared through the streets and troops swarmed over tourist sites, snapping photographs like giddy visitors.

Later, on a sentimental walking tour of the occupied city, the sight of old newspaper haunts added to Shirer's dark mood: the building of the *Petit Journal*, where in 1925 he had begun his newspaper work on the Paris *Tribune*; the Hôtel du Caveau, where he joined in Elliot Paul's food-and-drink galas; the Hôtel de Lisbonne, where he first lived in Paris, the building appearing as forlorn as ever but with a sign with the hardly credible news that a bath had been added. The sight of the city at night, "weird and . . . unrecognizable," was simply baffling:

> There's a curfew at nine p.m.—an hour before dark. The
> black-out is still enforced. The streets tonight are dark and

deserted. The Paris of gay lights, the laughter, the music, the women in the streets—when was that? And what is this?

German authorities housed the visiting correspondents in the Hôtel Scribe, and Shirer was delighted to find in the lobby two local American correspondents who had not followed the French government into exile, Walter Kerr and Demaree Bess of the *Saturday Evening Post*. The experienced Bess, whom Shirer had worked with in Germany, appeared his familiar stolid self while the younger correspondent, not unexpectedly for someone in an occupied city, seemed edgy. From the correspondents Shirer learned of the panic that had overtaken Paris with the flight of the government:

> Everyone lost his head. The government gave no lead. People were told to scoot, and at least three million out of the five million in the city ran . . . literally ran on their feet towards the south.

Yet nearly as swiftly as the city had emptied out, with the occupation it regained some semblance of its old self. Refugees trooped back, businesses reopened, citizens appeared on the streets, fishermen dangled lines in the Seine. Toward the end of his ten-day return, Shirer, having a drink at the Rotonde in Montparnasse, found

> the Dôme across the street as jammed with crackpots as ever, and in front of us a large table full of middle-aged French women of the bourgeoisie, apparently recovering from their daze, because their anger was rising at the way the little *gamins* . . . were picking up the German soldiers.

SCOOP. After the Berlin correspondents were transported back to Germany, Shirer, as a broadcaster, was allowed to stay behind, and was present when the armistice was signed with triumphant symbolism in the railroad car in the Compiègne Forest where the armistice of 1918 had confirmed German defeat in World War I.

From the site Shirer ad-libbed a broadcast on a line cleared for him to Berlin with the understanding the broadcast would be taped and held for the official release of the news in the German capital.

The following day he was awakened in his room in the Scribe by Walter Kerr with the startling information that he had scooped the world. Without press credentials from the Germans and unable to reach Compiègne, Kerr in the Paris *Herald* building had listened to shortwave rebroadcasts from New York and learned of Shirer's broadcast, for some hours the only news of the signing to reach America until correspondents released dispatches from Berlin. A switch mistakenly thrown in Berlin, Shirer later learned, had sent his broadcast to a shortwave transmitter that allowed it to be picked up live in New York.

By June 26 Shirer was back at his CBS post in Berlin, now awaiting what seemed the inevitable German invasion of Britain. Then, in August, Berlin was heavily hit by British bombers, and he recorded in his diary that "The Berliners are stunned. They did not think it could happen." As bombing raids intensified and German censorship increased, it became clear that he could no longer do his job as a correspondent. In October his wife and daughter left for Lisbon, and in December Shirer followed on a flight from Barcelona to Madrid to, as he joyfully wrote, "Lisbon and light and freedom and sanity at last!" Edward R. Murrow flew to Lisbon for a brief reunion, bringing with him encouraging news about British survival under German bombing, before returning to London. The following day, together with five other American correspondents, Shirer boarded a small ship, on his way home after fifteen years in Europe as a newspaperman, correspondent, and broadcaster.

STRANDED. Following the armistice Eric Hawkins, at his country property in Nérac, found himself just beyond the occupied zone of France—a location of relative safety for his French wife and children but not, as a British citizen, for him. He took up potato farming out of necessity and repeatedly sought a pass to Pétain's capital in Vichy to apply for an exit visa that would allow legal departure from France. Finally permitted into the town, he found the former provincial spa center jammed with journalist friends, all chomping at the bit under rigorous censorship that made their work all but impossible. "But Eric," said an astonished John Elliott when they met, "I thought you'd been caught by the Nazis and interned—or something worse." Over dinner they shared glum views of the future, including Elliott's doubt that the Paris *Herald* would ever publish again. Another dining companion was Gaston Archambault, Hawkins's old boss on the Paris *Herald*, the former editor of the *Paris Times*, and now reporting on the war for the *New York Times*.

While in Vichy Hawkins was offered the job of replacing the International News Service correspondent there, Kenneth Downs, who was eager to get to a scene of action. Hawkins was tempted but realized Vichy officials would hardly welcome the presence of a British citizen; more important, he felt a continuing tie to the *Herald Tribune*, and when he informed the New York office of the offer he was told that work awaited him in New York or London if he could leave France. When the visa at last came after some fourteen months of waiting, Hawkins left his family in Nérac and made the journey through Spain to Lisbon. From here a friend from Paris newspaper days carried word to the *Herald Tribune*'s London bureau that Hawkins was safe but stranded in Portugal, and after some months of uncertainty, and following American entry into the war, the British embassy informed him that he had a place on a flight to England.

SPARROW. The *Herald*'s editor and director, Laurence Hills, terminally ill, had elected to remain in Paris with his wife during the occupation, trying to protect the paper's building and machinery and vainly hoping to maintain some manner of business operation under occupation. A letter written to the *Herald Tribune* publisher in

New York, Ogden Reid, on February 3, 1941, reported frozen pipes and frozen ink in the scarcely heated building, and said Hills was preparing at last to depart, leaving his French aide and the paper's business manager, Renée Brazier, in charge. Before the letter reached Reid, Hills died in the American Hospital in Neuilly. In time, German authorities allowed his wife to leave Paris, and from Lisbon she returned to America.

Walter Kerr had also decided to leave for home. Early one morning he was in his office in the *Herald* building, gathering belongings, when Sparrow Robertson appeared, come to say goodbye. From Kerr, Paris *Herald* newsmen would later learn about the sporting columnist's life under occupation—news that, as Al Laney wrote, came as "reassuring and immensely heartening" amid the vast gloom when the curtain fell on the interwar world of Paris-American journalism.

In the period leading up to war Sparrow had carried on as if little was changed—in his column allowing only, as the Germans rolled into France, that some sporting affairs could possibly be affected by "events" or "somewhat unsettled conditions." With the coming of the occupation he remained in Paris and refused to recognize German rule, stubbornly keeping to his familiar rounds. Each day in his cramped cubicle in the *Herald* office he pecked out his column, dropped it on the copy desk of the deserted newsroom, and headed off to thirst emporiums. He had moved into the Hôtel Lotti in Rue Castiglione and was the sole remaining guest when German officers took over the rooms. On the first night of the building's occupation Sparrow was stopped at the door by a guard and informed it was past curfew. "Where do you get that *stuff*?" he shot back. A German officer appeared on the scene, one who happened to have met the columnist at the Berlin Olympic Games of 1936. Together they went out on the town.

During the winter of 1940–1941 Sparrow moved from the Lotti to the American Legion building just off the Champs-Elysées yet still came to the dark and now unheated office, sitting forlornly in the cold. Finally, at the urging of Renée Brazier, he agreed to retreat to a small property he owned in the village of Bois-le-Roi, close by the forest of Fontainebleau. He still ventured into Paris, and it was on a visit to the city that he appeared at the *Herald* to see Kerr off.

Kerr was touched by the wizened figure's presence yet troubled he would be picked up for breaking the German curfew. He urged Sparrow to take a taxi home. "Get away from me with that *stuff*," said Sparrow. "These swine don't worry me. I go anywhere, anytime." On June 10, 1941, returning from another Paris visit, he collapsed at the small train station of Bois-le-Roi. Two days later a few acquaintances from Paris buried him in the village cemetery.

RETURN. For one of these acquaintances, Renée Brazier, it was a last duty for a *Herald* staff member, but far from last for the paper's interests. Throughout the occupation she meticulously saw to the maintenance of the *Herald* building and equipment—and, so it is said, was waiting in Rue de Berri with the office keys upon the liberation of Paris in 1944.

On the day Eric Hawkins returned to the city to begin the slow process of resuming publication of the paper, riding in a Jeep in the company of Robert Moora, editor of *Stars and Stripes*, which planned to make use of the *Herald*'s printing plant, French Resistance fighters were still at work uncovering German snipers and gunfire echoed in the streets. "Moora and I did not stop," Hawkins recalled, and pushed ahead in the Jeep:

> We headed directly for the Rue de Berri. It was evening as we
> turned off the Champs-Elysées into the street of my
> memories, and in the twilight I could see clearly the six-story
> sign on the building's façade proclaiming: *Herald Tribune*.
>
> I choked a little on my emotions.

Acknowledgments

THE TITLE OF THIS BOOK comes from F. Scott Fitzgerald's "News of Paris—Fifteen Years Ago," an unfinished story written in the year of his death, 1940, and found among his papers. Arthur Mizener, who prints the story in his selection of uncollected Fitzgerald stories and essays, *Afternoon of an Author*, comments that the appearance of the manuscript, typed on yellow paper and triple spaced, indicates the writer meant to give it further work, filling out its sketchy scenes and pursuing a familiar theme of gain and loss in Paris of the twenties.

The central character, Henry Haven Dell, who "had been a romantic four years ago—right after the war" and now considers himself at age twenty-six a "contemptible drone," is waiting for a ship home. He whiles away the time saying goodbye to Ruth and having an afternoon fling with Bessie Wing, just freed from her engagement to another man. Before his ship leaves there is still time to see Hélène, a poor French girl he supported after the war by sending her to a convent school—and to experience a "surge of jealousy" toward a reporter on a Paris-American newspaper who has claimed her attention.

It is possible, says Mizener, to think of the story's blend of enchantment and disenchantment as Fitzgerald's final vision of what European experience had meant to his generation of Americans. Here I use the title to refer to a different sort of Parisian news—not literary news but the day-to-day news work that occupied many members of Fitzgerald's generation. Journalism as work edges into Fitzgerald's story in two places—in the reference to the newspaper reporter and to a Paris-American magazine—but life in its pages takes place in a glossy world of the Ritz bar, the Café Dauphine, the lobby of the Hôtel Crillon, Lipp's *brasserie*, and a fine apartment where, with a signature Fitzgerald touch, "peacocks on the draperies stirred in the April wind." In the pages of this book life is commonly lived around stuffy copy desks, in cramped hotel rooms, in cheap bars and restaurants. Yet the Paris-American world portrayed here is not wholly removed from the Fitzgeraldian news in that, inevitably, it shared fully in the grand back-and-forth ambiguities of expatriate life. When Hélène tells Henry Dell about her young reporter, he reproves her by saying "that one doesn't look very promising." "Oh, he is drunk now," the girl replies, "but at times he is all one would desire."

I am grateful for the help I received at several libraries. At the Bibliothèque Nationale de France staff members patiently guided me through its computerized retrieval system. The New York Public Library was pleasantly old-fashioned in comparison but equally efficient. Important help also came from the Lilly Library, Indiana University; the Library of Congress; and the libraries of Northwestern University, Princeton University, Wayne State University, Coe College, Knox College, Port Washington (New York) Public Library, and Velva (North Dakota) School and Public Library. The interlibrary loan service of the Hesburgh Library, University of Notre Dame, was superbly competent.

Friends and family members listened with what I took to be interest to many work-in-progress accounts of the book. The book's dedication is to my wife, who sat through most of them. My daughter, Andrea Weber, was my computer expert. In France, Samuel Abt responded promptly to inquiries about his edited publication of Waverley Root's autobiography. In the United Kingdom, Arnold Goldman graciously shared his extensive research on Elliot Paul. Ivan

Dee was both a perceptive reader and a fine editor. Others who gave key aid were Kenneth Kinslow, Joseph McKerns, John Twohey, Eric Gillespie, Dan Reasor.

A portion of Chapter Two appeared as an article in the *Virginia Quarterly Review*.

Notes and Sources

REFERENCES TO THE TEXT are indicated by the last words of a passage or by key words within a passage. Many references to newspapers and magazines are incorporated into the text and consequently not repeated below.

Prologue: *Jake's Work*

Epigraph: Ernest Hemingway, *The Sun Also Rises* (New York, 1926), 36.

page

3   "There you go": Hemingway, *The Sun Also Rises*, 114.

4   "Everything is very lovely": Hemingway to his family, December 8, 1921, *Selected Letters, 1917–1961*, ed. Carlos Baker (New York, 1981), 56.

4   "here we are": Hemingway to Sherwood Anderson, December 23, 1921, *Selected Letters*, 59.

4   "goddam newspaper stuff": Ibid., March 9, 1922, 62–63.

5   middle of the decade: Paris *Tribune*, September 10, 1924. The *Tribune* story is based on an article in a French newspaper drawing on figures assembled by the police. For the uncertainties involved in determining the Paris-American population see Al Laney, *Paris Herald: The Incredible Newspaper* (New York, 1947), 143.

5   "Paris in the winter": Hemingway, "Living on $1,000 a Year in Paris," *Dateline: Toronto, The Complete Toronto Star Dispatches, 1920–1924*, ed. William White (New York, 1985), 88.

5   "the centre of": Vincent Sheean, *Personal History* (Garden City, N.Y., 1937), 36.

5   five a day: Henry J. Greenwall, *Scoops* (New York, 1923), 211.

6   "led by newspapermen": Laney, *Paris Herald*, 76.

6   "to stay in Paris": Paul Scott Mowrer, *The House of Europe* (Boston, 1945), 392.

6   "used this way occasionally": Frederick J. Hoffman, *The Twenties: American Writing in the Postwar Decade* (New York, 1955), 29.

7   "as they saw it": Hemingway, "Papal Poll: Behind the Scenes," *Dateline: Toronto*, 99.

7   "lunch on Wednesday": Hemingway, *The Sun Also Rises*, 37.

7   "Big time at": Hemingway to Robert McAlmon, November 20, 1924, *Selected Letters*, 135.

7   "dinner was a great success": Harold E. Stearns, *The Street I Know* (New York, 1935), 239.

7   "tonight is the party": Harold Ettlinger, *Fair, Fantastic Paris* (Indianapolis, 1944), 214–216.

8   "A regular job": Stearns, *The Street I Know*, 359.

8   "I haven't told enough": Malcolm Cowley, *Exile's Return: A Narrative of Ideas* (New York, 1934), 289. The revised 1951 edition has a different epilogue.

9   "It was all right": Edmond Taylor, *Awakening from History* (London, 1971), 61.

9   "cluttering up the Dôme": Whit Burnett, *The Literary Life and the Hell with It* (New York, 1939), 92.

9   "I was working": Eric Sevareid, *Not So Wild a Dream* (New York, 1946), 85.

10 "journalism was a life": Mavis Gallant, Afterword to *Paris Stories*, selected by Michael Ondaatje (New York, 2002), 372.

10 "had the notes for": Kenneth Stewart, *News Is What We Make It* (Cambridge, Mass., 1943), 202.

10 "we were all trying": Eugene Jolas, *Man from Babel*, eds. Andreas Kramer and Rainer Rumold (New Haven, Conn., 1998), 68.

10 "Like all newspaper men": Frederic Joseph Svoboda, *Hemingway & The Sun Also Rises* (Lawrence, Kans., 1983), 134.

11 home and abroad: Janet Flanner, Introduction to *Paris Was Yesterday, 1925–1939* (New York, 1972), xvi.

11 was going there: For a discussion of the push (from America) and pull (to Paris) of the expatriate period, see—in addition to Hoffman's *The Twenties*—Malcolm Bradbury, *Dangerous Pilgrimages: Trans-Atlantic Mythologies and the Novel* (London, 1995), 330–339.

12 "have a try?": Laney, *Paris Herald*, 4–5.

12 "a passport to": Eric Hawkins with Robert N. Sturdevant, *Hawkins of the Paris Herald* (New York, 1963), 117.

13 below the surface: Stearns, *The Street I Know*, 298.

13 "exodus of the young": Ford Madox Ford, "Young Americans Abroad," *Saturday Review of Literature*, September 20, 1934, 121.

13 "I thought with satisfaction": Stearns, *The Street I Know*, 251–252.

13 "Paris mark on them": Sterling Noel, "Kirby & Barber," *Lost Generation Journal*, 1 (Fall 1973), 23.

14 "Continental glory": Whit Burnett and Martha Foley, "Your Home-Town Paper: Paris," *American Mercury*, 22 (January 1931), 24.

14 "grand display window": Morley Callaghan, *That Summer in Paris* (New York, 1963), 114.

15 Hart Crane: In *Americans in Paris: A Literary Anthology*, a 2004 Library of America publication, Paris-American journalists of the interwar years included are Waverley Root, Henry Miller, Janet Flanner, James Thurber,

and Hemingway. In the Introduction, the editor, Adam Gopnik, mentions two other Paris newsmen, Samuel Putnam and Elliot Paul, as notable omissions.

16   "From newspaper shops": Laney, *Paris Herald*, 11.

Chapter One: *The Dear Paris* Herald

Epigraph: *Gertrude Stein: Writings, 1903–1932* (New York, 1998), 803.

18   "baseball stories": Waverley Root, *The Paris Edition: The Autobiography of Waverley Root, 1927–1934*, ed. Samuel Abt (San Francisco, 1987), 156.

18   "amounted to nothing"; "a lively paper": Laney, *Paris Herald*, 92–93. With Laney and others, I call the paper by its familiar name, the Paris *Herald*. Properly it was the *New York Herald*, European Edition—and after the *New York Tribune* purchased the *New York Herald* in 1924, the *New York Herald Tribune*, European Edition. For the paper's history I draw, in addition to Laney's book, on Hawkins, *Hawkins of the Paris Herald*; Charles L. Robertson, *The International Herald Tribune: The First Hundred Years* (New York, 1987); Richard Kluger, *The Paper: The Life and Death of the New York Herald Tribune* (New York, 1986); and Bruce Singer, *100 Years of the Paris Trib* (New York, 1987).

18   "dear Paris Herald": Flanner, *Paris Was Yesterday*, 22–23.

19   "never very good": Laney, *Paris Herald*, 94.

20   "worse than any paper": Stewart, *News Is What We Make It*, 73.

20   "rather absurd": Sevareid, *Not So Wild a Dream*, 85.

20   "angora cat": Quoted in Flanner, *Paris Was Yesterday*, 23.

20   "up-State New York": Burnett and Foley, "Your Home-Town Paper: Paris," 27–28.

21   near at hand: Richard O'Connor offers this explanation in *The Scandalous Mr. Bennett* (Garden City, N.Y., 1962), 184.

22   "Black Beetles": Quoted in Robertson, *The International Herald Tribune*, 20.

24   "society news": Quoted in Alfred E. Cornebise, The Stars and Stripes: *Doughboy Journalism in World War I* (Westport, Conn., 1984), 4.

24   in the black: Cornebise, The Stars and Stripes, 170–172.

25   "Don't kid me": Hemingway, *The Sun Also Rises*, 15.

27   "collective bohemian life": Joseph Freeman, *An American Testament* (London, 1938), 165.

27   "placid sort of life": Laney, *Paris Herald*, 85.

27   "more English than American": Ibid., 90.

28   "serious drinkers": Quoted in Richard Lingeman, *Sinclair Lewis: Rebel from Main Street* (New York, 2002), 180.

28   "perpetual 're-write'": Stearns, *The Street I Know*, 216.

29   "in that respect": Ibid., 336.

29   "fulsome flop": Hawkins, *Hawkins of the Paris Herald*, 197.

30   "Don't change anything": John Weld, *Young Man in Paris* (Chicago, 1985), 20.

30 "savor the mayhem": Root, *The Paris Edition*, 143–144.

30 "met my old pal": Alex Small, *Chicago Tribune*, August 10, 1960. Small's recreation appeared in the "A Line O' Type or Two" column he was then conducting on the paper's editorial page.

30 "the greatest writer": Quoted in Arthur and Barbara Gelb, *O'Neill* (New York, 1962), 712.

30 "the paper stinks": Pound to Bill Bird, March 23, 1935. Bird papers, Lilly Library, Indiana University.

31 "get that *stuff*": Quoted in Hawkins, *Hawkins of the Paris Herald*, 207.

31 evolution was false: Raymond A. Schroft, *The American Journey of Eric Sevareid* (South Rayalton, Vt., 1995), 117. According to Al Laney, Bugeja was celebrated on the paper for having been excommunicated after transferring church property in Malta to the people. *Paris Herald*, 77.

31 Press Association gala: Bugeja's hiring and time on the *Herald* is recounted by Hawkins, *Hawkins of the Paris Herald*, 104–07, and Laney, *Paris Herald*, 77–78.

32 "the beginning": Hawkins, *Hawkins of the Paris Herald*, 103.

32 near-disaster as a newsman: For Barnes's career with the *Herald* I draw on Barbara S. Mahoney, *Dispatches and Dictators: Ralph Barnes for the Herald Tribune* (Corvallis, Ore., 2002), 15–33. Mahoney largely follows earlier accounts of Barnes by Laney in *Paris Herald* and Leland Stowe in *No Other Road to Freedom* (New York, 1941).

33 Lindbergh's Paris landing: Accounts vary about what took place that night. Below I mainly follow the accounts of Paris journalists who were on hand in the *Herald* office: Al Laney, *Paris Herald*, 218–230, and Eric Hawkins, *Hawkins of the Paris Herald*, 130–138. Richard Kluger also draws on Laney's account and supplements it with interview material from Laney and Leland Stowe in *The Paper*, 233–238. For a recent account, perhaps the most authoritative, see A. Scott Berg's biography *Lindbergh* (New York, 1998), 128–131. Berg says that Ambassador Herrick suggested to Lindbergh that he grant the late-night interview with reporters; that Herrick's son, Parmely, came downstairs to suggest to the *New York Times* representative that all the assembled reporters should be present; and that the interview lasted a brief seven or eight minutes. Lindbergh's own account of his arrival, published shortly after the flight, was succinct, but even more so was Fitzhugh Green's in an afterword to Lindbergh's book. Wrote Green: "Two French aviation officers extricated [Lindbergh] from the milling crowd at Le Bourget on arrival night and succeeded in getting him to the American Embassy where newspaper men located him at 1:30 a.m. The journalists naturally found the flier tired after having had practically no sleep for nearly sixty hours. But he was far from exhausted and he had no maudlin recital for the pencil-pushers who so eagerly surrounded him." Charles A. Lindbergh, "*WE*" (New York, 1927), 237–238.

34 "high and dry": Quoted in Hawkins, *Hawkins of the Paris Herald*, 138. In Laney's account, after Pickering reaches the office he wastes no time talking and immediately starts typing his story. *Paris Herald*, 223.

34 "Here is Lindbergh": Lindbergh, *"WE,"* 226.

35 "Write!": The exchange is recounted in Laney, *Paris Herald*, 228.

36 who had written it: Wilbur Forrest, *Behind the Front Page* (New York, 1934), 298ff. Forrest's account is persuasively challenged in Kluger, *The Paper*, 235–237.

37 "heathen rage": Hawkins, *Hawkins of the Paris Herald*, 143. For Laney's version of the Byrd story see *Paris Herald*, 231–239. Laney includes an office mix-up that caused the *Herald*, in one edition, to report that Byrd had indeed landed as planned at Le Bourget. Waverley Root provides an amusing account of how the Paris *Tribune* and the *Continental Daily Mail* capitalized on the *Herald*'s blooper in *The Paris Edition*, 83–86.

38 "second-day angle": Laney, *Paris Herald*, 116–119.

38 late-twenties newcomers: Burnett's and Foley's Paris days are recalled in Martha Foley, *The Story of STORY Magazine*, ed. Jay Neugeboren (New York, 1980), 61–81.

39 "only girl": Laney, *Paris Herald*, 253.

39 "uninhibited stag party": Foley, *The Story of STORY Magazine*, 48.

39 "Much of his talk": Ibid., 51.

39 "jaundiced eye": Hawkins, *Hawkins of the Paris Herald*, 118.

40 "pleasant Britisher": Burnett and Foley, "Your Home-Town Paper: Paris," 29.

40 "editorial strike": Foley, *The Story of STORY Magazine*, 67–68.

40 "concerted demand": Burnett and Foley, "Your Home-Town Paper: Paris," 28. Eric Hawkins makes no mention of a strike in his memoir.

41 "mighty synthesis": Foley, *The Story of STORY Magazine*, 72.

41 "quite at ease": Laney, *Paris Herald*, 160–162. In his book *Sylvia Beach and the Lost Generation*, Noel Riley Fitch repeats Laney's claim that Beach called on newspaper friends to type for Joyce but makes no further comment. In her memoir, *Shakespeare and Company*, Beach says nothing about Paris newspapermen as typists. Richard Ellmann reports in his biography of Joyce that Beach found Joyce typists for sections of *Ulysses* but mentions no newspapermen.

41 "laden with maledictions": Foley, *The Story of STORY Magazine*, 64.

42 "to go die": Ezra Pound, "After Election," *The New Review*, 1 (January/February 1931), 54. In the same column Pound allowed that the Paris *Tribune* had earlier produced a good weekly arts supplement but complained that for its present book reviewing it "spends money on printing and composition of features and booknews, and it could perfectly well afford to pay a little attention to what it uses. For twenty five dollars a week they could provide competent book-news service."

42 "we love his poems": Foley, *The Story of STORY Magazine*, 65–66. A recent biography, Clive Fisher, *Hart Crane, A Life* (New Haven, Conn., 2002), makes no mention of a role for Foley in the poet's release from prison.

43 appreciate wine!: Rosetti's oratory is recreated by Martha Foley, *The Story of STORY Magazine*, 76. Foley spells his name Rossetti. Harold Stearns called Rosetti an "authority on foods, wines, and political intrigue." *The Street I Know*, 294.

43 "remain green": Laney, *Paris Herald*, 80.

43 "an editorial assistant": Jolas, *Man from Babel*, 87. Jolas's wife and *transition* collaborator Maria Jolas recalled that Paul's salary allowed him to work fewer hours on the *Tribune* rather than leaving it completely. *Maria Jolas, Woman of Action: A Memoir and Other Writings*, ed. Mary Ann Caws (Columbia, S.C., 2004), 85.

44 parted company: Arnold Goldman gives a detailed account of Paul's involvement with *transition* in "Elliot Paul's *transition* Years: 1926–28," *James Joyce Quarterly*, 30 (Winter 1993), 241–275.

44 "unable to work": Ralph Jules Frantz, "Recollections of Elliot Paul." Unpublished typescript provided by Arnold Goldman.

45 "drawing for Picasso": Elliot Paul, *Understanding the French* (London, 1954), 19–20. The American edition of Paul's book, published by Random House in 1955, is an edited and rearranged version of the British edition.

45 "books, art and music": Burnett and Foley, "Your Home-Town Paper: Paris," 26.

46 "bubbling sense of humor": Laney, *Paris Herald*, 78.

46 before concerts took place: Ibid., 91.

47 "get off the paper": Pound, "After Election," *The New Review*, 54.

47 crafty solution: Elliot Paul, *That Crazy American Music* (Indianapolis, 1957), 128–129. The flap over Schneider is not mentioned in the memoirs of Hawkins, Laney, or Foley.

47 "unadvanced prose": Laney, *Paris Herald*, 153.

48 "So long, slaves": Quoted in Laney, *Paris Herald*, 257. Hawkins has a different account of Wertenbaker's leavetaking: "The late Charles Wertenbaker was plagued by the need for a walk two or three times a night. Once during an especially hectic flow of news he quietly arose at a particularly inconvenient moment and disappeared into the night without a word. When he returned I said, 'Enough's enough.' He merely nodded and left. The next time I saw him . . . he was one of the leading writers for *Time*. We argued the point of whether he had been fired. Wert maintained that he had quit." *Hawkins of the Paris Herald*, 113.

48 "romantics": Weld, *Young Man in Paris*, 14.

49 "up the ladder": Quoted in Ibid., 199.

49 a normal evening: Stewart, *News Is What We Make It*, 62–63.

50 terms of employment: Hawkins to Ned Calmer, November 8, 1930. Calmer papers, Wisconsin State Historical Society.

51 "quenchplace of thirst": Burnett and Foley, "Your Home-Town Paper: Paris," 28.

52 "alcoholic dream": "*Le New York*," *Time*, April 17, 1939, 67.

52 "chief problems": Laney, *Paris Herald*, 289.

52 "the presses rolled": Hawkins, *Hawkins of the Paris Herald*, 102.

52 "promptly fall asleep": Ibid., 112.

52 ongoing card games: Arthur Gelb, *City Room* (New York, 2003), 10–12, 21, 630.

52 "learned how to drink": Stewart, *News Is What We Make It*, 66–67.

52 "uncivilized about drinking": Harold Stearns, "Apologia of an Expatriate," *Scribner's Magazine*, March 1929, 340.

53 "I fire myself": Quoted in Laney, *Paris Herald*, 291–292.

54 wet oblivion: Burnett and Foley, "Your Home-Town Paper: Paris," 30.

54 basked in the sun: Burnett, *The Literary Life and the Hell with It*, 231–237. Martha Foley repeats the hospital story but says she was the one who saw Burnett's medical record. *The Story of STORY Magazine*, 66–67.

55 depression-era takers: For the *Herald*'s economic troubles in the thirties I mainly follow Robertson, *The International Herald Tribune*, 165–173.

56 "our initials in print": For Crawford's life and Mailbag career I draw on Charles L. Robertson's biography, *An American Poet in Paris: Pauline Avery Crawford and the Herald Tribune* (Columbia, Mo., 2001). All verse quotations appear in this work.

59 "no better off": Laney, *Paris Herald*, 303.

59 "gray little man": Ibid., 295.

60 "Big Beats in Europe": Quoted in Kluger, *The Paper*, 296.

61 "do something about it": Ibid., 304.

61 Walter B. Kerr: The correspondent is not to be confused with Walter F. Kerr, the influential theater critic of the *New York Herald Tribune* and later the *New York Times*.

61 he confused the: The explanation for the firing is Sevareid's in *Not So Wild a Dream*, 73. Other possible explanations are given in Schroth, *The American Journey of Eric Sevareid*, 106. Below I follow Sevareid's memoir for his newspaper work and start of his broadcasting career.

62 "nobody really cared": Sevareid, *Not So Wild a Dream*, 84.

62 "baleful silence": Ibid., 85–86.

62 "nature colony addict": Paris *Herald*, October 31, 1929.

63 "publicity saints": Paris *Herald*, November 16, 1938.

63 "think politically": Sevareid, *Not So Wild a Dream*, 90.

65 "like an animal pack's": Ibid., 92–93. Hawkins had a similar reaction to the crowd: ". . . I remember with revulsion the sickening sound of shrieks and cries of horror and vengeance that came from the massed spectators as the big knife fell." *Hawkins of the Paris Herald*, 192.

65 "executions by hanging": Webb Miller, *I Found No Peace* (New York, 1936), 155.

65 "meet it in Spain": Quoted in Sevareid, *Not So Wild a Dream*, 94.

66 depressing . . . "sheet": Quoted in Ring Lardner, Jr., *The Lardners, My Family Remembered* (New York, 1977; originally published 1976), 262. I draw on this memoir for James Lardner's time in Paris and Spain.

67 "Watch what I do": Quoted in Francelia Butler, "How Francelia Butler Lost Her Job in the '30s, Sailed to Paris and Found Happiness," *International Herald Tribune*, October 3–4, 1987.

68 "provide the honest news": Quoted in Sevareid, *Not So Wild a Dream*, 107.

68 "attract passing customers": Sevareid, *Not So Wild a Dream*, 107.

69 "don't worry about it": Quoted in Sevareid, *Not So Wild a Dream*, 107.

70 "we cannot see it": Ettlinger, *Fair, Fantastic Paris*, 250.

71 "built-in neurosis": A. J. Liebling, *Between Meals: An Appetite for Paris* (New York, 1962), 133.

72 miraculous escape: Schroth, *The American Journey of Eric Sevareid*, 154. The death toll is given as 250 in Alistair Horne, *Seven Ages of Paris* (New York, 2002), 348.

72 "a record business": A. J. Liebling, *The Road Back to Paris* (Garden City, N.Y., 1944), 82–83.

73 "will not print": Quoted in Robertson, *The International Herald Tribune*, 218.

73 historians would note: For one historian's view see Horne, *Seven Ages of Paris*, 348.

73 on no newsstands: Robertson, *The International Herald Tribune*, 219.

Chapter Two: *World's Zaniest Newspaper*

Epigraph: Stearns, *The Street I Know*, 287.

75 "drunk again!": Quoted in William L. Shirer, *20th Century Journey: The Start, 1904–1930* (New York, 1976), 232.

75 "really like": Quoted in Jolas, *Man from Babel*, 67–68.

75 "journal without peer": Shirer, *20th Century Journey: The Start*, 222.

75 "seldom ever reach": Stearns, *The Street I Know*, 335.

76 "almost entirely read": Shirer, *20th Century Journey: The Start*, 223.

76 in journalism history: There are no historical accounts of the Paris *Tribune* comparable to those of the *Herald* cited earlier. Beyond sections dealing with the *Tribune* in memoirs by Shirer, Stearns, Jolas, Ettlinger, and others, the most valuable resources are Root's autobiography and Hugh Ford's introduction and selections in *The Left Bank Revisited: Selections from the Paris Tribune, 1917–1934* (University Park, Pa., 1972). There are entries for several former *Tribune* staff members in the *Dictionary of Literary Biography* volume *American Writers in Paris, 1920–1939*, ed. Karen Lane Rood (Detroit, 1980). Here and in other chapters the *Lost Generation Journal* is an important source for articles by and about Paris-American journalists.

76 "boldest and bulkiest": Malcolm Cowley, review of William L. Shirer's *20th Century Journey: The Start, New York Times Book Review*, October 20, 1976, 244.

76 "awakened the broader circles": Samuel Putnam, *Paris Was Our Mistress* (New York, 1947), 220.

76 "sensational sweep": Paris *Tribune*, July 4, 1927.

77 "the local room": Putnam, *Paris Was Our Mistress*, 221.

77 "newspapermen's venture": Paris *Tribune*, May 25, 1930.

77 "the most prolific": Kay Boyle, *New York Times Book Review*, September 14, 1975. The remark comes in a review of Hugh Ford's *Published in Paris*.

78 "a little different": Robert Sage, "Farewell to Transition," *transition*, 19/20 (June 1930), 375.

79 by the War Department: For more about Hull as a correspondent see Wilda M. Smith and Eleanor A. Bogart, *The Wars of Peggy Hull* (El Paso, Tex., 1991).

79 "the comic side": Quoted in George Seldes, "My Decade with Col. Mc-Cormick," *Lost Generation Journal*, 2 (Fall 1974), 24.

80 "commandeered the rest": Ring W. Lardner, *My Four Weeks in France* (Indianapolis, 1918), 150–151.

80 redeem his pledge: The amount of francs was given in the *Tribune* editorial, "We Remain in France." Root reports a figure of 112,000 francs, or $2,240, in *The Paris Edition*, 51.

81 "red-blooded American": Shirer, *20th Century Journey: The Start*, 222–223.

81 "to spit in": Root, *The Paris Edition*, 51.

81 boldy forecast: Richard Norton Smith, *The Colonel: The Life and Legend of Robert R. McCormick, 1880–1955* (Boston, 1997), 233. In its 1923 editorial "We Remain in France," the *Tribune* noted that its "auditor's report shows a modest profit on operation [sic]."

82 "stroke of apoplexy": Shirer, *20th Century Journey: The Start*, 223.

82 "satisfied his conscience": Liebling, *Between Meals*, 115.

82 "left alone": Root, *The Paris Edition*, 60.

83 "frequent incompetence": Ibid., 64–65.

83 "rewrite and reprint": Burnett and Foley, "Your Home-Town Paper: Paris," 25.

84 "dim silence": Liebling, *Between Meals*, 115.

84 from the parent paper: Ralph Jules Frantz gives a detailed account of the *Tribune*'s news sources in "Recollections," *The Left Bank Revisited*, 311.

84 "a continual round": Elliot Paul, *The Amazon* (New York, 1930), 323–324.

85 typewriters for reporters: The newsroom layout is described by Ralph Jules Frantz in "Recollections," *The Left Bank Revisited*, 310. Frantz provides a drawing of the layout in "I Tell It This Way," *Lost Generation Journal*, 2 (Spring-Summer 1974), 19.

85 "other punctuation marks": Thurber to Hudson Hawley, July 27, 1954, *The Thurber Letters*, ed. Harrison Kinney (New York, 2002), 629–630.

85 "thrilling experiences": Paris *Tribune*, May 16, 1927.

86 "events in high society": Root, *The Paris Edition*, 160–161.

87 pair were told: I largely follow Shirer's account of the evening in *20th Century Journey: The Start*, 331–339.

87 "to use it": Quoted by Root, *The Paris Edition*, 34.

87 "he received me": *Chicago Tribune*, May 22, 1927.

87 "Lindbergh exclusive": Quoted in Root, *The Paris Edition*, 35. In his biography of McCormick, Richard Norton Smith acknowledges that Wales's "exclusive interview" was "in truth a pastiche of comments the Lone Eagle made to several reporters at the American embassy." *The Colonel*, 308.

88 with the report: Paris *Tribune*, June 5, 1927.

89 "a ship's list": *Chicago Tribune*, November 21, 1960, 14. A visit to Chicago by William L. Shirer opened a series of Paris recollections in the paper's "A Line O' Type or Two" column by Small, then conducting the column, that ran from November 18 to December 2.

90 perennial masterpiece: Taylor, *Awakening from History*, 65.

90 "erudite placer": Paris *Tribune*, November 30, 1934.

90   "hard boiled": Bravig Imbs, *Confessions of Another Young Man* (New York, 1936), 156.

90   "Paris audience": Stearns, *The Street I Know*, 291. For reasons unclear, Stearns refers to Alex Small as Adolph Strong.

91   wastrel or otherwise: Many of Bald's columns are reprinted in *On the Left Bank, 1929–1933*, ed. Benjamin Franklin V (Athens, Oh., 1987). Franklin's Introduction is a primary source of biographical information about Bald.

91   "telling all": Putnam, *Paris Was Our Mistress*, 82, 106–107.

91   "or the Surrealists": Ibid., 106.

93   unofficial hostess: For Gilliam's unique life in postwar Paris see Morrill Cody with Hugh Ford, *The Women of Montparnasse* (New York, 1984), 166.

94   "through the keyhole": Paris *Tribune*, September 8, 1924.

95   "and never was": Ibid., May 11, 1924.

95   "American reporting methods": Jolas, *Man from Babel*, 71.

95   "higher journalism": Ibid., 93.

96   "usually a necessity": Cody, *The Women of Montparnasse*, 9.

96   "and so long": Paris *Tribune*, November 30, 1934.

97   "with the translations": Quoted in Imbs, *Confessions of Another Young Man*, 37.

97   "struggling with copy": Paul, *Understanding the French*, 35.

97   Linotype machines: Ralph Jules Frantz makes this point about proofreaders in "Recollections," *The Left Bank Revisited*, 311.

97   "lower than mine": Imbs, *Confessions of Another Young Man*, 48–49.

98   "looked rosier": John Glassco, *Memoirs of Montparnasse* (Toronto, 1970), 50.

98   following day's work: Paul's *Tribune* exploits are recounted by Ralph Jules Frantz in an unpublished typescript provided by Arnold Goldman.

98   "disagreeable occupations": Paris *Tribune*, April 18, 1926.

99   into the stove: Quoted in Imbs, *Confessions of Another Young Man*, 138.

99   nothing more difficult: Ibid, 183–184.

99   "One humid day": Paris *Tribune*, February 15, 1927.

100   "mature experiments": Ibid., May 15, 1927.

100   "you begin there": Quoted in Gertrude Stein, *Autobiography of Alice B. Toklas*, in *Gertrude Stein: Writings, 1903–1932*, 895. Imbs adds some detail to Paul's contribution in *Confessions of Another Young Man*, 158–159.

101   "amazing job": Quoted in Dorothy Commins, *What Is an Editor?* (Chicago, 1978), 38.

101   "has disappeared": Quoted in Robert van Gelder, "An Interview with Mr. Elliot Paul," *New York Times Book Review*, March 1, 1942, 2, 23.

101   "bat away again": James Thurber, *Writers at Work: The Paris Review Interviews*, ed. Malcolm Cowley (New York, 1958), 89.

102   "straight reporting": Jolas, *Man from Babel*, 135.

102   "junior hanger-on": Quoted in Lyall H. Powers, "Leon Edel: The Life of a Biographer," *American Scholar*, Autumn 1997, 600.

103   "or a novelist?": Quoted in James Thurber, *The Years with Ross* (Boston, 1959), 30.

103   "never filed": Thurber to Hudson Hawley, July 27, 1954, *The Thurber Letters*, 629.

103 "were printed": Ibid., 629–630.
103 "North Pole": Thurber to Wolcott Gibbs, May 21, 1954, *Selected Letters of James Thurber*, eds. Helen Thurber and Edward Weeks (Boston, 1981), 161.
105 "I don't know": Ibid., 158. Elsewhere Thurber remarked about the Riviera edition that "stories were set up in 10-point type, instead of the customary 8-point, to make life easier for everybody, including the readers." "Memoirs of a Drudge," *The Thurber Carnival* (New York, 1945), 18.
105 "villas and yachts": Thurber to Hudson Hawley, July 27, 1954, *The Thurber Letters*, 630.
105 "Burmese monkey": Thurber, "Memoirs of a Drudge," 19.
105 "showers of protests": Paul, *Understanding the French*, 131.
105 seemed to notice: Virgil Geddes, *Country Postmaster* (New York, 1952), 117.
106 of murder: This version of the printed story appears in Shirer, *20th Century Journey: The Start*, 227. Bull's view of what happened and the *Tribune*'s response to embassy demands are in Hawkins, *Hawkins of the Paris Herald*, 109.
107 honor guard: Hawkins, *Hawkins of the Paris Herald*, 110.
107 "wouldn't hurt": Quoted in Root, *The Paris Edition*, 145. Harold Ettlinger recounts the same story but with a different aftermath in Fair, *Fantastic Paris*, 107–108. Ettlinger gives Paris newsmen fictitious names, with Egan here named Murphy.
108 "state of mind": Jolas, *Man from Babel*, 66.
108 "so independent": Ettlinger, Fair, *Fantastic Paris*, 100.
109 "a scoop": The story of Kirby's accident is told in Root, *The Paris Edition*, 175–177, and in Ralph Jules Frantz, "I Tell It This Way," *Lost Generation Journal*, 2 (Spring–Summer 1974), 18–19.
109 had been Kirby's: Sterling Noel questions the accidental nature of the death in "Kirby & Barber," 23–25, 34.
110 "'The,' said Thurber": Quoted in Shirer, *20th century Journey: The Start*, 217–228.
110 "silent Buddha": Shirer, *20th Century Journey: The Start*, 220. The phrase "There lies civilization in the United States" is from the revised 1951 edition of Malcolm Cowley's *Exile's Return*, 104–105, n.1.
111 "he was awake": Root, *The Paris Edition*, 119–120.
111 "the next evening": Shirer, *20th Century Journey: The Start*, 222.
111 amusement and wonder: Putnam, *Paris Was Our Mistress*, 29–30.
112 from the inside: Michael Reynolds, *Hemingway: The Paris Years* (New York, 1999), 222.
112 "never got around": Kay Boyle, *Monday Night* (New York, 1938), 244.
112 "and the ponies": Harold Stearns, "Racing in November," *Paris Comet*, I (12), 33. See notes to Chapter Five (point of work) for the magazine's dating system.
114 "going over to": Stearns, *The Street I Know*, 333–335.
115 "not lost faith": Paris *Tribune*, February 23, 1932.
115 "liberal attitude": Frantz, "Recollections," *The Left Bank Revisited*, 314.
115 "unpleasant business": Frantz to Ned Calmer, March 1, 1930. Calmer papers, Wisconsin State Historical Society.

115 "because it *was*": Stearns, *The Street I Know*, 287.

115 "no difference at all": Elliot Paul, *The Last Time I Saw Paris* (New York, 1942), 92.

116 "on the desk ordered": Freeman, *An American Testament*, 167.

116 by other means: Irene Corbally Kuhn, "Paris in the Twenties," *Remembrance of Things Paris*, ed. Ruth Reichl (New York, 2004), 4.

116 "those who worked": *Chicago Tribune*, November 22, 1960, 14.

116 "get up the stairs": Root, *The Paris Edition*, 172.

116 came to work: Ibid., 192.

117 "perhaps Ambrose Bierce": Taylor, *Awakening from History*, 65.

118 "on the copy desk": Ettlinger, *Fair, Fantastic Paris*, 109–110. In the passage Paul is Edward Carton, Small is Charles Perry.

118 spring of 1927: Samuel Abt recounts Root's background in his Introduction to *The Paris Edition*, viii.

118 "out for lunch": Root, *The Paris Edition*, 23.

119 "balance wheel": Ettlinger, *Fair, Fantastic Paris*, 105–106. In the passage, Root is Jim Plant.

119 "end in itself": Paris *Tribune*, July 4, 1932.

119 save New York: Ibid., August 14, 1927.

120 his Paris nightlife: Root's work routine is described in Ralph Jules Frantz, "Noted Author-Correspondent Waverley Root Is Legendary," *Lost Generation Journal*, 4 (Winter 1976), 16–17.

120 "the few pros": Frantz, "Recollections," *The Left Bank Revisited*, 308.

120 "in-and-out stars": Stearns, *The Street I Know*, 294.

120 hired a replacement: Frantz, "Recollections," *The Left Bank Revisited*, 312. Robert Ferguson has a somewhat different version of Miller's departure in *Henry Miller: A Life* (New York, 1991), 186.

121 "good sport": Ralph Jules Frantz, "I Did Not Fire Henry Miller," *Lost Generation Journal*, 1 (May 1973), 7.

121 "different milieu": Quoted in Ferguson, *Henry Miller*, 186.

122 "a better vehicle": Alfred Perlès, *My Friend Henry Miller* (London, 1955), 25. On pages 25–28 Perlès reproduces a Miller sketch. One of Miller's biographers, Jay Martin, says, "Miller placed a few articles in the *Tribune* under the names of regular staff writers and got a kickback from them." *Always Merry and Bright: The Life of Henry Miller* (Santa Barbara, Calif., 1978), 221.

122 "anonymous art": Henry Miller, March 10, 1931, *Letters to Emil*, ed. George Wickes (New York, 1989), 78.

122 dates and statistics: Henry Miller, *Tropic of Cancer* (New York, 1961; originally published 1934), 223.

122 "head guru": Taylor, *Awakening from History*, 63.

123 "Tant pis!": Miller, August 24, 1931, *Letters to Emil*, 81.

123 "newspaper files": Quoted in Ibid., 83.

123 As a joke: Brassaï, *Henry Miller: The Paris Years* (New York, 1995), 178.

124 "with his left hand": Perlès, *My Friend Henry Miller*, 21–22.

124 "between ourselves": Miller [no day or month] 1934, *Letters to Emil*, 152.

124   believed otherwise: Frantz, "Recollections," *The Left Bank Revisited*, 312. Jay
       Martin has it that Miller "occasionally wrote part of the column" for Bald for
       a fee of five francs. *Always Merry and Bright*, 210. Benjamin Franklin V dis-
       cusses the matter in his Introduction to *On the Left Bank*, xiv-xv.

124   signed on: Joan Mellen, *Kay Boyle, Author of Herself* (New York, 1994), 135.

124   Bedwell's name: Ibid., 180.

125   "unrequited love": Shirer, *20th Century Journey: The Start*, 236–237.

126   rising sun: Root, *The Paris Edition*, 106.

126   "of an oak": Hawkins, *Hawkins of the Paris Herald*. 149.

127   "stagger home": Shirer, *20th Century Journey: The Start*, 254.

127   "show much": Root, *The Paris Edition*, 107.

127   "old *bistrot*": Paris *Tribune*, May 12, 1929.

127   "riotous living": Root, *The Paris Edition*, 107, 109.

128   little eerie: Taylor, *Awakening from History*, 69.

128   actually printing: Root, *The Paris Edition*, 169. At the same time, Root noted,
       the *Herald* was claiming circulation of fifty thousand and printing twenty
       thousand.

129   "out of business": Miller, April [no date] 1932, *Letters to Emil*, 93.

130   "playfully set": Frantz, "Recollections," *The Left Bank Revisited*, 315.

130   "burned down": Waverley Root, "The Second 'Paris Tribune,'" *The Left
       Bank Revisited*, 305.

133   "on the boat": Wambly Bald, "The Sweet Madness of Montparnasse," *The
       Left Bank Revisited*, 289.

135   "alive and kicking": Quoted in Ford, *The Left Bank Revisited*, 283–84.

135   "at the price": Root, *The Paris Edition*, 205–208. Root gives a slightly differ-
       ent account of the new *Paris Tribune*, one that does not include his editorial,
       in "The Second 'Paris Tribune,'" Ford, *The Left Bank Revisited*, 303–307. In
       the article Root adds that, after the eight issues he published, he gave the
       weekly to James King of the former Paris *Tribune* staff, who brought out one
       or two more issues before closing down for good.

Chapter Three: *News in the Afternoon*

Epigraph: Hemingway, *The Sun Also Rises*, 46.

137   "by vocation": Quoted in Hawkins, *Hawkins of the Paris Herald*, 97. The ori-
       gins of the *Paris Times* are recounted in Hawkins, 92–103, and in Robertson,
       The International Herald Tribune, 116–117. The *Paris Times* is available in
       hard copy and microfilm in the Bibliothèque Nationale de France.

137   in earnings: *New York Times*, December 16, 1923, 85.

138   "sad memories": *The Boulevardier*, February 1930, 19–20.

138   "city on earth": Matthew Josephson, *Life Among the Surrealists* (New York,
       1962), 107.

139   "living in Paris": Laney, *Paris Herald*, 70. I change Laney's spelling of
       "Courtlandt." The *Paris Evening Telegram* is available on microfilm in the
       Bibliothèque Nationale de France, though during my time there only issues
       from 1923 could be viewed.

139   "engaging competitor": *Time*, April 17, 1939, 67.

139   "own prescience": Hawkins, *Hawkins of the Paris Herald*, 101.

140   better packaging: Whether the *Paris Times* had any cable or wire service, or had it consistently, is uncertain. Vincent Sheean (see below) refers to a cable service, but others who worked for the paper make no reference to it. Like the *Evening Telegram*, the *Times* seemingly did not subscribe to the French service Havas.

140   hire them: Root, *The Paris Edition*, 157.

140   "live on it": Quoted in Ibid., 20.

140   For women: Tom Wood, "Gaston Hanet Archambault," *Lost Generation Journal*, 7 (Summer 1983), 11.

140   "amply equipped": Hawkins, *Hawkins of the Paris Herald*, 97.

142   playing basketball: *Paris Times*, January 15, 1925.

142   Cody thought: Cody, *The Women of Montparnasse*, 173.

142   Hemmy paid: *Paris Times*, February 17, 1925.

142   "so many years": *Paris Times*, January 16, 1925.

143   "in the autumn": *Paris Times*, February 20, 1925.

145   "take it seriously": Imbs, *Confessions of Another Young Man*, 137.

145   "just the same?": Quoted in Ibid., 139.

145   "later each day": Ibid., 142.

146   "over from work": Sheean, *Personal History*, 306–307.

146   eating place: The restaurant is mentioned in an unpublished memoir of working on the *Paris Times* by Robert Collyer Washburn. Tom Wood, who published a sampling of the memoir in his *Lost Generation Journal*, calls the work, probably written in 1944, a "truncated history" and questions its reliability. *Lost Generation Journal*, 7 (Summer 1983), 2–7, 16–23.

147   unwilling to overlook: Bessie's Paris days and his later periods in Spain and Hollywood are recalled in Dan Bessie, *Rare Birds: An American Family* (Lexington, Ky., 2001), 94–96, 102–113, 222–224. Burnett mentions Bessie's firing in *The Literary Life and the Hell with It*, 93–94. Later, in *STORY* magazine, Burnett and Foley would publish a number of Bessie's stories.

148   Flanner remembered: Flanner, *Paris Was Yesterday*, xviii.

148   Crane biographer: Fisher, *Hart Crane*, 406.

149   The bastards: Harry Crosby, "Paris Diaries," *Americans in Paris: A Literary Anthology*, 343.

Chapter Four: *Short Cut to Paradise*

Epigraph: Taylor, *Awakening from History*, 73.

151   service was formed: William G. Shepherd, "Our Ears in Washington," *Everybody's Magazine*, 43 (October 1920), 73.

152   Press Association: Svoboda, *Hemingway & The Sun Also Rises*, 134.

152   "from New York": Ernest Hemingway, "New York Letter," *transatlantic review*, 5 (1924), 357.

153   "and evrything": Hemingway to Hadley Hemingway, November 28, 1922, *Selected Letters*, 73. The varied spellings of "everybody" and "everything" are Hemingway's.

153 believed himself: Charles A. Fenton notes the Mason-Krum connection in *The Apprenticeship of Ernest Hemingway: The Early Years* (New York, 1961; originally published 1954), 217 n. 8.

153 "fonder of him": Hemingway to F. Scott Fitzgerald, December 24, 1925, *Selected Letters*, 180.

154 "knows everybody": Miller, May 10, 1930, *Letters to Emil*, 49.

154 leaked document: I follow Frazier Hunt's account of the treaty scoop in *One American and His Attempt at Education* (New York, 1938), 168–171. For somewhat different versions see Lloyd Wendt, *Chicago Tribune: The Rise of a Great American Newspaper* (Chicago, 1979), 441–444, and Smith, *The Colonel*, 219. In 1922 Frazier Hunt, now writing for Hearst magazines and acting as a Hearst talent scout in Europe, praised Hemingway's story "My Old Man" and told him he was sending it to *Cosmopolitan* for consideration. Reynolds, *Hemingway: The Paris Years*, 78.

155 "wanted froth": Quoted in Fenton, *The Apprenticeship of Ernest Hemingway*, 101.

155 praised him: Foley, *The Story of STORY Magazine*, 122.

155 "were all right": John Dos Passos, *The Best Times* (New York, 1966), 154.

156 "printer's ink": Ford Madox Ford, *It Was the Nightingale* (New York, 1975; originally published 1933), 299.

156 "a nice job": Svoboda, *Hemingway &* The Sun Also Rises, 134. In the published version of the novel, Jake checks his bank balance, which shows he has $1,832.60. He is doing pretty well, in other words. In 1921 Malcolm Cowley and his wife found they could live in Paris in modest comfort on $1,000 a year.

157 travel pieces: George Seldes, *Lords of the Press* (New York, 1938), 283.

157 freest figures: Seldes devotes a shrewd and sardonic chapter to the stature and work of foreign correspondents in *Lords of the Press*, 283–293. For more detail about the American press abroad in the prewar and postwar periods see Robert W. Desmond, *Windows on the World: The Information Process in a Changing Society, 1900–1920* (Iowa City, Ia., 1980).

158 "peaceful backwater": Miller, *I Found No Peace*, 120.

158 "to Paradise": George Slocombe, *The Tumult and the Shouting* (New York, 1936), 66–67.

159 "best-seller appearances": Seldes, *Lords of the Press*, 290.

159 "try it a year": Mowrer, *The House of Europe*, 129. I follow Mowrer's account of his Paris period in this memoir.

160 with Chicago?: Quoted in Ibid., 129–130.

161 "very fully": Lilian T. Mowrer, *Journalist's Wife* (New York, 1937), 18.

162 constructive purpose!: Mowrer, *The House of Europe*, 345.

163 "newspaperman desire?": Ibid., 439–440.

164 "jolly times": Ibid., 553.

164 second wife: Following Ernest Hemingway's death in 1961, his fourth wife, Mary, asked Paul Scott Mowrer to write the authorized biography rather than Carlos Baker. Mowrer declined. Gioia Diliberto, *Hadley* (New York, 1992), 278.

165 on his staff: The writing Mowrers included Edgar's British-born wife Lilian.
165 a heroic portrait: Seldes, *Lords of the Press*, 285.
166 "Damascus blade": *New Republic*, February 20, 1935, 50.
166 "newspaperman's mind": Stewart, *News Is What We Make It*, 198–199.
166 "of the imagination": Sheean, *Personal History*, 26. I follow this memoir for Sheean's Paris days and his time with the *Chicago Tribune* foreign service.
167 "fill the hours": Ibid., 35.
167 70 percent: Smith, *The Colonel*, 233.
168 genuine Americans: Seldes, "My Decade with Col. McCormick," 28.
168 from his boss: Ibid., 25.
168 wired back: Quoted in Root, *The Paris Edition*, 75.
169 from Timbuktu: Seldes, "My Decade with Col. McCormick," 26.
169 "damned foreigners": Quoted in Ibid.
170 ending his days: Sheean, *Personal History*, 116. McCormick's version of how Sheean's days ended was sharply different. Sheean, he said, was "a liar, disloyal and dishonorable," and charged the correspondent with misconduct during an assignment in Italy. Smith, *The Colonel*, 304.
171 He had written: Sheean, *Personal History*, 280–281. "My Old Man," a short story, was written by Hemingway in 1922 and first published in his *Three Stories & Ten Poems* in 1923.
172 "they participate in": John Gunther, "Potential Battlegrounds," *Saturday Review of Literature*, November 14, 1936, 7.
172 Gunther was: I follow Gunther's account of his work as a correspondent and the writing of *Inside Europe* in *A Fragment of Autobiography* (New York, 1962), 1–23.
172 "picked up dust": Gunther, *A Fragment of Autobiography*, 5.
172 "to tell me?": Quoted in Foley, *The Story of STORY Magazine*, 103.
173 agreed to the book: A different account of the meeting with Canfield is given in Foley, *The Story of STORY Magazine*, 103–104.
173 a million copies: The figure is given in Gunther's *American National Biography* entry.
174 "widely-selling book": Paris *Herald*, July 2, 1939.
174 "foreign correspondent": Shirer, *20th Century Journey: The Start*, 282. I follow this work and the second volume of Shirer's three-volume memoirs, *20th Century Journey: The Nightmare Years, 1930–1940* (Boston, 1984), for his time with the *Chicago Tribune*'s foreign service and his later radio work with CBS.
175 "give me a hand": Quoted in Shirer, *20th Century Journey: The Start*, 332.
176 "room for you": Ibid., 339.
176 "only a dancer": Ibid., 318.
176 waited in the rain: Flanner, *Paris Was Yesterday*, 34.
177 "doing badly": Shirer, *20th Century Journey: The Start*, 423.
178 Take Over: Quoted in Ibid.
178 "for a while": Ibid., 427.
179 "produce literature": Foley, *The Story of STORY Magazine*, 86.
179 "drink and talk": Burnett, *The Literary Life and the Hell with It*, 269.

179 "I'm sending you": Quoted in Shirer, *20th Century Journey: The Start*, 488.
180 "gave me Vienna!": Ibid., 489.
181 "not been satisfactory": Quoted in Shirer, *20th Century Journey: The Nightmare Years*, 55.
181 the mistake trivial: In his biography of McCormick, Richard Norton Smith says the mistake was more serious than Shirer allows. He also points to another incident, not mentioned in Shirer's memoirs, that figured in his firing. *The Colonel*, 307–308.
181 was in order: Quoted in Shirer, *20th Century Journey: The Nightmare Years*, 56.
182 "What a contemptible": Ibid., 57.
182 "square deal": Quoted in Smith, *The Colonel*, 307.
182 "to try it": Taylor, *Awakening from History*, 57. I follow Taylor's account in this memoir of his *Chicago Tribune* career.
183 "Montmartre nightclubs": Ibid., 78.
183 "robot gestures": Ibid., 84.
184 "shorter English sentences": Taylor relates the story of the trip in Ibid., 88–91.
184 "vanished civilization": Ibid, 87.
184 terse cable: Quoted in Ibid., 172.
185 "bedtime story": Quoted in Smith, *The Colonel*, 388.
185 Rest Cure: Quoted in Taylor, *Awakening from History*, 174. John Tebbel has it that McCormick was protesting a Taylor dispatch predicting that German-Russian collaboration would result in an attack on Romania. When Taylor defended the dispatch, McCormick replied: "Your fantastic Rumanian story, hysterical tone, and your recent cable and other vagaries indicate you, along with Knickerbocker, Mowrer and others, are victims of mass psychosis and are hysterically trying to drag U.S. into war. Suggest you join Foreign Legion or else take rest cure in sanitarium in neutral country until you regain control of your nerves and recover confidence in yourself. Until then file no more." *An American Dynasty* (Garden City, N.Y., 1947), 156.
185 in my own: Taylor, *Awakening from History*, 211.
186 "something better": William L. Shirer, *Berlin Diary: The Journal of a Foreign Correspondent, 1934–1941* (New York, 1941), 3.
187 prominent broadcaster: Smith, who had been a Rhodes Scholar at Oxford before joining the United Press, left the agency in Berlin to begin broadcasting for CBS news. This period of his life was recounted in 1942 in *Last Train from Berlin*.
187 "not people": Foley, *The Story of STORY Magazine*, 213.
188 Meet Me: Quoted in Shirer, *20th Century Journey: The Nightmare Years*, 273.
189 "Okay": Quoted in Ibid., 280.
189 "news firsthand": Ibid., 303. See author's note on this page referring to William S. Paley's memoir *As It Happened*.
189 "do it?" Quoted in Ibid., 304.
190 "So much so": Quoted in Ibid., 308.
191 "allowed to stay": Shirer, *Berlin Diary*, 450.
191 "for a while": William L. Shirer, *20th Century Journey: A Native Returns, 1945–1988* (Boston, 1990), 326.

192   "loyal friend": Stowe, *No Other Road to Freedom*, 247.

192   "to Ralph Barnes": Ibid., 250.

193   "about my 'book'": Quoted in Mahoney, *Dispatches and Dictators*, 148. Barnes's book was never published.

Chapter Five: *A Smart Little Magazine*

Epigraph: F. Scott Fitzgerald, "News of Paris—Fifteen Years Ago," *Afternoon of an Author*, notes and introduction by Arthur Mizener (Princeton, N.J., 1957), 221.

194   had met before: Jed Kiley, *Hemingway: An Old Friend Remembers* (New York, 1965), 19–33. The memoir appeared as articles in *Playboy* magazine in 1956 and 1957; book publication followed Kiley's death in 1962.

195   smacks of fiction: When Kiley sent him the manuscript of his memoir in 1954, Hemingway responded: "A gag is a gag and a fantasy is a fantasy, but the Ms. you sent me . . . is a long series of untruths, misstatements and falsehoods which I could not allow you to use even if it was labelled a fictional nightmare." Quoted in Jeffrey Meyers, *Hemingway: Life into Art* (New York, 2000), 143.

196   "lighter side": Paris *Tribune*, May 26, 1927.

196   American edition: Theodore Peterson, *Magazines in the Twentieth Century* (Urbana, Ill., 1956), 108. *True Story* circulation figures are given in Robert Ernst, *Weakness Is a Crime: The Life of Bernarr Macfadden* (Syracuse, N.Y., 1991), 76–77.

197   "class publication": Edna Woolman Chase and Ilka Chase, *Always in Vogue* (Garden City, N.Y., 1954), 161.

197   "seasonal mode": Janet Flanner, "Mainbocher," *An American in Paris*, 259.

198   a staff member: Pauline Pfeiffer's background, journalistic work, and affair with Hemingway are recounted in Bernice Kert, *The Hemingway Women* (New York, 1983), 171ff.

198   "write me": Quoted in Ibid., 187. The "write me to" phrasing is Pfeiffer's.

199   "lady-writer stuff": Lillian Hellman, "The Art of the Theater I," *Paris Review*, 9 (33), 67. The stories are mentioned but titles are not given by Hellman biographers or in a bibliography of her work.

200   point of work: Quoted passages above come from the *Paris Comet*, vol.1, no. 12. Through its opening two volumes the magazine listed issues on its masthead only by volume and number. With vol. 3, no. 1 it began running a table of contents that also identified the now monthly issues by month. In the few places the *Comet* comes in for mention, it is usually said to have begun publication on October 12, 1927—a confusion possibly stemming from the fact that available microfilm begins with this issue. The October 12, 1927, number was the eleventh issue of the then fortnightly magazine.

203   "business man": Sisley Huddleston, *Back to Montparnasse* (London, 1931), 139.

205   week's pay: Hawkins, *Hawkins of the Paris Herald*, 111–112.

205   Kiley returned: Information about Kiley is given in a publisher's introduction to *Hemingway: An Old Friend Remembers*, 5–10. Here the Rue Fontaine club is called Kiley's. It is given as Le Palermo in Arlen J. Hansen, *Expatri-*

ate Paris: A Cultural and Literary Guide to Paris of the 1920s (New York, 1990), 131, 268.

206 "read with pleasure": Paris *Tribune*, March 8, 1928.

206 "sign me up": Kiley, *Hemingway: An Old Friend Remembers*, 49.

206 "you must go": Paris *Tribune*, October 14, 1930.

207 Boswell of: Basil Woon, *The Paris That's Not in the Guide Books* (New York, 1926), 269.

207 "ideas and tastes": Gilliam recalled the Paris years with Moss in a two-part article, "My Years with Arthur Moss," *Lost Generation Journal*, 2 (Fall 1974), 10–13, 32, and 3 (Winter 1975), 39–42.

207 book about clowns: Basil Woon thought *Slapstick and Dumbbell: A Casual Survey of Clowns and Clowning* by Moss and Hiler Harzberg (New York, 1924) would "probably go down as a classic on a subject that has been surprisingly little touched upon." *The Paris That's Not in the Guide Books*, 269.

210 "was celebrated": Flanner, *Paris Was Yesterday*, xvi.

210 "damned decent": Hemingway to F. Scott Fitzgerald, December 31, 1925–January 1, 1926, *Selected Letters*, 185.

211 to his friends: Hemingway to F. Scott Fitzgerald, March 31, 1927, *Selected Letters*, 249.

213 "got guts": Kiley, *Hemingway: An Old Friend Remembers*, 31–33.

213 "your block off": Quoted in Jeffrey Meyers, *Hemingway: A Biography* (New York, 1985), 592 n. 10. Hemingway himself reportedly said that the article "was written partly by me, mostly by my wife, and re-written by . . . Arthur Moss." Quoted in Charles M. Oliver, *Ernest Hemingway A to Z* (New York, 1999), 277.

213 "kill a sparrow": *The Boulevardier*, April 1929, 62.

215 "insignificant rates": Carol Weld, "Viva Ric!", *Lost Generation Journal*, 2 (Fall 1974), 30.

215 "monthly rag": Paris *Tribune*, January 26, 1932.

Chapter Six: *Countless Reams of Stuff*

Epigraph: See note below ("$40 per").

217 "some Toronto newspaper": Anderson to Lewis Galantière, November 28, 1921, *Letters of Sherwood Anderson*, eds. Howard Mumford Jones and Walter B. Rideout (Boston, 1953), 82–84. Charles A. Fenton takes note of Anderson's use of "letters" in *The Apprenticeship of Ernest Hemingway*, 99–101, though his point is the term was an effective way of describing the loose, informal feature stories the *Star* wanted from Hemingway.

218 "regular correspondent": I follow Leon Edel's account of James's newspaper venture in *Henry James: The Conquest of London, 1870–1881* (Philadelphia, 1962), 195–245, and in the introduction to Henry James, *Parisian Sketches: Letters to the New York Tribune, 1875–1876*, eds. Leon Edel and Ilse Dusoir Lind (New York, 1957), ix–xxxvii. The latter work reprints all James's Paris letters as well as correspondence concerning the letters between Whitelaw Reid and James.

219   "I can write"; Ernest Hemingway, "Pamplona Letter," *transatlantic review*, 2 (September 1924), 300.

219   "labor pains": For Gingrich's reference to the "Pamplona Letter" see Ronald Weber, *Hemingway's Art of Nonfiction* (New York, 1990), 63–65.

219   "fine writer": Hemingway to Arnold Gingrich, March 13, 1933, *Selected Letters*, 383.

220   "great playmates": Anderson to Lewis Galantière, November 28, 1921, *Letters of Sherwood Anderson*, 83.

220   "last person": Stearns, *The Street I Know*, 212.

223   Sundays included: *Town & Country*, November 1, 1923.

223   "Paris press": Ibid., November 1, 1922.

223   "to be hysterical": Ibid., May 15, 1925.

223   "it paid well": Stearns, *The Street I Know*, 212–213.

224   "of his royaties": Fitzgerald to Ernest Hemingway, December 28, 1928, *A Life in Letters*, ed. Matthew J. Bruccoli (New York, 1994), 160–161. "Royaties" is Fitzgerald's spelling.

225   "time you wanted": Stearns, "Apologia of an Expatriate," 340.

225   in her hand: *Town & Country*, May 1, 1922. For Flanner's relationship with McMein see Brenda Wineapple, *Genêt: A Biography of Janet Flanner* (New York, 1989), esp. 43–44. I mainly follow this work for biographical detail about Flanner.

225   among the latter: Gardner Botsford, *A Life of Privilege, Mostly* (New York, 2003), 82.

226   "less than less": Janet Flanner, "Then and Now," *Paris Review*, 9 (33), 169. The remark appeared in a printed account of a 1964 Paris symposium on the expatriate tradition.

226   "famous writer": Flanner, Introduction to *Paris Was Yesterday*, vii.

226   "emotional crises": Paris *Tribune*, December 28, 1924.

227   "not writing fiction": Quoted in Cody, *The Women of Montparnasse*, 159–160.

227   "sphere of inaction": Liebling, *The Road Back to Paris*, 17.

227   "gay and attractive": Jane Grant, *Ross, The New Yorker, and Me* (New York, 1968), 223.

227   "$40 per": Grant's letter is among her papers at the University of Oregon. The letter was available online as part of a University of Oregon Libraries exhibit devoted to Grant. Portions of the letter are reprinted in Wineapple, *Genêt*, 97.

228   gloomy coverage: Wineapple, *Genêt*, 103.

228   Ross inspiration: Gardner Botsford says Flanner suggested Flâneuse, an idler. *A Life of Privilege, Mostly*, 182.

229   "the French think": Quoted by Flanner, "The Unique Ross," Introduction to Grant, *Ross, The New Yorker, and Me*, 7. Within the book, page 223, Grant says Ross's "only admonition" to Flanner was to "remember that *The New Yorker* is a magazine of reporting and criticism." Flanner comments briefly on the manner of her column as it developed over the years in her introduction to *Paris Was Yesterday*, xix–xx.

229   "the writer's mind": Flanner, *Paris Was Yesterday*, xix.

229 "off the faucet": Botsford, *A Life of Privilege, Mostly*, 183–184.
230 "extreme jabberwocky": Flanner, *Paris Was Yesterday*, 20.
230 "carrier pigeon": Ibid., 22–23.
230 "stuffed-bird-loving Bill": Ibid., 12.
230 "brain wants": "Paris Letter," *The New Yorker*, January 2, 1926.
230 for correction: Botsford, *A Life of Privilege, Mostly*, 174.
231 "a somnambulist": Flanner's "Tourist" is reprinted in *An American in Paris, Profile of an Interlude Between the Wars* (New York, 1940), 265–282.
231 "as a practice": *The Little Review*, May 1929, 32–33.
232 ten thousand words: Flanner, author's note to "Führer: A Document," *An American in Paris*, 374.
232 "huntsmans reporting": Quoted in Shari Benstock, *Women of the Left Bank: Paris, 1900–1940* (Austin, Tex., 1986), 133.
233 "from low-life": Liebling, *The Road Back to Paris*, 18.
233 "one-war category": Ibid., 10–11.
233 "he looked it": Botsford, *A Life of Privilege, Mostly*, 200.
234 "hies me to Paris": Thurber to Elliott Nugent, January 22, 1921, *The Thurber Letters*, 81–82.
235 $90 payment: Burton Bernstein, *Thurber, A Biography* (New York, 1975), 142–143.
235 "sells his gleanings": Root, *The Paris Edition*, 23.
236 Rosemary wrote: Charles A. Fenton, *Stephen Vincent Benét: The Life and Times of an American Man of Letters, 1898–1943* (New Haven, Conn., 1958), 191.
236 "salary check": Kuhn, "Paris in the Twenties," *Remembrance of Things Paris*, 7.
238 "timely articles": Ida M. Tarbell, *All in the Day's Work* (New York, 1939), 100. For Tarbell's Paris period I follow this memoir. I also write about Tarbell in Paris in Ronald Weber, *Hired Pens: Professional Writers in America's Golden Age of Print* (Athens, Oh., 1997), 142–143.
238 "stray journalist": Ibid., 141.
239 "mutilated land": Ibid., 343.
239 "of her articles": Quoted in Peter Kurth, *American Cassandra: The Life of Dorothy Thompson* (Boston, 1990), 48. I follow this biography for Thompson's early career.
240 "those notes!" Ibid., 52.
240 haven't I talent?: Ibid., 57.
241 some mention: William Holtz, *The Ghost in the Little House: A Life of Rose Wilder Lane* (Columbia, Mo., 1993), 91–92.
241 "to shake you": Quoted in *Dorothy Thompson and Rose Wilder Lane: Forty Years of Friendship*, ed. William Holtz (Columbia, Mo., 1991), 24–25.
242 "no risk involved": Quoted in Kurth, *American Cassandra*, 59.
242 "speak German": Vincent Sheean, *Dorothy and Red* (Boston, 1963), 2.
242 "you can imagine": Quoted in Kurth, *American Cassandra*, 71.
243 "to the hilt": Ibid., 83.
243 "woman newspaperman": Ibid., 86.
243 "very important fellows": Ibid., 95.

244 "no other woman": Ibid., 85.
245 "writing is easy": Mary Knight, *On My Own* (New York, 1938), 51. I follow this memoir for Knight's work with the United Press.
245 "take me on:" Ibid., 67.
246 "to unlearn you": Quoted in Ibid., 77.
246 "stuff like that": Ibid., 84.
246 "staff reporter": Ibid., 93.
248 "get going!" Quoted in Ibid., 157.
248 "flagpole sitting": Ibid., 93.
249 "lecture platform": Robert van Gelder, *New York Times Book Review*, April 24, 1938, 25.
249 "write my way": Quoted in Caroline Moorehead, *Gellhorn: A Twentieth-Century Life* (New York, 2003), 33. I follow this biography for Gellhorn's time in Paris and beyond.
250 "What the hell": Ibid., 33.
251 ruined her skin: Ibid., 107.
251 "with the boys": Quoted in Ibid.

Chapter Seven: *Stories of Paris*

Epigraph: Miller, February 16, 1931, *Letters to Emil*, 73.
254 "farewell forever": Thurber, *The Years with Ross*, 30.
254 "his Paris years": Wickes, *Americans in Paris*, 251.
255 had he wished: Putnam, *Paris Was Our Mistress*, 6.
256 a news agency: Aaron Latham recounts Fitzgerald's efforts to adapt his story to the screen in *Crazy Sundays: F. Scott Fitzgerald in Hollywood* (New York, 1971), 245–258.
256 "being grotesque": "Hollywood Paris," *Nation*, 154 (April 25, 1942), 491.
257 "go to Paris": Quoted in Putnam, *Paris Was Our Mistress*, 47.
257 "even a best-seller": Ibid., 112–113.
258 Miller's story: Ibid., 232. Alfred Perlès says the scheme was foiled when printers sent galley proofs to Putnam, who in turn wired them to kill some of the changes. *My Friend Henry Miller*, 35. A different conclusion is given in Mary V. Dearborn, *The Happiest Man Alive: A Biography of Henry Miller* (New York, 1991), 136.
258 "Are you game": Miller, *Tropic of Cancer*, 50–53. Here applied to Miller, "Joe" is an all-purpose nickname among Miller, Carl, and Van Norden. After one exchange of the name with Van Norden, page 102, Miller explains: "I call him Joe because he calls me Joe. When Carl is with us he is Joe too. Everybody is Joe because it's easier that way. It's also a pleasant reminder not to take yourself too seriously."
259 "promise you that": Ibid., 139.
259 a final edition: Ibid., 146–147.
259 lot in life: Ibid., 150–152.
261 "precautions I took": Ibid., 175–176.
261 "luxury by comparison": Ibid., 154–155.

261 "to flow": Ibid., xxxii. According to Mary V. Dearborn, ". . . he [Miller] wrote the essay [preface] himself and had Nin sign it (she no doubt had something to do with its composition as well)." *The Happiest Man Alive*, 117.

262 "like hair": Ibid., 166.

262 "on the blink": Ibid., 101.

262 "feel anything": Ibid.,145.

262 "superfluous to mention": Ibid., 133.

262 "the world shrinks": Ibid., 132.

263 "storytelling genius": Wambly Bald, "I Remember Miller," *Lost Generation Journal*, 2 (Fall 1974), 41.

263 "what a book": Miller, October 14, 1932, *Letters to Emil*, 108.

263 "make economies": Miller, *Tropic of Cancer*, 186.

263 "there's the rub!": Miller, November [no date] 1931, *Letters to Emil*, 89.

264 "once-a-week souls": Miller, *Tropic of Cancer*, 55.

264 "place to sleep": Miller, November [no date] 1931, *Letters to Emil*, 90.

264 funds if needed: Carlos Baker, *Ernest Hemingway, A Life Story* (New York, 1969), 257–258, and Scott Donaldson, *By Force of Will: The Life and Art of Ernest Hemingway* (New York, 1977), 44.

264 European correspondents: Calmer was originally employed at CBS by Paul White rather than Murrow, a distinction of some importance among broadcasters who worked with Murrow. For details see Stanley Cloud and Lynne Olson, *The Murrow Boys: Pioneers on the Front Lines of Broadcast Journalism* (Boston, 1996).

265 "longest gangway": Edgar Calmer, "Paris Interlude," *STORY*, 4 (February 1934), 56.

266 "Radiantly drunk": Ned Calmer, *All the Summer Days* (Boston, 1961), 18.

266 "or ignored": Ibid., 38.

266 "or whatever": Ibid., 20.

266 "stay that way": Ibid., 40.

267 "and the hotel": Ibid., 108.

267 "some kind friend": Ibid.,19.

268 "drinking and sex": Ibid., 145.

268 "French girl": Ibid., 287–288.

268 "praises of himself": Ibid., 112.

269 "so many of us": Ibid., 300–302.

270 "so alone": F. Scott Fitzgerald, "Babylon Revisited," *The Short Stories of F. Scott Fitzgerald*, ed. Matthew J. Bruccoli (New York, 1989), 633.

271 master and student: Ned Calmer, "The Last Time I Saw Elliot Paul," *Virginia Quarterly Review*, 55 (Winter 1979), 99.

271 "at a bar": Adam Gopnik, Introduction to *Americans in Paris: A Literary Anthology* (New York, 2004), xxi.

271 "read French": Freeman, *An American Testament*, 167–168.

271 "runaway" colonies: Putnam, *Paris Was Our Mistress*, 247–248.

272 "of evanescence": Stein, *The Autobiography of Alice B. Toklas*, 894.

272 "rotund and bewhiskered": Sage, "Farewell to Transition," 373.

272 "any gathering": Jolas, *Maria Jolas, Woman of Action*, 84.

272 "lose his temper": Root, *The Paris Edition*, 133.
272 severe depression: The diagnosis is Arnold Goldman's in an article relating a journey to Ibiza to investigate the factual accuracy of *Spanish Town*. "The Town That Did Not Die," *Journal of American Studies*, 25 (April 1991), 71–72.
272 "disorderly life": Paul, *The Last Time I Saw Paris*, 171.
273 I owe them: Elliot Paul, *The Life and Death of a Spanish Town* (New York, 1937), 3–4.
273 "find tranquillity": Ibid., 9.
274 "and depressed": Ibid., 288.
274 "in a dream": Ibid., 337.
274 "above ground": Ibid., 427.
274 "started tapping": Elliot Paul, "'Whodunit,'" *Atlantic Monthly*, 168 (July 1941), 37.
275 breakfasting one morning: *Paris* (Chicago, 1947), n.p.
276 "torch of civilization": Elliot Paul, *The Mysterious Mickey Finn, or Murder at the Café du Dôme* (New York, 1939), 45–46.
276 had a gun: Ibid., 93.
276 "appropriate seriousness": Ibid., 250.
277 "fire him": Ibid., 74.
277 turned detective: For more on Paul's mysteries see Arnold Goldman, "Elliot Paul's Interwar 'Whodunits,'" *Joyce Studies Annual*, 6 (Summer 1995), 19–38.
277 "to know them": Putnam, *Paris Was Our Mistress*, 71.
277 "I found Paris": Paul, *The Last Time I Saw Paris*, 16. Paul says he first saw the Rue de la Huchette in 1923, presumably during a European trip. He came to Paris to live and work for the Paris *Tribune* in 1925.
278 each bound volume: Ibid., 134–136.
278 "all coming to": Ibid., 237.
279 "local color": Ibid., 389.
279 "breath of freedom": Ibid., 414.

Epilogue: *Curtain Fall*

Epigraph: Hawkins, *Hawkins of the Paris Herald*, 219–220.
281 shut down: Paris *Herald*, June 19, 1940. I correct typos in Kerr's account.
281 Kospoth's fate: Sevareid, *Not So Wild a Dream*, 87; Robertson, *The International Herald Tribune*, 187.
282 Mailbag poet: A new Crawford poem appeared in the Mailbag in the initial post-occupation issue of the *Herald* on December 22, 1944. In 1946 Crawford began her own weekly column, "Our Time in Rhyme," sharing it with other versifiers.
282 "broadcasting feats": Quoted in Sevareid, *Not So Wild a Dream*, 163.
282 turning to broadcasting: Root's post-*Tribune* career is recalled in Frantz, "Noted Author-Correspondent Waverley Root Is Legendary," 16–19. Ring Lardner, Jr., quotes a letter from his brother Jim saying that the UP "lost its only two customers in Berlin as result of [Root's] story." *The Lardners*, 262.

283 "hit the horn": Quoted in Raymond Sokolov, *Wayward Reporter: The Life of A. J. Liebling* (New York, 1980), 139.

283 "smell of tuberoses": Liebling, *The Road Back to Paris*, 99.

284 "left in Europe": Ibid., 104.

284 "had not come": Shirer, *Berlin Diary*, 409.

285 what is this?: Ibid., 413.

285 towards the south: Ibid., 411.

285 the little *gamins*: Ibid., 431.

286 live in New York: In his memoirs Shirer speculates on the possibility the broadcast was intentionally allowed to go out via shortwave. *20th Century Journey: The Nightmare Years*, 542–543.

286 "it could happen": Shirer, *Berlin Diary*, 486.

286 "sanity at last!": Ibid., 599.

287 "something worse": Quoted in Hawkins, *Hawkins of the Paris Herald*, 224.

288 Hills died: Robertson, *The International Herald Tribune*, 220. Hills's obituary in the *New York Times* on March 29, 1941, said he had left Paris for Vichy, where his death was announced.

288 "immensely heartening": Robertson's last days in Paris are recounted in Laney, *Paris Herald*, 322–325. In 1950 Kerr would return to Paris as European editor of the *New York Herald Tribune*, operating from the bureau in the Herald building and working closely with Eric Hawkins on the Paris paper.

289 was waiting: Laney, *Paris Herald*, 322. For more on Renée Brazier's dedicated wartime efforts on behalf of the *Herald* see Robertson, *The International Herald Tribune*, 228–229.

289 on my emotions: Hawkins, *Hawkins of the Paris Herald*, 244.

Index

A NOTE ON THE AUTHOR

Ronald Weber's nonfiction books include *Hemingway's Art of Nonfiction*, *The Midwestern Ascendancy in American Writing*, and *Hired Pens: Professional Writers in America's Golden Age of Print*. He has also published short stories and novels. He is professor emeritus of American studies at the University of Notre Dame.